Positive Psychology at Work

Positive Psychology at Work

*How Positive Leadership
and Appreciative Inquiry Create
Inspiring Organizations*

Sarah Lewis

A John Wiley & Sons, Ltd., Publication

This edition first published 2011
© 2011 Sarah Lewis

Wiley-Blackwell is an imprint of John Wiley & Sons, formed by the merger of Wiley's global Scientific, Technical and Medical business with Blackwell Publishing.

Registered Office
John Wiley & Sons Ltd, The Atrium, Southern Gate, Chichester, West Sussex, PO19 8SQ, United Kingdom

Editorial Offices
The Atrium, Southern Gate, Chichester, West Sussex, PO19 8SQ, UK
350 Main Street, Malden, MA 02148–5020, USA
9600 Garsington Road, Oxford, OX4 2DQ, UK

For details of our global editorial offices, for customer services, and for information about how to apply for permission to reuse the copyright material in this book please see our website at www.wiley.com/wiley-blackwell.

The right of Sarah Lewis to be identified as the author of this work has been asserted in accordance with the UK Copyright, Designs and Patents Act 1988.

Library of Congress Cataloging-in-Publication Data

Lewis, Sarah, 1957-
  Positive psychology at work : how positive leadership and appreciative inquiry create inspiring organizations / Sarah Lewis.
       p. cm.
  Includes bibliographical references and index.
  ISBN 978-0-470-68320-0 (cloth)
  1. Leadership. 2. Positive psychology. 3. Organizational change. I. Title.
  HD57.7.L49 2011
  158.7–dc22   2010039783

A catalogue record for this book is available from the British Library.

This book is published in the following electronic formats: ePDF 9781119990406; Wiley Online Library 9781119990390

Set in 10.5/13 pt Minion by Toppan Best-set Premedia Limited

1   2011

To Stewart Smith, my husband,
whose gift of love sustains me

Contents

About the Author

Sarah Lewis is a fully qualified chartered psychologist, an Associated Fellow of the British Psychological Society and a founder and principal member of the Association of Business Psychologists. She holds a master's degree in occupational and organizational psychology, attained with distinction, and a certificate in systemic consultation. She is a specialist Appreciative Inquiry practitioner and an expert at facilitating large group events.

She is the managing director of Appreciating Change and is an experienced organizational consultant and facilitator. She has been actively involved in helping people and organizations change their behaviour for 25 years. Her clients include local government, central government, not-for-profit organizations and private sector clients, particularly in the manufacturing, financial and educational sectors.

When positive psychology burst onto the scene, Sarah quickly realized that work in this area both chimed with her practice and offered robust theoretical support to Appreciative Inquiry as an approach to organizational change. She integrates these two approaches in her work and is delighted to be able to extend, explore and share this connection in this book.

Sarah has lectured at postgraduate level and continues to be a regular conference presenter in the UK. She writes regularly for publication and is the lead author of *Appreciative Inquiry for Change Management: Using AI to Facilitate Organizational Development*, published by Kogan Page in 2007.

Sarah's work can be viewed on her website (www.appreciatingchange. co.uk) and she can be contacted at ++44 (0)7973782715 or by emailing sarahlewis@appreciatingchange.co.uk

Book Contributors

Alastair J. M. Arnott, Subject Leader of Performing Arts – St Paul's Way Trust School, MSc Applied Positive Psychology postgraduate student, Results Certified Coach Level 1. www.alastairjmarnott.com; alastairarnott@hotmail.co.uk

James Butcher, owner of Work Without Walls. Specializes in appreciative learning – helping people learn from their strengths and successes. www.work-without-walls.co.uk, ++44 (0)1303863581, ++44 (0)7976898782. Based in Kent, UK

Wendy Campbell, Founding (1989) and Managing Director of The Glastonbury Company Pty Ltd, Creator of The Resilient Leadership Program for Community Change Leaders. wendy@glastonbury.com.au, ++61 (0)893828071

Kate Coutts is a head teacher in Unst, Shetland, and has background in research. She also works in the private and public sector on leadership development. metasaga.wikispaces.com; katecoutts@shetland.gov.uk

Jane Filby, Director of Planning and Resources, Aston Business School, Aston University, Birmingham, UK. Expertise in load and financial models in HE, management of HE and reward structures. j.l.filby@aston.ac.uk

Ewa Francis, learning and development professional, specializing in designing and facilitating people development solutions: personal effectiveness workshops, management development, coaching, mentoring. Eva_Francis@postmaster.co.uk; ++44 (0)7800546291. Based in Surrey, UK and Poland

Mario Gastaldi, owner of Brain Team Consulting. Specializes in designing and facilitating spaces and conversations, live and on-line, leading to engaged change and collaboration. mg@mariogastaldi.com; www.mariogastaldi.com, ++39 (0)3489330978

Karena Gomez, C.Psychol. FCIPD. Consultant at KPMG. Specializes in unlocking organization and individual learning to deliver whole-system change. karena.gomez@kpmg.co.uk, ++44 (0)7919808452. Based in Leeds, UK

Helen Higson, Professor of Higher Education Learning and Management and Pro-Vice-Chancellor, Aston University, Birmingham, UK. Specializes in employability competences and intercultural learning. h.e.higson@ aston.ac.uk, ++44 (0)1212043191

Clive Hutchinson, Company Leader of Cougar Automation. Trained as an engineer and then a manager, Clive now devotes himself to helping people become free to play to their strengths

Louisa Jewell, MAPP, Consultant and Facilitator specializing in creating positive and productive workplaces. www.positivematters.com, louisa@ positivematters.com, 1-416-481-8930. Based in Toronto, Canada

Joep C. de Jong, CEO at Van Harte & Lingsma. Co-founder of AI Consultancy and has expertise in the practical, daily use of Appreciative Inquiry, special interest in Appreciative Leadership. joep.dejong@h-l.nl, ++31 (0)715191600; ++31 (0)654396936

Leif Josefsson, Metaspace facilitator, coach, networker. Explorer of new technology and thinking. On a learning journey, whether it's with his two-year-old grandchild or Maasai partner Rafael. www.metaspace.se. Based in Stockholm, Sweden

George Karseras is a chartered occupational psychologist and a Director of Leap Partnership, a boutique consultancy specializing in aligning organizational mindsets to organizational strategy. www.leappartnership.co.uk, ++44 (0)7976789366

Vanessa King, Master Applied Positive Psychology, University of Pennsylvania. Partner, ChangeAble Consulting LLP. Specializing in leadership development, positive change, and creative thinking. www.changeable. org.uk, ++44 (0)7989337083. Based in UK, works internationally

Martin Leavy, Training Development Manager, Dublin City University. Specializes in the design, delivery of training and development interventions together with supporting organizational change. www.dcu.ie, ++353 17005147. Based in Dublin, Ireland

Alex Linley, Founding Director of Capp, the leading people management consultancy specializing in strengths approaches. www.cappeu.com, ++44 (0)2476323363

Liz Martins, strengths-based change, psychosynthesis and open space practitioner, working with individuals, organizations and communities. lizmartins2@gmail.com, ++44 (0)1225858406; ++44 (0)7977932066. Based in Bath, UK

Lesley Moore, Director of MooreInsight Ltd, consultant and facilitator of strengths-based change with individuals, public organizations and community networks. www.mooreinsight.co.uk ++44 (0)7813197657; ++44 (0)1959569980. Based in Kent, UK

Nick Moore, Director of MooreInsight Ltd, specializing in co-creating seismic quality and efficiency enhancements in children's social care, with public and independent organizations. www.mooreinsight.co.uk, ++44 (0)7779082631; ++44 (0)1959569980. Based in Kent, UK

Shannon M. Polly, MAPP, President of Accentuate Consulting, facilitator and consultant specializing in communication/presentation skills and increasing organizational productivity and wellbeing. www.accentuate-consulting.com, spolly@accentuate-consulting.com, 1-917-449-1789. Based in Washington, DC

Ann Shacklady-Smith, Senior Fellow, Manchester Business School, Chair Community Empowerment Network St Helens, thrives doing Appreciative Inquiry research, appreciative coaching and whole-system change. ann.shacklady-smith@mbs.ac.uk; info@censthelens.org.uk, ++44 (0)1744759390

Tim Slack, Co-Director Appreciating People, Appreciative Inquiry and whole system OD practitioners. www.appreciatingpeople.co.uk, ++44 (0)1514271146; ++44 (0)7986515237. Based in Liverpool UK

Stewart Smith, artist and cartoonist. www.darkhorseart.co.uk. stew@darkhorseart.co.uk, ++44 (0)2083051862. Based in London, UK

Ceferi Soler, PhD in Psychology, Barcelona University. Associate Professor ESADE Business School. ceferi.soler@esade.edu

Professor Michael West, Executive Dean, Aston Business School, Birmingham. His areas of research interest are team and organizational innovation and effectiveness, particularly in relation to the organization of health services

Lesley Wilson, Founder of Dreamcatchers, an organization development consultancy specializing in strengths-based change. Designer of leadership learning journeys and Metasaga guide. dreamcatcherglasgow@hotmail. com, ++44 (0)7980449135

Preface

Every book written I am beginning to realize poses certain questions, the key one being: Who is it for? In this case the answer is that it is written for its author: it is the kind of book I like to read. I like books that tell me about new, exciting ideas and theories in a clear, easily understood way; that are prepared to recount in some detail key interesting research, but don't insist I follow every twist and turn of the academic debate; and that give me ideas about how all this interesting new knowledge might be used in the field.

So this is the book I have attempted to write: the key ideas, research and pragmatics of positive psychology at work drawn together into one reader-facing volume. I have also attempted to illuminate the application of positive psychology in different workplace settings and cultures so that many different readers will find an example that resonates with their workplace or work challenge. My aspiration is that it will be interesting and useful to leaders and managers, students and consultants, and people at work interested in how things could be improved.

I have attempted to make the text lively and interesting as well as informative and scholarly. To achieve this balance I have had to make some choices and I want to say a few words about these.

Accounts

I have chosen to insert short accounts of practice as supplements so that they don't break up the flow of the main chapter narrative and you can read them at a point in your reading that suits you.

Summaries and Key Points

I have chosen occasionally to pull out the key points of the discussion in the text to help readers keep the big picture of the discussion, or a map of the main points, to hand.

Stories

I have included occasional stories from my own experience, some work-based, some more personal, to illuminate arguments in the text. I have done this on the basis that sometimes a story aids understanding and also to leaven the dough of academic exposition. I realize that these are as likely to annoy as to charm. In my defence I can only say I road-tested them with my contributors, and those included passed the squirm test. Feel free to skip them if they are not to your taste.

Cartoons

I have also included some cartoons. My hope is that these will illustrate points in a dramatic way and also that they offer a little light relief.

Referencing

I thought long and hard about the level of referencing in this book. An organizational leader who read an early draft made it clear that too many references really interfered with his pleasure in reading the text. On the other hand, I get really annoyed reading under-referenced books or foot-noted texts, where I can't easily see where the information came from.

So my compromise is this: key pieces of research that I explain in some detail are properly referenced as the primary source. Elsewhere I have given as the reference the book, or book chapter, from which I have gleaned the information I am presenting. Further, in a slight departure from best academic practice, I haven't constantly re-referenced my source with 'ibid.'. Instead, unless I introduce a new name or clearly switch to my own observations, you can assume the information continues to come from the same source until told otherwise.

In addition, I have added some further reading at the end of the chapters for those who want to explore a particular area or idea further, with a few notes about the nature of the text. I hope this will help readers find the kind of books they like to read among the ever-growing selection available.

So that's it. I have learnt a huge amount researching and writing this book and have enjoyed the journey tremendously. I can only hope that you buy this pristine volume and rapidly deface it with underlining, exclamation marks, question marks, comments, dog ears and coffee stains. Such, to me, are the signs of a useful book.

Acknowledgements

In 2007, along with my colleagues Jon Passmore and Stefan Cantore, I wrote a book called *Appreciative Inquiry for Change Management.* I enjoyed the experience so much that when Wiley-Blackwell asked me to write a book about positive psychology and Appreciative Inquiry I leapt at the chance.

From the beginning my ambition was to comb the ever-widening field of positive psychology research and theory for that most relevant to the challenges of leading, or working in, organizations. I wanted to combine that theory with examples of how it is being put into practice across the world, as people ask 'So what?' and play with 'What happens if … ?' I am blessed that so many colleagues, friends and contacts were kind enough to put pen to paper, and it is the unfailing support of the positive psychology and Appreciative Inquiry community that I wish to acknowledge.

Each contribution is clearly acknowledged in the text and details can be found on page xiii. My contributors have all been unfailingly patient with me as my ideas for the book have developed and so my ideas of what I want from them have changed. The text is immeasurably enriched by the generosity of my contributors who come from the UK, Australia, America, Canada, Italy, Poland, Spain, Holland, Sweden and the Republic of Ireland. I thank them all.

I wish also to thank my husband, Stewart Smith, who has provided the cartoons that appear in the text. Working to my very inexact briefs he has somehow managed to produce simple and impactful images that illustrate, with humour and wit, the points I am attempting to make.

My eldest son, Jem, also deserves my thanks for his extensive help with the part of the whole project that I find the hardest: the final detailed checking of text and referencing. He has been diligent in his efforts and any mistakes which remain are entirely my own.

There are a number of people who not only made contributions but who also took the time to read and comment on earlier drafts of various chapters. They are Clive, Martin, Ewa, Shannon, Helen, Mario, Ceferi and Karena. My grateful thanks go to them all.

I wish particularly to thank Clive Hutchinson who alerted me very early on to the danger of writing an over-referenced academic text that was of little interest to active and pragmatic organizational leaders. I hope I have successfully diverted the course of this book to avoid this outcome!

Karen Shield and Darren Reed of Wiley-Blackwell were kind enough to approach me to write this book and have been unstinting in their efforts to help me get it right.

The Short Version of This Book

To create positive and inspiring workplaces

1. Create a workplace that feels good.
2. Play to everyone's strengths.
3. Recruit for attitude.
4. Encourage positive deviation.
5. Build social capital.
6. Make sense together.
7. Be an authentic leader.
8. Create conditions for change.
9. Create reward-rich environments.
10. Be appreciative.

To learn how to do these things, read this book.

1

Introduction to Positive Psychology

Positive Psychology at Work: How Positive Leadership and Appreciative Inquiry Create Inspiring Organizations, First Edition. Sarah Lewis.
© 2011 Sarah Lewis. Published 2011 by John Wiley & Sons, Ltd.

Positive Psychology is Not Positive Thinking

This distinction is important, but unfortunately there is a certain amount of confusion about these two ideas. We shall first examine positive thinking to enable it to be distinguished from positive psychology, before going on to consider positive psychology in its own right. Positive thinking has a history all of its own, brilliantly traced by Barbara Ehrenreich in her 2009 book *Bright-sided: How the Relentless Promotion of Positive Thinking Has Undermined America*. This book traces the origin of positive thinking to a particular human malaise prevalent in the United States in the mid-nineteenth century, which took the form of unexplained fatigue and mysterious physical symptoms. It occurred at the time when a Calvinist doctrine of joyless, work-oriented, fearful, sin-avoidant living was in the ascendant. While this religious perspective and its accompanying prescriptions of hard work and sobriety contributed to, and supported, the work ethic that helped make the US the country it is, it also reduced the amount of positive emotions in life, such as hope, joy, passion, interest and happiness. From our perspective we might suspect this malaise to have been a form of depression.

The recommended cure was frequently complete bed rest without stimulation – no reading, no company, bland food and in a darkened room. With the benefit of hindsight we might question the wisdom of such a prescription. At the time few did until Phineas Quimby came on the scene. Quimby had little respect for the medical profession and set himself up as an alternative healer. He identified Calvinism as the source of the problem, arguing that it was oppressive guilt that was laying his patients low. He eschewed the depression-inducing prescriptions and instead developed a talking cure 'through which he endeavored to convince his patients that the universe was fundamentally benevolent' (Ehrenreich, 2009, p. 85). He suggested to his patients that they were essentially at one with this benevolent mind and that, through this power of connection, they could use the power of their mind to cure their own ills.

Such magical thinking, a belief that you can influence things by thinking, is not new. To anthropologists it is known as sympathetic magic and is prevalent in native, or unscientific, cultures; hence, perhaps, the close association between promoters of the benefits of positive thinking and shamanistic, Native American or other Native culture practices. Such an association isn't always benign. In 2010, three people died and 20 more were injured in a Native American steaming ritual run by self-styled spiritual guru James Arthur Ray (Harris, 2010). In addition to these sweat-lodge deaths, there is a history of people being injured by fire-walking, such as the 20 managers of the KFC fast-food chain in Australia who, in 2002, received treatment for burns caused by fire-walking (Kennedy, 2002). Again in July 2010 eight employees in Italy had to go to hospital with foot injuries from fire-walking, which were expected to take up to 10 days to heal (Hooper, 2010).

Sensible people try these forms of magical thinking or sympathetic magic because they offer hope and because they bypass other, harder routes to achieving what they want. But this isn't to say that, as with many things, there isn't some truth in it. Visualization does have an effect on human behaviour, but through the medium of our actions, not through the medium of the magic of our thoughts. It is unfortunate that positive thinking and positive psychology both contain the word 'positive' and that both make reference to the power of positive visualization. However, it is possible to distinguish the two fields.

How Positive Psychology Differs from Positive Thinking

The main difference is that positive psychology is subject to the rigours of scientific experimentation and endorsement, suggesting that the phenomena discovered are reliable and repeatable: if it worked in the studies, then under the same circumstances, it is likely to work again. Positive thinking deals more with the realm of anecdote and exhortation. It also takes up the tautological position that, if it didn't work, it's because you weren't positive enough (Ehrenreich, 2009). Positive psychology is about accruing a body of knowledge that is useful to people who want to live good, long, happy and productive lives, while positive thinking is about persuading people that what happens to them is their own fault. (Of course, this is usually presented in more upbeat fashion – that what happens to them is under their own control!)

Positive psychology literature can also be distinguished from positive thinking literature in that it accommodates the reality, and necessity, of negativity: it not only accommodates the reality of negative events, emotions, behaviour, and so on, but also recognizes their importance to human wellbeing. Negative emotions and outcomes are recognized and accommodated by positive psychology in at least three ways. First, within positive psychology there is a recognition that bad things happen to people through no fault of their own; there is such a thing as randomness. It is possible to live a life free from carcinogens (tobacco, alcohol, red meat or exposure to toxic agents) and still contract cancer at an early age. Bad luck if you will. Second, negative emotions can serve a useful purpose. Fear, anger, sadness, anxiety, stress, and so on are essential for alerting us to threats to our wellbeing so that we can do something about them. They are necessary to our survival. Finally, it is clear that some well-intended behaviour has adverse outcomes, due to a basic inability of people to understand all the causal relationships within which they operate. In other words, we are all susceptible to making mistakes with unforeseen negative consequences. That's life.

Positive psychology is further distinguished from positive thinking by the fact that it has 'body of knowledge' structures such as collegiate bodies, university departments, professors and rigorous accredited academic courses that work to collate and share information. It has all the paraphernalia of scientific discourse with peer-reviewed journals and academic conferences. Its practitioners apply to respected scientific bodies for research grants. Assertions made as fact can be checked, verified or refuted by others. People build on other's work and acknowledge their debts to them. Traditionally, within the scientific establishment this has meant that the discoveries made often remain within the ivory towers of academia, only seeping slowly into public consciousness. Now something different is happening.

Interestingly, in contrast to other lines of inquiry in psychology, and possibly in response to the changing world, the founding mothers and fathers of positive psychology undertook from the beginning to make a conscious effort to get the information they were gaining over the wall of the cloistered world of academia. They felt that what they were thinking about, learning about and discovering how to practise was too fundamentally important to human life to be isolated within a small closed community: the world needed to know. Accelerating the rate of transmission of knowledge from the specialist community to the general public is not without risk.

In attempts to make work more accessible to the public a fine line has to be trodden between the danger of 'dumbing down' the message and producing something in the style of an academic paper, with the attendant danger of discouraging potential readers by detailing the scientific journey in too great a depth. This is a point that Barbara Held raises in her critique of positive psychology, where she notes the over-reliance on a few key, and not entirely satisfactory, research events for statements of a causal relationship between happiness and longevity (2004, p. 16). Held also notes a lack of attention to mixed or contradictory findings and an emphasis on clear, simple messages for the public. Clearly, there are dangers associated with bringing an embryonic science to the public too quickly.

Such caveats notwithstanding, the field is demonstrating a commendable rigour in pursuing both an academic and a more general reading public. As I write a range of texts already exists. Those aimed at the general reader include, for example, *Positivity* (Frederickson, 2009), *Authentic Happiness* (Seligman, 2002) and *Now, Discover Your Strengths* (Buckingham and Clifton, 2002) – all aimed squarely and pragmatically at helping people improve their lives. Accompanying these on the positive psychology bookshelves are texts aimed more at practitioner or academic markets. These include *Positive Psychology Coaching* (Biswas-Diener and Dean, 2007), *A Primer in Positive Psychology* (Peterson, 2006) and *Positive Psychology in a Nutshell* (Boniwell, 2008) – all excellent integrated texts. For readers who like their academic information straight from the horse's mouth, there are rigorously referenced edited texts that pull together expert papers, most recently *The Oxford Handbook of Positive Psychology and Work* (Linley, Harrington and Garcea, 2010). High on academic standards, they are richly referenced and make for dense reading.

This book aims to complement the existing field. Working to bridge the gap between academic rigour and accessibility, it hopes to avoid the Scylla of dumbing down and the Charybdis of interruptive referencing. This text aims to offer a guided read through the science from this developing field pertinent to the challenges of running, leading, managing and working in a workplace organization. It aims to illuminate the science with useful anecdotes, practical examples, top tips and the occasional cartoon. In this way it aims to present a central argument that positive psychology can lead us to a new era of organizational understanding and practice. Much of the research comes from the US, which leads this field. However, the research has spread remarkably quickly and people all over the world are picking up these ideas and working on how to develop them. I have tried to incorporate examples of practice from Europe and the US and beyond. I have also tried to demonstrate how these findings are relevant to public and private, large and small organizations.

So this book needs to be read within a series of caveats: the science is young; it is more soft than hard science; there is an ever-present danger of over-eager interpretations of preliminary results; there is a tendency within the field to over-generalize and over-extrapolate findings; there can be a glossing over of the null hypothesis findings; and there are slips from established correlations to speculative causality. This text is not designed to be a critical academic text and I shall not be taking the reported findings from positive psychology and subjecting them to rigorous scientific criticism; that is a job for the academic community. Instead, I am offering the best information that is currently available about what seems to distinguish the more virtuous, beneficial, flourishing and inspirational workplaces from the average or worse, to boost your chances of ensuring that your practice within your organization promotes the best that organizational life can offer.

Many managerial texts seem to be written from an unquestioned position that what is good for the organization is good for the workers; that practices that increase productivity need no particular ethical justification. Little consideration is characteristically given to the impact on the worker. These books are written from a managerial perspective, where the unspoken aim is to get more, the best, out of employees. I have always felt slightly uneasy about this assumption and would be wary of adding a book to that cannon.

The Ethical Bias of This Book

The justification for this book, one that I also hope further distinguishes it from its positive-thinking cousins, is the clear reference to an ethical base. Cameron, Dutton and Quinn (2003), discussing their work on positive organizational scholarship, a sub-branch of positive psychology if you will, note that positive organizational scholarship is not value neutral:

> It advocates the position that the desire to improve the human condition is universal and that the capacity to do so is latent in most systems. (Cameron *et al.*, 2003, p. 10)

They also suggest that this school of organizational studies, while recognizing the importance to organizational life and survival of goal achievement and making a profit, chooses to prioritize for study that which is 'life giving, generative, and ennobling' (p. 10). In other words, they hold a firm belief that organizational life is neither inherently good nor bad. Rather, it contains the potential to be both and it is a worthwhile and ethical endeavour, in which they are engaged, to discover how to help organizations unleash their potential for good.

From a slightly less lofty position, I start from the observation that most people are obliged to earn a living by working in an organization. Given this, anything we can do, as psychologists, to help that experience be life-enhancing rather than spirit-deadening is a good thing. For all those hours on someone else's payroll, to add to the sum of good things in someone's life, to increase their sense of a life well lived and to enhance their capacity to experience positive emotional states are good things. So this book is not about trying to get more out of people in terms of hours or effort, although this is often a side-effect of a growth-enhancing working life, such may be the occasional benefits; it is about pursuing wellbeing at work as an ethical endeavour in its own right.

Throughout this text, then, you will find reference to the ethical basis for suggesting a particular practice or intervention. We shall be constantly referring to the bedrock science of positive psychology, which is about what it means to be a good person and to live a good life. A positive psychology-based understanding of aspects and elements of organizational life offers us an ethically viable choice about how to be leaders and managers. Without this compass we can get waylaid by the snake oil salesmen and find ourselves submitting our colleagues and workers to humiliating and even dangerous juju practices, as we saw earlier.

Ehrenreich suggests that one of the reasons why positive thinking-based activities took such a hold during the last years of the twentieth century was the undermining of the power of rational management techniques by the speed of change. It was no longer sufficient to accumulate a depth of knowledge of your organization and your business to prepare you for senior leadership. Your knowledge was too quickly outdated. Ehrenreich credits Tom Peters, of *In Search Of Excellence* fame (Peters and Wasserman, 1982), as one of the first to create the bandwagon of constant downsizing and renewal as he began to appreciate the speed of world change. And it is undoubtedly true that the world is, competitively speaking, a smaller place, that innovation offers a shorter market lead-time and that ideas spread at the speed of the internet. Does that mean organizations have to abandon any rationality in their attempts to manage or lead and resort instead to charlatanism and magical thinking to forge new paths? Is it possible to offer leadership based on authenticity, integrity and an ethical base, as well as detailed knowledge and skills? Increasingly, the research shows that this is not only possible but also productive.

There is an inherent paradox in a lot of the research in the area. Virtuous practices are consistently found to produce good results for people and organizations. Yet to simulate virtuous practices to produce the good results can lead to a lack of authenticity that is quickly detected and so undermines the intended outcomes. As John Lennon famously said: 'Life is what happens to you when you are busy making other plans.' So positive psychology suggests that good organization results happen to you when you are busy making your organization a good place to be. There is no shortcut. If you as a leader don't practise what you preach, don't live by the values you espouse for the organization, are unable to show humility as well as pride, sorrow as well as delight, then people will quickly spot the 'authenticity gap' and into that gap cynicism will flow. Entrenched organizational cynicism can undermine the best efforts at organizational improvement.

Key Themes of the Book

As I have researched and written this book a number of themes have emerged. These are threaded through the chapters. The reference to an ethical basis for science shared and advice given has already been mentioned. Throughout the book we shall be treating organizational change as an ethical and moral act.

You will also find continual references to the power of positivity, or 'feeling good'. It is worth reiterating that positivity is not a brand of positive thinking. It is not about pretending bad things don't happen or that people never feel down. Rather, it refers to the balance of positive emotions against negative ones in people's lives. It is becoming clear that this ratio profoundly affects both individual and organizational wellbeing. The more positive emotions are studied, the clearer it becomes that they are hugely important and powerful factors in human wellbeing. Interestingly, one of the most powerful approaches to organizational change, Appreciative Inquiry (Cooperrider *et al.*, 2001), which developed independently of the school of positive psychology (although they are now coming much closer together), incorporated an early recognition of the power of positivity in achieving organizational change: one of the key principles of Appreciative Inquiry is the principle of positivity.

Appreciative Inquiry is another theme that is present in this book, along with other whole-system interventions. When I started to write I didn't appreciate quite how much backing the research would give to the importance of thinking and intervening at a whole-system level in organizations. Yet time and again the implication from the research is that piecemeal, or linear, interventions are unlikely to be as successful as whole-system approaches. These are explained in more detail in Chapter 8, which was added to the original book plan as it became apparent that many paths of inquiry led to them as a practical way forward. The link is that these methods invariably build social capital.

The importance of social capital to organizational life and wellbeing is another theme. The terms 'social capital' and 'relational reserves' refer to the quality of relationships and interactions within the organization. They profoundly affect organizational capability. Key to building good reserves of social capital is an affirmative bias within organizational life, and the importance of this is another of the book's key themes. Together, these ideas – positivity, ethical actions, affirmative bias and whole-system approaches – hold out the exciting and tantalizing possibility of building sustainable, flourishing, inspirational organizations for the next stage of organizational development. Organizations are living entities within a living world. This means that we need to give up our ideas of organizations as dead machines and instead understand them as complex, adaptive systems.

Understanding organizations as complex, adaptive systems is the final unifying theme of the book, along with an important idea that stems from this way of viewing organizations, that of the value of ambivalence. Complex adaptive systems are explained in Chapter 2 and will be referred to as a frame of reference for understanding organizations throughout the text. The value of ambivalence has been another interesting discovery on the path to writing this book. Organizations have a tendency to regard clear, unambiguous statements and positions as the basis for strong, clear organizations. Increasingly, research is indicating that the best organizations incorporate, rather than attempt to banish, the ambivalence inherent in human life. At a fundamental level the existence within the brain of both an approach and an avoidance behaviour system (Pickering and Gray, 1999) suggests that we need ambivalence to survive. Organizations, it seems, also benefit from an ability to hold two opposing ideas, thoughts and approaches in their repertoire of behaviour. We explore this more fully in Chapter 4.

Given the collapse of the world financial markets following the unbri-dled pursuit of profit and the proliferation of unedifying unethical prac-tices, the time has come to take a look at the evidence suggesting that organizations can be built on virtuous and ethical principles and still be profitable and sustainable. This book brings together the various parts of the jigsaw of research, theory and practice from positive psychology and Appreciative Inquiry to explore how this can be achieved and sustained.

2

Positive Workplaces

In 2009 I ran a series of large group events at a manufacturing organization. The organization was about to introduce a new Enterprise Resource Planning IT system and needed to help everyone become aware of the changes in behaviour needed to get the best of the new system, particularly the need to enter very accurate data. The investment in this new IT was symbolic of a wider shift in the culture of the organization. One of the events we ran was a simulation of both the 'real' movements of goods through the manufacturing process and the 'virtual record' of these movements. Each part of the process – goods inwards, production, sales, pick, customer service, pack, assembly, planning and the client – had a stand in a large circle. Each stand was the equivalent of a computer terminal. They also had the kit needed to run the simulation: cardboard boxes, labels and a few specific bits of product. We had some people in another room who were the central processing unit (CPU): they were wholly dependent in their decision-making and planning on the data that came to them on cards about what was going on. In other words, they couldn't see what was physically happening. In this way we assembled all the disparate parts of the production process, normally spread out over a 42-acre site, in one, very long room. Now they were in a much better position to see the normally hidden patterns of interdependence.

We ran three rounds to simulate a three-month time period. Each round focused on effecting the delivery of an order from its receipt to the dispatch of the goods. However, between each round we introduced a 'glitch', a departure from procedure that would happen for the best possible reason. For example, we arranged for someone to 'borrow' some product from a location to solve the problem of an urgent order that was being fast-tracked. We arranged for

Positive Psychology at Work: How Positive Leadership and Appreciative Inquiry Create Inspiring Organizations, First Edition. Sarah Lewis.
© 2011 Sarah Lewis. Published 2011 by John Wiley & Sons, Ltd.

someone to 'solve' the problem of a lack of the exact specified product to fulfil an order by using some other product that could act as a substitute. All of these glitches were agreed by the planning team to be exactly the sort of immediate, local, pragmatic problem-solving activity that resulted in stock changes not being properly entered on the virtual system. If this sounds complicated, it was. One thing the planning team learnt in devising this event was how complex the links and problems were within the existing system of production. Our 'model' of the process for the exercise was highly simplified.

The exercise was a great success. Over the course of the three rounds the gap between the reality and the record grew as 'small' discrepancies led to further errors. By the end we had a CPU issuing production orders that production couldn't meet because the product was either not where the CPU insisted it was or, if it was there, the quantity was insufficient. We had people improvising like mad to try to make up orders and we had a customer threatening to take their business elsewhere as they got part or late deliveries. By the end of the third round very small errors in the computer information were about to result in the loss of an account worth £500,000 p.a.

The event was highly illuminating. Those present were able to see and experience how ad hoc *decisions that made good sense in their local context were highly damaging in the context of the whole. They could see how their small problem-solving decisions, if left unrecorded or uncommunicated, could escalate further downstream into huge problems and frustrations. They could see how if they didn't tell the computer exactly what they were doing, it would start to tell them to do things they couldn't do. They saw the connection between tiny daily decision-making in their areas and £500,000 worth of business. In other words, they gained a much deeper understanding of the systemic nature of the production system and its relationship to the virtual world of the computer system. Their mental model of the world changed significantly. At a deep level they understood the importance of ensuring that the computer system had accurate data, and of informing other parts of the production process about what was happening in their section that could have impact elsewhere. In terms of creating learning, heightening awareness and inspiring changed behaviour, it was a great success. However, the proof of the pudding would be in the eating when the new system came in.*

Various things happened after this that meant I didn't have any contact with the site for the next year. When I returned to the site on other business I bumped into one of the event planning team members, who is now on the troubleshooting team for the new IT system, which is now installed. Other changes have taken place on the site, including the merger of some workers from another site. He mentioned in passing that 80% of his time is spent sorting out problems with the workers who have come across from the other site, who only make up 20% of the total production team. I asked what these errors were about – had they had less training, for example? He thought it was about attitude. Workers from the other site weren't as engaged and willing to try to sort things out. They weren't as forgiving of the teething issues. They weren't as willing to work with the problems to ensure the data entered were accurate; they were more willing to blame the IT system. It would seem that the collective experience of discovering the interdependencies of the virtual and real system created a culture of shared awareness, engagement and ownership among the group we worked with that is delivering dividends now. By working together in a way that mimicked the way they would need to work together to successfully embed the new system, the exercise helped them create a positive experience of how things could be: creating a more positive workplace for themselves.

Introduction

In this chapter we explore what characterizes a positive workplace and the processes that create and support such cultures. We suggest that it is helpful to view organizations as complex adaptive systems and to view culture as organizational patterns of behaviour. We conclude by briefly outlining Appreciative Inquiry as an appropriate approach to creating positive workplaces.

What is a Positive Workplace?

What is a positive organization? Is it possible for an organization to be run and managed in such a way that it is good for people and good for business? What are the secrets of positive workplaces?

When Martin Seligman first coined the term 'positive psychology' in 1999 he suggested that this new domain would have three key areas of study: positive emotions, positive traits and positive institutions, the third being those where people flourish. At the time he identified as positive institutions democracy, strong families and free inquiry, which suggests he was thinking more of societal institutions than commercial organizations. However, a growing field of research known as positive organizational scholarship is developing which integrates positive psychology and organizational research. The particular quest of this field of research is to understand better the characteristics of the most positive workplaces. The key question they are investigating is: How does an organization within which people are able to flourish differ from those in which they merely survive, or indeed languish?

The best workplaces are defined as those that achieve exceptional organizational performance, that is, where outcomes dramatically exceed common or expected performance. In particular the researchers have studied organizations that recover exceptionally quickly from downsizing, or indeed escape altogether the negative consequences, outlined in Supplement 2.1. Gittell, Cameron and Lim (2006) found that these exceptional organizations behave in qualitatively different ways from their competitors before, during and after downsizing. In particular, it transpires that by their habitual behaviour they have built up a reservoir of social and financial capital, organizational resilience and goodwill that allows them both to downsize

---

Supplement 2.1   The Dirty Dozen Negative Effects of Downsizing

These are the commonly observed effects of downsizing on organizations.

1. Employee loyalty decreases.
2. Team work deteriorates, people feel more isolated.
3. Decision-making is pushed up the organization.
4. Many of the best people leave.
5. Morale declines.
6. Organizational politics and coalition formation increases.
7. Conflict escalates.
8. Both employees and managers develop a short-term orientation.
9. Experimentation and creativity decline.
10. Criticism, scapegoating and complaints directed at top management increase.
11. People are more resistant to change.
12. People are less willing to communicate openly and share information.

(Cameron *et al.*, 1987)

differently and to recover from the negative effects more quickly. At such difficult times they reap the benefit of having an abundance culture which they have nurtured and developed over time.

Three things make up an abundance culture: positive deviance, virtuous practice and an affirmative bias (Cameron, 2009).

1) Positive deviance

A positively deviant organization is one that is flourishing, benevolent, generous and honours people and their contributions. It is focused on creating an abundance of good and positive things (see Figure 2.1). By contrast, most organizations are primarily focused on preventing bad things from happening, on narrowing the deficit gap rather than building the abundance bridge. This distinction is subtle but highly significant. All organizations want excellence, but it is how they go about trying to achieve it that makes the difference. Organizations with a deficit orientation are focused on achieving consistency by solving, or preventing, errors and inefficiencies; they aim to maintain a minimum standard. Organizations with a positive deviance orientation, while not ignoring problems, focus on growing towards excellence and exceptional performance; they aim to exceed a normal standard. Organizations that display positive deviance are likely also to display a high level of virtuous actions and practices.

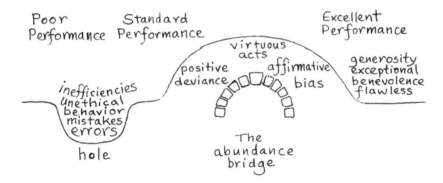

The Deficit Gap and the Abundance Bridge

Figure 2.1 Abundance bridge.

2) *Virtuous actions*

Virtuous actions have a positive impact on others and are undertaken regardless of reciprocity or any reward beyond that which is inherent in the act. Acting virtuously might be helping a stranger in difficulty, forgiving someone who has done you wrong or offering wise counsel even though you won't benefit from the outcome. Increasingly, research is demonstrating how good it is for us to behave in these ways towards others. Take forgiveness: the ability to demonstrate forgiveness is associated with broader and richer social relationships; a greater sense of empowerment; better health; faster recovery from disease; and less depression and anxiety. Being compassionate, fostering hope and optimism, and acting with integrity have similar benefits (Cameron, 2003).

A key factor in bridging the abundance gap is the presence in the organization of lots of virtuous interactions, such as being helpful to each other and generous, sharing information and forgiving people when they make mistakes. These individual acts can be encouraged and supported by virtuous organizational practices such as strengths-based performance appraisals and appreciative ways of working. Many examples of such practices are given throughout this book. A culture characterized by these benevolent and forgiving processes allows people to be fully themselves at work, so they don't need to put as much effort into defending themselves against unjust accusations or into justifying mistakes, fearing they won't be forgiven. Energy instead goes into working out what went wrong and how to improve things. When known for their strengths, people can acknowledge their weaknesses rather than trying to disguise them for fear of being found lacking. The contrast between a workplace characterized by these ways of interacting and the perhaps more familiar context where weaknesses are exposed and criticized is evident. It seems such positive ways of behaving are not only good for us but are also good for business.

Cameron and colleagues found that the perceived level of virtuousness (trust, optimism, compassion, integrity and forgiveness) in an organization is positively correlated with the perceived performance (innovation, quality, turnover and customer retention) of the organization. In addition, this perceived performance is positively correlated with more objective measures of organizational performance, such as the profit margin. This finding effectively means that organizational virtuousness and performance are positively related (Cameron *et al.*, 2004). More recently, in an investigation into the financial services sector, 45% of the variance in six measures of financial performance was accounted for by the implementation of positive practices, again supporting the strong relationship between virtuous behaviour and business success (Cameron and Mora, 2008). In another very important study, the speed and robustness of a return to financial viability in the airline business after the destruction of the World Trade Center on 11 September 2001 were found to be significantly related to the virtuousness of the downsizing strategies (Gittell *et al.*, 2006). We look at this fascinating research in more detail in Chapter 5. Taken together these results point to an unexpected finding: virtuous processes are highly correlated with excellent business performance. One form that virtuous organizational practice might take is to emphasize growing strengths rather than correcting weaknesses. This practice would also be an example of the general affirmative bias displayed by these flourishing organizations.

3) Affirmative bias

To have an affirmative bias means focusing on the best rather than the worst. Organizations that display an affirmative bias demonstrate an emphasis on strengths, capabilities and possibilities rather than threats, problems and weaknesses. Clive Hutchinson's account (in Supplement 2.2) illustrates the positive effects for individuals and organizations of cultivating an affirmative bias. Every element of organizational life can reflect this bias: leadership, relationships, communication, meaning, energy and organizational climate (Cameron, 2008a). Such an affirmative bias doesn't discount or exclude negative events – as we saw in the introduction, positive psychology as a whole recognizes the importance of negative events and emotions to human experience – rather, it is that affirmative organizations have a way of incorporating negative events without being pushed by the threat they pose into a typical simplistic and rigid response (Cameron, 2008b). Such responses can come into play remarkably quickly when a traumatic event occurs, as I experienced when I worked as a residential social worker.

One evening, when I was off-duty, an adolescent unit where I worked had a very bad night. It was described as a riot. Furniture had, reportedly, been picked up in threat. I went to work the following morning to find a serious proposition that the furniture in the lounge somehow be secured to the floor. This is a typical, simplistic and rigid response to a negative event. We know that in the face of negative emotions people's choice of action narrows right down; their ability to process complex thought is

Supplement 2.2   Highlighting Successes

We have come to learn the power of highlighting the successes of our people, how acknowledging the great things people do every day makes them feel better about themselves and better about us as a company. I remember being very struck a couple of years ago when someone who had recently joined the company told me how different the email messages were compared to his previous employer's. He said that in his previous company all the messages from managers to staff were about the need to improve, highlighting mistakes that must be avoided in the future and blaming people for things that had gone wrong. He compared this to the messages he saw at Cougar Automation, which all seemed to be celebrating successes, praising people and thanking people.

Now, I recognized his description of his former employer. We used to be like that too. But somehow, as we've changed our approach to running the business, the nature of these messages has changed. I remember one of the earliest conscious changes we made to achieve this was in our team briefing meetings. In these meetings everyone in an office gets together and managers talk about what is going on, as well as plans for the future. Pretty standard stuff and something we had been doing for a long time. But what made the difference was when we asked managers to base their briefing on praising their team members. So, when they planned what they were going to say, instead of making a list of things that were happening in their area, they made a list of what individuals had achieved. The result was that they still talked about what was going on, but the focus changed from activities to people and their achievements.

At about the same time a great trainer called Peter Taylor taught us about a playing card model for giving feedback. Clubs was just telling people they had done badly, with no reasons. Spades was negative feedback but with specific information on what was bad. Hearts was praise, but without saying specifically what was good. And Diamonds was praise with specific information about what was good. This simple model revolutionized our approach to positive feedback. Previously, many people had said they disliked giving positive feedback; it felt false. Through this model we realized why. Naturally, we had been trying to give 'Hearts' feedback: simply saying things like 'that was great work'. When we started to experiment with Diamonds feedback things changed dramatically. Before giving the praise we had to ask ourselves what specifically was good in what the person had done before we could say something like: 'I thought the way you asked the customer exactly what she wanted worked really well.' It was harder to do because we had to stop and think, but instead of feeling uncomfortable about giving praise, we now felt good about it. Not only that, but we started to appreciate more the great things everyone did every day. Just by taking the time to notice how people did things, we started to see how good they were.

Contributed by Clive Hutchinson

much reduced. For those shocked and scared by the events of the previous evening securing the furniture to the floor appeared to be the only right response. In this instance the furniture was not screwed to the floor although it took a lot of work to help both the staff directly affected and those infected by the negative emotions of the affected staff to see how this negative-emotion-driven, short-term response would only make matters worse and that there were alternative, effective ways of proceeding. On a grander scale Her Majesty's Revenue & Customs' response in 2007 to the revelation that a huge database of personal data had escaped into the public

domain was to ban the use of USB sticks or non-authorized computers on their premises. Since people routinely used USB sticks or their personal laptops to increase their flexibility at work, this simplistic and rigid response reduced work performance at a stroke. Organizations with a strong affirmative bias are better able to avoid this kind of rigid threat response.

How Does Positive Organizational Behaviour Turn into Positive Organizational Performance?

The virtuous practices, affirmative bias and positive deviance associated with flourishing organizations are increasingly being recognized as a cause rather than an outcome of abundance. In other words, while it might seem likely that organizations that are 'doing well' can afford to be virtuous in their dealings with their staff and community, it increasingly looks as if it works the other way round. Through the work of Cameron, Fredrickson and others, we are beginning to understand the processes at play that create this association between positive organizational behaviour and performance. Virtuous behaviour in particular is associated with three positive outcomes: it helps to create positive emotions; it makes people more likely to help each other; and it creates social capital. In turn, it seems there are two key processes that convert virtuous, positive orientation into abundant performance. These are the creation of virtuous circles of positive emotions among groups of people, and the creation and accumulation of social capital in organizations.

1) Upward virtuous circles of positive emotion

Virtuous acts produce positive emotions, that is, doing good makes us, and the recipient of our action, feel good. Feeling good in turn has two positive effects: it makes us more likely to do good and it increases personal wellbeing. Interestingly, this virtuous spiral of feeling good and doing good can also be triggered by observing others being exceptionally generous, helpful, humble, self-effacing or wise. An entire organization can be influenced in a positive way by such virtuous behaviour, especially when it is displayed by leaders. Recently, many leaders at KPMG in the UK volunteered to take a 20% pay cut to help with the organizational wage bill during the economic recession, some still working full-time. This clearly virtuous behaviour contrasts sharply with the more common scenario during an economic downturn of wage cuts and pay freezes being imposed on the lower orders, while the bonuses-as-usual scenario continues to play out at the top. KPMG is consistently voted one of the best places to work in the *Sunday Times'* Best Companies Annual Awards. Such an accolade from staff is an expression of a high level of social capital in the organization.

2) Social capital

Social capital is a term used to refer to the value within the social networks of the organization. It reduces transaction costs through the trust in the network. Trust is both priceless and frequently much undervalued. Social capital creates a platform that allows speedy, coordinated, responsive and flexible action or reaction. It facilitates communication and cooperation, it enhances employee commitment and fosters individual learning. It strengthens relationships and involvement, and ultimately enhances organizational performance (Alder and Kwon, 2002). Positive interpersonal relationships are a good sign of the presence of social capital. Virtuous acts help to create social capital. People are attracted to virtuous actors, they want to join them and build on each other's contributions. Organizations function better when people experience trust and feel positive towards each other. Social capital is a great asset during difficult times.

With high levels of social capital come organizational resilience and solidarity. Together, high levels of social capital and virtuous practices help create a buffer against the negative effects of trauma. On an individual level, they act as inoculation agents against psychological disorders, addiction or dysfunctional behaviour, while at an organizational level, they help organizations to remain connected, optimistic, proactive and effective. Virtuous acts and social capital add their organizational value through the interactions of individuals. Ceferi Soler's account of the Mondragón Corporation in Spain helps to illuminate the connections between positive behaviour and organizational performance (see Supplement 2.3). By considering how the actions of individuals can affect organizational performance we are starting to engage with the idea of organizational culture. Figure 2.2 illustrates the connections between organizational behaviour and performance outcome in an abundance culture. Organizational culture is a hugely important idea that creates as much heat as light when we are attempting to understand organizations. It is helpful to understand organizational culture as a collective phenomenon that can be collectively influenced.

Supplement 2.3 Mondragón: A Sustainable Virtuous Business

Introduction

Mondragón Corporation was founded in 1957 in the Basque country in Spain at the instigation of Father José Maria Arizmendarrieta. Mondragón Corporation is made up of 130 functional cooperatives in Spain, elsewhere in Europe, Asia and Brazil. Together, they employ 90,000 people in the industrial, retail, financial, insurance and educational sectors.

Over the last 20 years we, at the Escada Business School in Barcelona, have found it an invaluable case study of a virtuous organization. At our Business School we study their practices, values and competences which make up their corporate culture. Interestingly, the founder never had a direct hand in the running of the cooperatives he helped set up, yet his philosophy, based on democracy, empowerment, self-reliance and positive influence between the employees, has been developed throughout every one of the functional cooperatives.

What Makes it Different?

Virtually all of the leaders we interviewed at Mondragón spoke about their belief in their fellow human beings. Several noted that, as young workers, mentors had demonstrated faith in them beyond the faith that they had in themselves. These appreciative leaders are now replicating that behaviour in working with their employees.

They are strongly values-driven. This is an authentic congruence of belief, values and action. The employees recognize every year the power of the positive inquiry, seeking answers from what has worked and developing the best in people.

Mondragón promotes members' economic participation and ownership: members, on being hired by a cooperative, lend a set amount to the cooperative's capital: €15,000. The dividends that accrue from their shares of the capital are reinvested in the cooperative. Members can only cash in their dividends when they leave or reach retirement.

Mondragón has a policy of wage solidarity that imposes a maximum pay differential of 6 : 1 between the top and bottom of the pay scale. The average CEO in the US makes 531 times as much as the average blue-collar worker (O'Reilly and Pfeffer, 2000).

How Successful is it?

Despite the fact that competition and economic efficiency are not the primary purposes of Mondragón it has still managed to succeed as a business in terms of survival and growth with sustainability. The various cooperatives were federated in 1988 under Mondragón Cooperation. It is a co-coordinating body for all the worker-owned cooperatives in the Basque community, which include a research company, a technical college and private university, a cooperative savings bank and a network of supermarkets.

How Does it Work?

The management model is based on Team Appreciative Leadership. There is a belief that leadership capabilities reside in the team and not in the designated leader. There is an explicit acknowledgment that individuals alone do not have all the answers. The teams are working in the affirmative bias model of values and competences as 'Envision, Inspire, Holistic and Collective discovery of the way forward' with the awareness that this worldview is not only about being inclusive; it is also good business, and has been since 1957.

What they do there is nothing except trust the community and the cooperation within it.

Contributed by Professor Ceferí Soler

Organizational Culture

In April 2002 I was in a room with about 70 other facilitators being trained to deliver a two-day leadership development programme for what would be the largest UK Government department. This department had been newly created by the merger of two separate departments. The programme was to be delivered to 100 people at a time. One of the stated aims was to create culture change. The plan was to help the new department be people- rather than paper-oriented, customer-focused rather than status-conscious and creative rather than hidebound. To this end we were going to deliver a series of events across the country that would touch every manager in the new department.

We had finished the training and were moving on to the logistics of delivery when the internal team suddenly realized they hadn't addressed the problem of allocating facilitators to specific events. Clearly, it made little sense for us to be criss-crossing the country at random, but they had failed to ask us where we were all located. Their response to this was highly illu- minating: 'We'll email you all to ask where you come from. Then we'll go

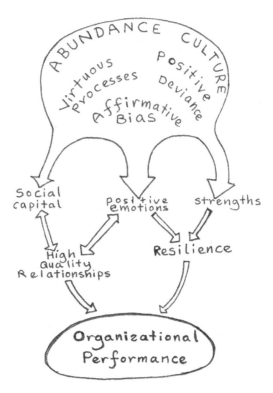

Figure 2.2 Abundance culture.

away, set up a spreadsheet and work it out.' I had a suggestion. Since we were all there, we could organize ourselves by location, each corner of the room being a compass point, and then write a note of who was in each corner and their place of residence. Job done. This bit of self-organization was thought to be a risky and difficult idea but worth a try, so I labelled the corners of the room and issued the instruction. Initially, it looked chaotic as people decided on where to position themselves, forgot which corner was which and found themselves in the wrong place. Quickly though, as I knew it would, the confusion resolved itself into order and the job got done. It was responsive, fast and effective, the very behaviour the organization believed it wanted to increase. It was also messy and relied on self-organization rather than command and control organization: it was these factors that ran so counter to the institutional way of doing things.

"Don't panic I'm a facilitator!"

What struck me so forcibly at the time was that the people within the organization, with the best will in the world, were unable to step outside their usual way of doing things even as they were working to change the culture. The culture was so powerful and exerted such an influence that even the people keenest to bring about change were unable to escape it; they found themselves bound by the very culture of which they were part. The essential paradox has remained with me since and I have observed it many times: the impossibility of using the current culture to introduce a new one. For example, it is not uncommon to find, as here, a bureaucratic organization using bureaucratic means in an attempt to reinvent itself as a dynamic, fleet of foot, entrepreneurial entity, or to find an organization with a fire-fighting culture working to introduce a more farsighted, strategic, calm culture through a burst of frenetic, all-hands-to-the-pump activity. It seems we cannot act outside of the cultural milieu of which we are part, but this doesn't stop us trying. What is it about culture that seems so resistant to change? Is it possible to step outside the culture of which you are part? Can something new be created by the existing culture?

On one level organizational culture is a simple concept expressing a widely shared understanding of the 'feel' of an organization. We can quickly pick up the feel of any particular organization and contrast it with others in which we have worked or that we know. We have shorthand expressions that work to capture the essence of the organizational cultures we encounter most frequently. For example, we talk of 'a can-do culture', 'a blame culture' or 'a bureaucratic culture'. At the same time, culture is a complex, paradoxical and slippery concept. It is intangible, yet you can bump up against it. It is a faint background hum that conveys loud and clear messages about what is and isn't permissible. It has a big impact on all attempts at organizational change, yet is highly resistant to change itself. The study of self-organizing natural systems has begun to offer some ideas, by analogy, on how culture might be created, maintained and changed in organizations. These systems, such as the eco-system of the African savannah or the cellular organization of a body, are known as complex adaptive systems and they throw a very useful light on the nature of organizational culture.

The Organization as a Complex Adaptive System

The study of complex adaptive systems from the natural world, systems such as swarms of bees, flocks of birds or herds of animals, has illuminated how the group as a whole and its members are influenced by, and influence, each other. Pursuing questions such as 'How do birds flock?' and 'How do bees swarm?' has led scientists to investigate how individual elements act within the context of the whole. For example, how do individual birds act within the bigger context of the flock or bees within a swarm? Flocking occurs when individual birds fly together in such a way that they form a discrete entity, what we call a flock. The remarkable thing is that they do this without any lead bird directing each bird's individual action. They do it without bumping into each other, while maintaining similar speeds; and they do it in close proximity. Indeed, they perform rather like the Red Arrows' flying formation, except that there are a lot more of them and they don't get 10 years' specialized training. How do they do it?

Close observation suggests that they achieve these feats of coordination by adhering to some very simple rules in their local environment: each bird makes moment-to-moment decisions by following these few behavioural guidelines in its own immediate context. Through computer simulations these have been identified as being: try to maintain a minimum distance from other objects in the environment, including other birds in the flock; try to match your velocity with that of other birds in your proximity; and try to move towards the perceived centre of the mass of birds. In computer simulations where dots on the screen follow these instructions, the visual results look remarkably like flocking behaviour (Reynolds, 1987). It seems that in complex adaptive systems, individual birds behave as if they were following these rules, and the result is the graceful behaviour of flocking birds.

Some important features of complex adaptive systems

1) Emergence
In this way flocking is understood as an emergent phenomenon from the behaviour of a mass of individual birds acting in concert and in context. What is interesting about this idea of emergence – the idea that the flocking behaviour emerges from very different individual behaviour – is the dual nature of influence. The emergent phenomenon, flocking, is created by the individual actions of each bird, yet the individual action of each bird is influenced by the emergent phenomenon of the flock. They form a complex adaptive system. Viewing the organization as a complex adaptive system gives us a means of understanding how people create culture and how culture affects people. Thinking of the organization as a complex adaptive system, we can view people as independent agents and organizational culture as an emergent phenomenon they collectively create.

In this way, complex adaptive systems offer a wonderful analogy of how culture operates in organizations and so allows us to explore how organizational culture might, by analogy, grow, develop and change. It suggests that organizational change is not due to planned change or leadership choice, but to changes in the nature of the interaction and relationship between people. It suggests that as the interactions between people change, so does the organization. Working with this analogy we might suggest that organizational culture is the emergent global phenomenon created by people behaving in recurring patterns in a local environment, and that the organizational culture created by this in turn influences each individual's behaviour at a local level. Viewing organizations in this way makes it clear that no one agent is in control of the system's evolution, whatever their job description might say. Rather, the control lies in the patterns of the system. Change the patterns of the system, which is achieved by agents simultaneously mutating their patterns of interaction, and the system changes. Complex adaptive systems contain both change and stability in their evolutionary pattern.

2) Consistency and change
Effective complex adaptive systems feature both a degree of consistency and an ability to adapt. For example, the flock consistently flies around the

features found in the environment, yet it adapts its behaviour to the inconsistent nature of these features, which means the pattern of each bird's flight, and the flight path of the flock, are different every time to achieve the same result: avoiding bumping into things. It is the patterns that emerge from the individual agents' behaviour that have both sufficient consistency and stability to be a reliable phenomenon, and yet contain enough diversity to be adaptive. These patterns contain both stability and change. It is interesting here to note the ambivalence contained by the system. It is neither stable nor changeable: it is both, prioritizing each feature at different times. The ability to contain ambivalence has been demonstrated to be very important to adaptive behaviour in human systems, a point we return to in more detail in Chapter 4. Here, we can note that learning, growth and change in the system come from changes in the simple rules each agent follows in its local environment. As the local rules evolve, so does the system. If the rules change, the system changes. Change occurs at a local level due to the micro-diversity contained within the system. Nature contains variety. A slight chance change can lead to system learning. System learning means a shift has taken place in the understanding of the world: we might say a new mental model of the world has emerged.

3) Mental models and system learning

A change in the pattern of the behaviour of the system is accompanied by a shift in the mental models the complex adaptive system holds of the world: understanding the world differently, the members of the system therefore behave differently in it. There are many examples from the natural world of changes in the complex adaptive system's mental models. For example, flocks of seagulls no longer only look for food in the sea: they seek it out behind tractors or on landfill sites. Indeed, there is even a suggestion that they are learning to snatch it from the hands of small children on the beach. Clearly the seagull system's mental map of the world has expanded to include new sources of food. Essentially, of course, this is what we call learning. If mental models don't change, learning doesn't occur. Mental models, or maps of the world, change when interactions with the wider system change: as we have different experiences, so we learn to view the world differently and so we are inclined to act differently. This was the kind of learning experienced by the participants in the simulation described at the beginning of the chapter. Learning and change are about our experience in the world. Learning can be an inefficient process, for it involves trial and error, and stepping into the unknown. For a system to have the facility to accrue this adaptive learning, it needs some built-in redundancy.

4) Usefulness of redundancy

A counterintuitive notion that arises from considering organizations as complex adaptive systems is that redundancy, as in duplication or overlap of effort or resource, is very important to the organization's stability and resilience, particularly at a time of great change. Complex adaptive systems need a certain amount of redundancy. This stands in stark contrast to the normal organizational emphasis on efficiency and the striving to achieve the minimal duplication or overlap in organizational roles, tasks and boundaries. For example, my process for establishing the geographical origin of 70 facilitators was highly redundant: everyone was involved in solving the problem, there was a certain amount of milling around in circles and no one could really focus on achieving anything else. One could say it involved a major duplication of effort. How much more efficient, one might say, to have one person focus on solving that issue and to have everyone else work on something different. Consider, though, how much less effective, how much less adaptive to the challenge in hand, such a solution, as was originally proposed, would be. By all moving at once we created new patterns. By changing our physical pattern of relationship we produced new system information immediately.

Efficiency is all about reducing redundant effort. In my experience this clash between an unquestioning ideological acceptance of the virtue of efficiency and the inbuilt redundancy necessary to change whole systems is one of the more durable obstacles to managers and leaders being able to engage with processes such as Appreciative Inquiry or Open Space. They see them as inefficient. It is not necessary to get all those people off the line at once, they argue. There are more efficient methods, for example using representatives. But if the pattern of the whole system is made up by all the individuals, then changing the whole system, the objective with culture change, requires that all the agents be influenced and influence what is happening. It is through the recurring patterns of organizational life that we can have influence on organizational culture. However, when organizational culture change first gained ascendancy, this point was missed. It is useful to review the history of the idea of organizational culture as it helps to explain some of the persistent errors encountered as organizations attempt to positively influence their culture.

Supplement 2.4　Key Points from Considering Organizations as Complex Adaptive Systems

- Change comes from changing the patterns of interaction amongst members.
- Ambivalence is an important system feature for adaptive behaviour.
- Mental models of the world, borne from experience, are key to behaviour.
- Redundancy is a virtue in complex adaptive systems.

What an organisation becomes emerges from the relationships of its members rather than being determined by the choices of individuals. (Stacey, Griffin and Shaw, 2000, p. 123)

The concept of organizational culture entered mainstream organizational study and theory in the early 1980s. Peters and Wasserman's *In Search of Excellence* (1982) was a huge bestseller with its key finding that a strong culture, among other things, distinguished the best from the rest. At the same time, Pascale and Athos (1982) published *The Art of Japanese Management: Applications for American Executives* and Deal and Kennedy (1982) offered a comparative analysis of organizational cultures in *Corporate Cultures: The Rites and Rituals of Corporate Life*. These books fostered enthusiasm among organizations to emulate the apparently successful cultures identified in the texts. At this time 'creating a new culture' became the leading edge answer to the perennial organizational challenge of maintaining a competitive advantage. And so a thousand culture change programmes were launched. While some undoubtedly were successful, many clearly weren't, with some research suggesting 90% of culture change efforts were unsuccessful (Carr, Hard and Trahant, 1996).

Organizations discovered that trying to change their culture was hard, took a long time and did not guarantee results. My suggestion is that many organizations failed to achieve their desired goals because they were focused on culture as a form rather than as a living process. In effect they thought that if they looked like one of these successful organizations, they would be like them. So they imported the water-coolers and the standing meetings and the open-plan office without understanding that it was the organiza-

Supplement 2.5   Why Culture Change Efforts Often Fail

- They regard culture change as a shift in state from state A to state B.
- They work with surface form rather than deep patterns.
- They fail to fundamentally shift people's experience of the world and so their mental models.
- They are limited by existing world beliefs in the system.

tional processes and the patterns of interaction that enabled these features to function so well, not the features that created the organizational processes. What often happened was a reversion to established behaviour: water-coolers languished in rarely traversed corridors; people learnt to bring chairs with them to the meetings (which ran on as long as ever) to spare their tired legs; and office dividers proliferated to recreate the fondly remembered individual workspace. If a pattern emerges it is that leaders are often very keen to change their organizational culture, and that it is an exceptionally hard outcome to achieve.

Why is Culture so Hard to Change?

Our understanding of organizations as complex adaptive systems offers some clues as to why culture change programmes so often fail to deliver the culture change required. We have seen that it suggests that behaviour in a system is predicated on the mental models held by its members: as we understand the world so we act into it. These models, or maps of the world, are constructed from past and present experience and from both personal and shared experience. They also contain projections of the future, what we expect to happen when we act in a certain way. They create a sense of predictability. The group must have a different experience of the world, experience the world differently, if their mental maps are going to adapt. Simply being told about the need for a new culture is not normally sufficient to change established worldviews or organizational patterns and dynamics. Frequently, the mental models in place are sufficiently robust that the group is able to absorb the regular announcements of dynamic culture change plans into its experience of the world and to adapt to them within the existing organizational dynamic. In some organizations this means such announcements result in a flurry of paperwork which is largely ignored, while in others a positive storm of passionate rhetoric and hot air is released; meanwhile nothing really changes.

Culture is created, maintained and transmitted through the social dynamics of the group, suggesting that the focus for change needs to be on the social dynamics of the organization rather than on the formal structure. An emphasis on changes of surface phenomena, such as uniforms, letter-heads, value statements, strap-lines or seating plans, will not impact on these patterns that hold the culture in place. Or rather the patterns will strongly reassert themselves in the face of expected change. For example, an organization may arrange itself so finance and marketing now share an open-plan office space in the hope that they will work more closely together. But if no other work is done and they still hold antagonistic views of each other, then it is likely that their views will only be reinforced by the evidence of the other group's misdemeanours to which they are now exposed on a daily basis. Indeed, the relationship problem may worsen rather than improve. The surface picture has changed, but the recurring patterns of belief and action have barely been touched. Culture change is not an easy fix.

How might an organization work to achieve change at this deep level of patterns of interaction, relationship and communication? Recently, a number of large group change processes have been developed that work with the organization as a complex adaptive social system (see Supplement 2.6). These approaches recognize and respond to a need to affect the whole pattern of organizational life, not just parts of it. They all recognize that sustainable development is embedded in changes to the deep patterns of interaction. They recognize that achieving change at this level requires a different experience of the world. (The essential difference between these change approaches and more conventional change approaches is explored more fully in Lewis, Passmore and Cantore, 2007.) Essentially, the difference is that these changes are focused on the interactions between people rather than on producing change in specific individuals *per se*. It is when the pattern of organizational life is brought into focus and exposed to different experiences that a sustainable change in ways of relating is achieved.

Cameron's work, discussed earlier, illuminates the nature of the processes and interactions that characterize flourishing organizations: they are virtuous, encourage deviation in a positive direction from the normal

Supplement 2.6   Some Large Group
Approaches to Change: In Brief

Appreciative Inquiry

Focuses on illuminating hidden resource in the organization to enable it to imagine and create more resourceful futures. Appreciative Inquiry works through the power of appreciation, inquiry, story, imagination, positive emotion and group dynamics. It is a highly versatile approach which can be incorporated into all aspects of organizational life. It is often run as an event known as an Appreciative Inquiry Summit.

Open Space

Focuses on directing energy to good purpose in conversation to create a large amount of movement on areas of organizational life in a short amount of time. Open Space works through the power of interest, dialogue and self-organization. It is a very scalable approach which can be used when you want high quality discussion and decision-making.

World Café

Focuses on discursive, exploratory and creative or generative conversation that allows nuances, hidden solutions, resources and perspectives to combine to create new ways forward. World Café works through the power of inquiry, connection, attention, mindfulness and conversation. World Café produces high quality exploration and consideration of areas of organizational life from a carefully structured process.

Future Search

Focuses on connecting the past, present and future to create common ground for diverse groups connected around a topic to find fruitful ways forward. Future Search works through the power of commonality, story, inquiry, connections, conversation and a particular emphasis on ensuring that energy is directed towards areas of agreement, not sidetracked in the irresolvable.

See Further Reading at the end of Chapter 8 for where to find more on these and other approaches.

towards the exceptional and affirm all that is good in the organization. These findings fit very well with the suggestion from complex adaptive systems theory that it is the daily patterns of interaction that make up organizational culture. These might be small personal things, such as how, or even whether, we greet each other in the morning, or they might be larger organizational processes, such as how we do performance management. Together these influence, and are influenced by, the organizational culture.

The ethics of attempting to change organizational culture

Before going on to consider Appreciative Inquiry (Cooperrider and Whitney, 2001) as an approach to organizational change, we might take a moment to remind ourselves that change is a moral act. A deliberate attempt at organizational change is not a value-free consequence of logic, although it is often presented that way; it is a moral decision. Inherent in any idea of change, or enhancement, is the idea that something is better than something else: it involves judgements of good and bad, right and wrong. Attempting to influence organizational culture is a moral act: we are acting in an attempt to make things better. The decision of what is good or right, what signifies an improvement, is a moral judgement. Judgements about culture are precisely that, human judgements. We are wise to involve all actors in this deliberation since none of us has a monopoly on moral or ethical judgement. Appreciative Inquiry does this and is particularly well suited to the challenge of creating positive workplaces. One approach is to use Appreciative Inquiry to help the organization recognize and build on its existing positive core of values, strengths, resources, positive experiences, relationships and abilities. In this way the positive workplace culture can be grown from the inside out rather than being unsuccessfully imposed from the outside in.

How to Create Positive Workplaces

Appreciative Inquiry is a positive change methodology that helps organizations identify the root causes of their success, release the positive potential of the organization and its processes and create positive change. As the positive core becomes more visible and acknowledged, it grows in strength, allowing negative elements or weaknesses to be rendered increasingly irrelevant and impotent. By liberating positive emotions such as joy, passion, excitement and pride, and by creating conscious images of a better future based on an expansion of the existing positive core, Appreciative Inquiry creates an impetus for action that can transform organizations. It offers a methodology that perfectly matches method to outcome: it is a positive change methodology for growing a positive workplace. No one is telling the organization 'how' to be or how to build a positive culture; it is finding out for itself. There are many books that explain how to do Appreciative Inquiry in some detail; these are cited at the end of the chapter. I have included here the key principles (see Supplement 2.7) and the 4D

Supplement 2.7   Principles of Appreciative Inquiry

- The **anticipatory principle** is about the power of imagination to pull systems towards attractive futures. When we create a picture of the future that is imbued with our energy, aspiration and hope, we are drawn to do things that make the realization of that future more likely. It refers to the inspiring and directing effect of a powerful dream.
- The **positive principle** refers to the power of positive emotional energy to sustain change. Fredrickson's work is increasingly demonstrating the capabilities, capacities and energy created and released by people, and particularly groups, experiencing positive emotions.
- The **constructionist principle** reflects the importance given to the joint making of meaning. This is a reflection of the understanding of the organization as a complex adaptive system, created and enacted by those within it. It is based on an understanding of the social world as being socially and collectively constructed by those who form it.
- The **simultaneity principle** encapsulates the idea that things happen together: to change the pattern of relating is to change the system. This reflects a complex adaptive system understanding of organisations with its patterns of recursive dynamics.
- The **poetic principle** notes that an organization is a living human system where communication and conversation are the fabric of the organization.

(Cooperrider and Whitney, 2001)

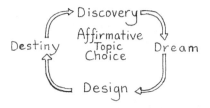

Figure 2.3   4D model.

methodology (Figure 2.3) for easy reference. In addition, we make reference to Appreciative Inquiry throughout this book, but in particular in Chapters 6 and 8. Below, James Butcher's work with a London borough illustrates how collecting and creating images and stories of the organization at its best reveals the values that form the positive core of the organization; and how this allows an attractive future to be built on the best of a successful present and past, with commitment and enthusiasm (see Supplement 2.8).

Supplement 2.8   The Borough at its Best

A local authority wanted to translate the abstract nouns of their statements of vision and values into a more tangible picture of their aspirations for the area and the communities they served. And pictures are exactly where we started: a week before we were to work together, each member of the Cabinet and the Corporate Management Team was given a disposable camera and asked to take photographs of what for them represented their borough at its best.

When we gathered together, each person displayed their photos and explained what was important about them. There were pictures of people and buildings and open spaces, and stories to go with them, of how the photos came to be taken, some planned, some fortuitous, and of what the pictures represented.

People then shared stories of when they had experienced the council's values in action. We wanted examples, no matter how small, of people working just as the vision and values challenged them to do. We asked the group to think about the factors that made these examples of success possible: 'Good to look at positive achievements for a change', commented one participant.

The group then began to identify themes that described what seemed to be significant in the photos and the stories they had shared. From these themes came statements capturing the essence of the borough at its best, statements that were both a celebration of existing strengths and successes, and an aspiration for living those strengths and values more fully. The power of such statements lies in the collaborative process through which they are derived, and in the knowledge that each element can be traced back to a tangible experience of success. As one person observed: 'This has given us a greater sense of working together.'

The next stage was to identify ways of bringing their picture of the future to life: what changes needed to be made to the organization, to its structures, processes, roles and relationships? What did they need to do more of, give greater emphasis to? What were the offers, commitments and requests each person would make as their contribution to change?

In reviewing the session there was a strong sense of a different atmosphere to the day – a refreshing sense of celebrating success rather than focusing on shortcomings. The Leader described the session as 'a hugely positive experience', while the Chief Executive described it as 'a creative, collaborative day'.

Reproduced by permission of James Butcher

Summary

In this chapter we have reviewed Cameron and colleagues' research into what makes flourishing organizations successful. We have considered how viewing the organization as a complex adaptive system helps us to understand how organizational culture is held in daily patterns of interaction, relationship and communication. We have considered why many attempts at culture change fail to achieve deep-rooted change. We have noted that any attempt at producing change is a moral act and needs to take place within a clear ethical frame. We have suggested that Cameron's work on flourishing organizations and Cooperrider's work on appreciative organizational change offer a suitable ethical frame. We have noted that Appreciative Inquiry in particular works in an affirmative way with the organization, recognizing it as a complex adaptive social system.

Further Reading

For more information on complex adaptive systems and organizations:
Stacey, R. D., Griffin, D. and Shaw, P. (2000) *Complexity and Management: Fad or Radical Challenge to Systems Thinking?* London and New York: Routledge.
This is a dense and highly informative book, theoretical and academic in tone.

For more information on Appreciative Inquiry:
Lewis, S., Passmore J. and Cantore, S. (2007) *Appreciative Inquiry for Change Management: Using AI to Facilitate Organizational Development.* London: Kogan Page.
This is a well-informed practical 'how to' text, written from experience.

Cooperrider, D. and Whitney, D. (2001) A Positive Revolution in Change: Appreciative Inquiry. In D. Cooperrider, P. F. Sorenson, Jnr., T. Yaegar and D. Whitney (Eds.) *Appreciative Inquiry: an Emerging Direction for Organizational Development.* Champaign, IL: Stipes.
This is a great resource of original papers and case-studies.

For more information on Cameron's work on positive leadership and positive organizational scholarship:
Cameron, K. (2008) *Positive Leadership: Strategies for Extraordinary Performance.* San Francisco: Berrett-Koehler.
This is an inexpensive, practical paperback offering guidance on how to be a positive leader.

Cameron, K. S., Dutton, J. E. and Quinn, R. E. (Eds.) (2003) *Positive Organizational Scholarship; Foundations of a New Discipline.* San Francisco: Berrett-Koehler.
This is a collection of academic papers in this area.

For more information on large-group change methods in general:
Holman, P., Devane, D. and Cady, S. (2007) *The Change Handbook: The Definitive Resource on Today's Best Methods for Engaging Whole Systems.* San Francisco: Berrett-Koehler.

3

Positive Engagement and Performance

As a naïve 16 year old I got a temporary Saturday job in Boots the Chemist in our local town. One of the regular full-time employees was a woman called Dot. She was old enough to have grandchildren and had worked on her feet in retail most of her life. Dot was a confirmed smoker. Dot was also tired. Dot didn't believe in unnecessary energy expenditure.

Dot could get me to do anything for her, for example, running to find things in the stockroom; stacking the low shelves so she didn't have to bend down; covering for her while she spent 10 minutes having a cigarette in the toilets. I didn't mind at all; in fact, I was only too pleased to do these things for her. Why? Because she knew how to make me feel good about myself. Because she allowed me to feel helpful. Because she enabled me to feel competent and strong. Because she was appreciative of these small things I did for her and it was obvious the appreciation was genuine: I could see it in her face. Because, although she could order me to do things, she never did. She always asked, 'If you've got a moment and don't mind, could you possibly …?', to which I would invariably reply with a willing 'Of course'. Because she said 'Thank you', as if I had done her a favour when I had only done what the job demanded. Dot was an excellent supervisor who knew exactly how to get the best out of me.

A life in retail was not for me. A few months later I happily gave it up to revise for exams. Yet in my brief time as a Boots Saturday girl Dot worked miracles in helping to make the endless, repetitive challenge of keeping the shop stocked and the customers served relatively engaging and enjoyable.

Positive Psychology at Work: How Positive Leadership and Appreciative Inquiry Create Inspiring Organizations, First Edition. Sarah Lewis.
© 2011 Sarah Lewis. Published 2011 by John Wiley & Sons, Ltd.

Introduction

In this chapter we shall look at positive engagement at work and explore the research to see what it has to say about what facilitates positive engagement. We shall also look at the impact on engagement of the rewards available to employees in a particular context. We shall look at the impact of the manager on engagement, particularly their skill (or otherwise) in setting goals and creating motivation. We shall also outline some strategies the research suggests individuals, organizations and leaders can employ to assist engagement. Along the way, we shall consider such questions as: What is an engaged employee and what makes one? Is it good for people to be positively engaged in their work? How much difference does it make to your business if your employees are engaged? What makes engagement at work more or less likely? How can we encourage engagement at work?

Employee engagement is rapidly becoming a key focus of human resource activity. There is a growing realization that the returns on ensuring that present employees are giving of their best might be greater than those accruing from the costly process of recruiting new, shinier employees. There is mounting evidence that the level of employee engagement makes

Supplement 3.1 Some Benefits of Positive Engagement at Work

- On average engaged employees take fewer than three days a year sickness leave (actively disengaged average more than six days a year).
- On average there is a 4% difference in employee turnover between organizations in the top and bottom quartiles on employee engagement. This may not sound much, but it equates to $120,000 per business unit per year.
- Employees who are most committed perform 20% better and give a 57% increase in discretionary effort.
- A one-point (on the measurement scale) increase in employee commitment can lead to a *monthly* increase of $200,000 per store.
- There is a 2.9% difference in customer satisfaction between organizations in the top and bottom quartiles on employee engagement, equating to millions of dollars of sales revenue per organization per year.

From Stairs and Gilpin (2010)

a huge different to organizations' effectiveness, profitability and productivity. Stairs and Gilpin (2010) found evidence that employee engagement is positively related to wellbeing and attendance, employee retention, effort and performance, quality, sales performance, income and turnover, profit, customer satisfaction, shareholder return, business growth, and success (see Supplement 3.1 for more detail). It's little surprise then that working out how to engage employees is rapidly becoming an organizational holy grail. There is certainly room for improvement as it is estimated that currently only 19% of employees are highly engaged in their work (Stairs and Gilpin, 2010, p. 162). Before considering these exceptional few, we might ask what the other 81% are doing?

In his book *The Living Dead* David Bolchover (2005) has brought together research showing that the estimated 19% of employees who are actively disengaged, and probably some of those 62% neither actively engaged nor disengaged, spend their time *at work* taking drugs (1 in 3 workers), having sex (1 in 5), accessing internet pornography sites (70% of these hits occur during working hours), visiting theme parks (1 in 3 midweek visitors is 'off work sick') or constantly surfing the net (1 in 5). This disengaged activity is costly to organizations. Gallup estimated in 2003 that it cost the UK economy between £37.2bn and 38.9bn a year (Flade, 2003) and there is no indication that things have improved since then. Neither organizations nor national economies can afford to lose this kind of income.

Active Engagement at Work

There is no universally agreed definition of employee engagement. However, Britt and colleagues have defined it as 'feeling responsible for, and committed to, superior job performance, so that job performance matters to the individual' (2007, p. 144). This seems adequate, conveying as it does a sense of focus, emotional investment, effort and a concern for outcomes. When engaged in our work we are more likely to feel good and competent, and to have a sense of belonging. We are also more likely to have a sense of control and of being able to make things happen (Bateman and Porath, 2003). In other words, active engagement is associated with positive feelings that have physiological and long-term benefits. By its association with positive emotions we can say that it is a beneficial state for individuals, and therefore there is no moral dilemma in promoting it.

The various definitions of employee engagement all agree on two key things: that engagement resides with the person not the job; and that it is a state rather than a trait. This means that the level of engagement will vary among individuals in the same job, and that for any one individual their level of engagement will vary from task to task and from day to day. Within a particular job or role any individual is likely to find some aspects of the job more engaging than others and will be more engaged on some days than on others. It also means that greater engagement at work can be developed, the question being not whether but how. One of the findings that is emerging from positive psychology research is that being able to use unique strengths and talents at work makes a huge difference to the likelihood of being engaged at work.

Strengths and Talents

1) Seligman's character strengths

One of Martin Seligman's earliest positive psychology research interests was character strengths. He wanted to create a taxonomy of strengths that would act as a counterweight to the taxonomy of human frailty developed over the postwar years: the extensive categorization system for mental dysfunction or illness known as the DMS (*Diagnostic and Statistical Manual of Mental Disorders*, fourth edition (DSM-IV)). Having recruited Peterson, they researched extensively across human history and culture to identify aspects of human character consistently recognized as inherently worthy, virtuous or good. It is their view that there is a discrete number of human character strengths that are acultural, ahistoric, universal and quantifiable. At present they have identified 24 virtues under six character strengths which fit their criteria (Peterson and Seligman, 2004).

Almost everyone has some character strengths. Signature strengths are the positive traits that a person owns, celebrates and frequently exercises. Research in this area suggests that knowing your signature character strengths and using them frequently are the path to a fulfilling life. Some strengths, such as zest, hope, curiosity, gratitude and love, positively predict happiness and life satisfaction across the lifespan (Seligman, 2006). We might all do well to cultivate these strengths. Meanwhile, it has fallen to other researchers to examine the relationship between strengths and work in more depth.

2) Gallup's talents

For over 25 years Gallup researchers have focused on identifying the factors that lead to management success. Their most important finding was that successful managers do not treat everyone in the same way. Indeed, they do the opposite: they treat everyone as a unique individual. And the point of this attention is to identify each individual's unique talents and to make sure their job fits those talents. Consciously or otherwise they invert the normal order of things where a role exists and a person must be found, or made, to fit it and instead focus on moulding and creating jobs to fit people, or on moving people to jobs that fit them better. This isn't the only factor that distinguishes the most successful managers, but it is one of the most significant (Buckingham and Coffman, 2001).

In contrast to Seligman's idea of a finite and strictly classifiable system of strengths, the Gallup group regards talents as almost infinite. They define an individual's talents as their 'unique and natural gifts' (Hodges and Asplund, 2010) the important point being that talents, more than skills or knowledge, form the basis for consistently high levels of performance and achievement. With development investment a talent can be transformed into a strength, which is defined as 'the abilities to produce near perfect performance on a specific task' (Hodges and Asplund, 2010, p. 213; Rath, 2007). Strengths, according to the Gallup group, are a composite of skills, knowledge and talent.

Talent is seen as behaviour that is an expression of our brain 'wiring'. As we mature, our brains become uniquely wired as a result of our original genetic endowment and subsequent experience. Any thought or action that we experience repeatedly develops into a well-trodden groove in our mind. This is a low resistance neural pathway, that is to say, electrical brain signals can travel along the path quickly and smoothly. For our purposes we can think of these pathways as the things that are very easy for us to do.

More controversially, these researchers suggest that greater performance improvement at work comes from the further development of an already existing talent than from rectifying a weakness. Their argument is that if we haven't developed a particular facility to a certain level by adulthood, we are unlikely to get much return on our efforts to improve. Science backs this up. It is clear that our brains are much more active at developing and growing new connections before we reach adulthood. Amazingly fast when we are young, our brain growth rate progressively slows down, except for a late spurt in adolescence, reaching its mature state around the early twenties. Initially highly flexible and fluid in its development, our brain pattern progressively solidifies. We continue to develop more connections but at a slower rate. The core, we might say, of our unique brain design is in place by the time we are young adults, and the suggestion is that we are better off devoting our energies to working out what we have and how best to use it than trying to fundamentally change it.

Their research, like Seligman's, demonstrates that we feel much better in ourselves when we are using our talents or strengths. This is partly because using our strengths or talents is clearly related to success, achievement and performance, but also because it is related to feelings of positivity. When we are doing what we do best, we feel good. Struggling to do things for which we have no aptitude or which don't play to our strengths is often at best uninspiring and at worst demoralizing. Another way of looking at it is to say that using our strengths or talents is a life-enhancing experience, while working against them frequently produces a 'losing the will to live' feeling.

We can use this to help us identify talents. Buckingham and Coffman (2001) very helpfully suggest that an indication of talent can be that which you almost cannot *not* do. In other words, the expression of a talent is so easy it is not only effortless, it is almost irresistible. I, for instance, have to stop myself interfering every time I'm waiting in a queue and I hear people misunderstanding each other. I itch to help by (for want of another way of expressing it) facilitating their conversation. The urge is strong and physical: I notice it and consciously have to override it. I have a friend who no sooner arrives at my house than she is tidying things up and away. She barely knows she is doing it. Mostly I appreciate this, but on more than one occasion it has caused some friction. In this way shall we know our strongest talents.

There are other clues. Hodges and Asplund suggest that areas of talent are indicated by a sense of yearning to do something. They describe it as 'an internal force that leads one to a particular activity or environment time and again' (2010, p. 214). Similarly, rapid learning reveals talent through the speed at which one anticipates the steps of a new activity, acquires a new skill or gains new knowledge. We all have friends who join in a sport we have practised for years and who in no time at all excel at it or who can pick up any instrument and get a tune out of it. Another clue is the sense of satisfaction we experience when successfully meeting challenges that engage our strongest talents. When we are using our talents we feel energized. And when we are engaged in exercising our talents we often lose the sense of time passing; if we are 'clock watching' we are probably not exercising our talents.

3) Linley's performance strengths

However, talents alone are not enough to ensure good performance; we need to develop them into strengths to get the best from them. Linley's excellent book *Average to A+* (2008) presents a performance-oriented view of strengths that seems to pull together the best of the ideas that emerge from the two approaches outlined above. He defines a strength as 'a pre-existing capacity for a particular way of behaving, thinking or feeling that is authentic, energizing to the user, and enables optimal functioning, development and performance' (p. 9). He accepts Seligman's strengths as universal strengths, and then suggests that humanity has also developed niche strengths, of which he and his team have identified over 100. He suggests that any individual is likely to possess elements of both and that, while there may be a finite number of strengths, how they are expressed is infinite, as each person brings a unique combination of strengths, experience and personality to any particular context.

Linley characterizes most organizations' development activity as resulting in 'the curse of mediocrity', which suggests that mediocrity is the best that can be expected from the overt focus so many organizations put on addressing their employees' weaknesses while ignoring their strengths. He notes how this curse of mediocrity is present in schools as pupils are encouraged to devote their energies to scraping grades on their poorest subjects rather than spending the time on the subjects they love. This orientation continues at work, supported by competency frameworks that suggest everyone should be equally good at everything. Linley suggests an alternative approach to organizational development, based on identifying and building strengths (see Supplement 3.2). This approach is likely to have the benefit of improving engagement as well as performance.

Linley is very clear on the three-way relationship between strengths, engagement and authenticity. It seems that this sense of authenticity, being the real me, relates to the ease of use of brain pathways. Using the well-established pathways in our brain correlates with feeling natural, good and right – what we call authentic. And being authentic is good for us, for it is

Supplement 3.2   The Fundamentals of the Strengths Approach

The Approach

1. Focuses on what is right, what is working, what is strong.
2. Recognizes strengths as part of our basic human nature; therefore, every person in the world has strengths and deserves respect for their strengths.
3. Believes our areas of greatest potential are in the areas of our greatest strengths.
4. Believes we succeed by addressing our weaknesses only when we are also making the most of our strengths.
5. Believes using our strengths is the smallest thing we can do to make the biggest difference.

How to Spot Strengths

These are some of the signs of when you are using a strength. A sense of energy and engagement when doing certain things:

*   losing the sense of time passing;
*   very rapid learning;
*   repeatedly successful performance;
*   good completion on tasks;
*   an attraction towards certain tasks; and
*   a real pleasure in performing some tasks.

From Linley (2008)

associated with enhanced wellbeing, better health, reduced psychological distress, better relationships, greater self-esteem and higher levels of happiness, gratitude, emotional intelligence and positive energy.

Like other practitioners in the area, Linley notes that strengths can cause difficulties if they are unrecognized and underused (and also if they are overused). Indeed, he notes that an unacknowledged strength is often a source of frustration; if we have a particular strength in something, it comes as a constant surprise to us that others can't do it just as well as we do! At the same time, an unrecognized strength overplayed can cause unintentional or unhelpful results. I remember watching one young man during a discussion in a development centre becoming so animated about a point he was making that he was almost crawling across the table in his attempts to connect with the other side. His voice was loud, his gestures expansive, his face alive and animated. I saw enthusiasm, albeit rather over-played; the other assessors saw aggression and intimidation. In feedback I suggested to him that his unbridled enthusiasm to communicate was overpowering in some settings, so he might need to conceptualize a control knob he could use to turn his enthusiasm to communicate up or down. In a hall of a 100 people the performance we had just seen would be electrifying, but to a small group with no escape it was intimidating. He needed to adjust his expression of this aspect of himself accordingly. Linley also uses this analogy to help people understand that they need to dial their strength up or down to achieve what he labels 'the golden mean', that is, 'the right strength, to the right amount, in the right way, at the right time' (2008, p. 58), as we can see in his account (Supplement 3.3) of how he helped David gain control of his perfectionist strength so that it was an asset at work and unobtrusive at home.

The evidence is mounting that when people are able to use their strengths they are more likely to be engaged, energized, authentic and feel generally at their best; at the same time it is becoming clear that taking a strengths-based approach is profitable as well as pleasurable (see Supplement 3.4). Linley suggests that realizing strengths can be seen as the smallest thing that is likely to make the biggest difference to workplace performance because of its positive impact on so many aspects of sustainable improvement (see Supplement 3.5). This concept of realizing strengths, as well as that of active engagement, links to intrinsic motivation. Intrinsic motivation is the idea that we do things because we enjoy doing them rather than because we are being motivated by some external factor, such as a parent's approval, a pay bonus or the chance of a seat on the board of directors. When we are

Supplement 3.3   Perfectionism – But Not Done Perfectly

There is always one person who stays in my mind when I think about the golden mean of strengths use. David was one of the members of the SMT at a large aviation company and was responsible for keeping aircraft flying. As someone who flies regularly, I appreciate that. So I wasn't too disappointed to find that David was an absolute perfectionist when it came to his job – in fact, I was downright pleased. When somebody is responsible for something so critical, something that is literally a matter of life and death, it's good to know that they're obsessive about getting it right, by making sure that everything is perfect.

David's challenge, however, was that while that was fine at work, it wasn't fine at home. At work, he had been rewarded and promoted for making sure that everything was perfect and this recognition had fed his obsession. At home, however, when he opened up, it was a different story. His wife could never live up to what he expected of her and his children suffered in the same way. Their grades were never the perfect list of A*s which would have told him there was nothing more they could do; they were not winning every sporting event they entered; they were not the beacons of the school which David would clearly have liked, even expected.

Yet as we spoke, it was clear that David recognized this, in some ways, for the dysfunction that it was. While his perfectionism was great at work, it wasn't what he – or his wife and children – needed at home. He was struggling, though, because it had become so hard-wired in his working life that he had lost sight of how to turn it off.

'Turning it off' is a common misconception about strengths overplayed. It can be a real challenge, because it feels like we have to stop doing the thing that has helped us to be successful – and that seems like a disastrous step, undermining everything that we have worked so hard to achieve.

But dealing with strengths overplayed is not about 'turning it off' – rather, it's about 'turning it down'. We think of strengths as having a volume control – you can turn them up or down according to the situation. This idea of a volume control transforms how we can think about strengths overplayed, because rather than being an 'on/off', 'yes/no' decision, it becomes a 'how much?' calibration.

This simple recognition transformed David. He suddenly saw that he didn't have to stop being a perfectionist at work in order to stop being a perfectionist at home. (If he did stop at work, I'd probably stop flying!)

Instead, he could turn his perfectionism dial right up at work, because that was what the situation needed – that was his role and what he was rewarded for doing. But at home, he could be different. He could turn the perfectionism dial down and give his wife and children some slack. He started enjoying them for who they were, letting go of the unrealistic pressures and expectations that had distorted his experience of them until now. In doing so, he transformed his home life and changed his own life massively for the better.

David started to see things more clearly, making the right judgements about what needed to be perfect and what didn't. In this way, and using the golden mean of strengths use, he could recognize that what was right for one situation wasn't necessarily right for another, and to know – and practise – that difference. The difference for David was, quite simply, transformational. He became an even better leader at work and a far better husband and father at home. As these two areas of his life worked out more of an appropriate balance, he was happier than he ever had been. A lot of the pressures and frustration melted away, and David grew into the exceptional individual he had always strived to be.

Key elements of this case study have been changed to protect anonymity.

Contributed by Alex Linley

Supplement 3.4   Evidence of the Benefits of Strengths-Based Working to Organizations

An employee whose supervisor focuses on her strengths is over 2½ times as likely to be engaged as one whose supervisor focuses on her weaknesses (Rath, 2007).

Hodges and Asplund (2010) analysed some of the extensive Gallup data and found:

- Among employees receiving some strengths feedback turnover rates were 14.9% lower than for those employees receiving nothing.
- Those units where managers received strengths feedback showed 12.5% greater productivity post-intervention compared to those units where the manager received nothing.

Continued

Supplement 3.4 *Continued*

• Among those employees receiving a strengths feedback, productivity improved by 7.8% compared to employees who didn't.

Harter, Schmidt and Hayes (2002) found that work units that offered their people a higher than usual opportunity to use their strengths everyday were significantly more engaged, which was linked to a strong likelihood of better performance on customer loyalty and employee retention and productivity.

The Corporate Leadership Council showed that focusing on performance strengths increased performance by 36.4%, while focusing on performance weaknesses made performance decline by 26.8%.

Supplement 3.5   The Smallest Thing to Make the Biggest Difference

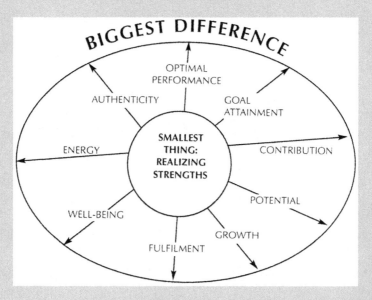

Reprinted courtesy of Alex Linley from, Linley A. (2008)
From Average to A+: Realising Strengths in Yourself and Others.
Coventry, UK: CAPP Press

intrinsically motivated to do something, it is probably related to the opportunity that it offers us to use our strengths and experience a state of flow.

Flow

Flow is a term used by Csikszentmihalyi (2002) to describe the state experienced by people when they are so fully engaged and absorbed in what

Supplement 3.6 The Flow State

The flow state is characterized by a number of things:

- There is high concentration, a complete immersion in what we are doing. The concentration becomes like breathing; attention is focused on a very limited area.
- There is a temporary cessation of the concerns and anxieties of daily life.
- There is a sense of control; a freedom from worry about failure.
- We are likely to forget about ourselves; being lost in the moment, unselfconscious of what others may think. We might lose awareness of hunger or aching muscles.
- There is a sense of transcendence, of having moved beyond our limitations.
- There is a distortion of time: a minute lasts forever, an hour passes in a flash; we exist in an extended present.
- The goal of the activity is to do it.

Certain conditions make the experience of flow more likely:

1. There is clarity about 'in the moment' goals, for example the next note to be played, ball to be hit, sentence to be spoken or concept explained. The long-range goals – for example, finishing the song, winning the game or concluding the session – aren't why one is performing the task.
2. There is an immediacy of feedback – for example, a good or sharp note, a successful or otherwise return, a look of enlightenment or puzzlement.
3. What can be done and what one can do are in balance: there is a more or less one-to-one ratio between challenges and personal skill.

they are doing that time ceases to matter, any sense of self-consciousness or ego disappears and the person and the activity become as one. It is a highly rewarding state, although emotionally neutral, for which some people will risk life, health and career to achieve and repeat. Consider, for example, mountain climbers who can only account for their obsession with the explanation 'because it's there' or artists who neglect to eat or sleep, caught up in the challenge of their creation. While most of us may not be caught up in these extremes, we will have some activities that give us the chance of experiencing flow.

Flow can be achieved in one of two ways. Sometimes activities are structured to induce flow: music, games, sports and rituals tend to work like this; and some people can induce flow regardless of the external conditions. There are stable individual differences in the ability to experience flow, and developing the skill starts young. Flow is good for us. It has been demonstrated that flow experiences have physiological correlates: the smile muscle is active (although the smile may not be visible), breathing is deeper and more even, the heart rate slows and blood pressure is reduced (Csikszentmihalyi, 2010). Flow is inherently connected to growth: as we achieve mastery at one level of the activity, we need to stretch ourselves to the next. The experience of flow correlates with the personality trait of perseverance and with the state of mindfulness.

Mindfulness

Mindfulness is about the conscious directing of attention. Entering flow is largely a function of how attention has been focused in the past and is being focused in the present. Interests developed in the past will encourage us to notice opportunities in the present for exercising our skills against enticing challenges. In this way we can begin to see the relationship between flow, mindfulness and strengths: our pattern of attention over the years contributes to our strengths pattern; together they contribute to experiences of flow and when I am in a flow state I am also in a state of mindfulness. Our opportunities to experience being engaged, use our strengths or experience flow at work are highly influenced by management activity, usually designed to increase work productivity, particularly goal setting.

Management Influence on Engagement and Productivity at Work

Much management activity is devoted, intentionally or not, to manipulating the context in such a way as to encourage employees to be productive. Managers work to control the contingencies that operate in a particular context in an attempt to influence behaviour. So they try to control what happens when a person achieves their targets, when they are late to work or when they spend too long talking rather than working. Contingencies are about the relationship in the environment between what is going on, what people do and what happens next. It is through experiencing contingencies that people learn about the world. So at a simple level, when I am thirsty after playing sport (what is going on), I turn the tap (what I do) and water flows for me to drink, which relieves my thirst (what happens next). If taps never produced water, I would soon give up turning them when I'm thirsty.

This basic relationship translates to work situations. If, after I have produced a report and am keen for appreciation of my effort (what's happening), I go to my boss (what I do) and the report is lying on the desk unread or it returns with nothing but corrections (what happens next), I shall soon learn not to look to my boss to get my need for appreciation met. These local workplace contingencies are highly important and influential. We know that people's decisions to stay in or leave jobs are based on their assessment of their job against four criteria: first, they want an interesting job; second, they want to be fairly paid; third, they want to know if they are growing or progressing; and fourth, and most importantly since it massively affects the others, they want a good quality, local work environment (Harter and Blacksmith, 2010). The assessment of the local work environment is essentially an assessment of the contingencies operating in that environment, which are very dependent on the behaviour of the local manager.

Most managers have very little understanding of their influence on the quality of life of their employees and consequently on their intention to stay or go, never mind their levels of positive engagement at work. They also have very little understanding of the power of contingencies to influence behaviour and engagement. Instead they rely on the power of instruction to influence those around them. Daniels (2000) estimated that managers spend about 85% of their time telling people what to do or deciding what to do because employees have not done as they told them. Telling people what to do is rarely sufficient to get them to do it, especially if the contingencies operating in the area support different behaviour. To influence behaviour positively we need to make sure the contingencies in play support what is required. The most favoured organizational technique for attempting to align behaviour and consequences is goal setting. However, using goals effectively to encourage engagement and performance is not as straightforward as half-day courses on setting SMART goals might lead us to believe (Lewis, 2008).

Goal Seeking

Before examining goal-setting behaviour in *organizations*, I want to review goal-seeking behaviour in *organisms*. To do this I want to introduce some important neuroscience research that underpins much of what we shall consider later. This research has revealed, among other things, that the brain contains two behavioural systems: a behavioural activation system and a behavioural inhibition system (Pickering and Gray, 1999). These can be characterized as approach and avoidance systems. They are independent of each other and only one can be activated at any one time. Differences in the responsiveness of these systems in individuals go a long way to explaining reliable behaviour differences, which in essence are what we know as personality differences. For example, it seems possible that extraversion may be related to patterns of activation of the behavioural approach system and that neuroticism may be related to differences in the activation of the behavioural inhibition system (Patterson and Newman, 1993). These two systems also help to explain differences in our day-to-day patterns of behaviour. These daily patterns are an expression of our accumulated learning about the world: its rewards and dangers. Our past experience affects what we find engaging and what we recognize as a rewarding goal. It also affects what we experience as punishing. Our accumulated learning about the punishing aspects of life is reflected in the activation of the behavioural inhibition system.

1) The behavioural inhibition system

Typically, the behavioural inhibition, or avoidance, system is activated by encountering new things or by encountering things known to be punishing or non-rewarding. In other words, we are inclined to treat unknown new things with caution and are inclined to withdraw from things we know to be painful, punitive or frustratingly non-rewarding. If we generally experience our environment as frustrating, punitive and prone to sudden surprises, we are likely to be more inhibited in our behaviour. This literally means our behavioural repertoire shrinks: we do less. An observer would note more caution, more restricted patterns of behaviour, less innovation, less exploratory behaviour and a slowness of response to new things, as we stick to behaviour and environments known to be safe.

2) The behavioural approach system

The behavioural activation or approach system is, in turn, activated by reward or by release from a punitive situation. This suggests that if we believe our environment to be essentially safe and rewarding, we will be inclined to exhibit more behaviour, especially goal-seeking behaviour. An observer might note that we are more active in seeking and exploring, more interactive, more communicative and quicker to respond to new things in the environment. We are active in our environment, seeking to achieve our goals, and we are willing to push the boundaries of our knowledge to do so. We will venture beyond the known repertoire of what it is safe to do and where it is safe to go. Goal-seeking behaviour can be thought of as reward-seeking behaviour. To understand this we need to understand something about how achieving our goals becomes rewarding, and how rewarding experiences become goals.

At a basic level all organisms have life-oriented goals – essentially, to survive and to reproduce. This basic drive for life is expressed in a number of important recurring goals, to find food, shelter, water, a social group and a mate, for example. These are known as primary goals and reinforcers: achieving them is inherently rewarding and so reinforces the likelihood of us repeating the behaviour that led us to them. In almost all societies these needs are now negotiated through the medium of money, and if not, through barter. I don't wish to discount romantic love, of course, or fellow feeling, however we are talking here in evolutionary terms. Through the possession of money we can meet these life goals: put food and water on the table, rent a home, woo a companion, do things with friends.

We get money from working. However, contrary to the prevalent belief among managers, generally on a moment-to-moment basis we aren't working for the money. We turn up for the money. But we work, or not, for far more immediate goals and far more immediate rewards. These immediate goals are likely to be rewarding because they have become conditioned reinforcers by association with primary rewards. Over a lifetime most people acquire many conditioned reinforcers, or things they find rewarding, and therefore will actively seek to achieve.

Remember the glow you experienced as a child when you got a gold star, a Brownie or Cub badge or a tick on your work. In themselves these things have no value, they are not inherently reinforcing or rewarding. But they become rewarding through association with things that we do find inherently rewarding: approval, affection, social bonding, status, chocolate, pleasure, love, and so on. In time, through their association with these other things that give us a warm glow of good feeling, they also give us that little glow of feeling good. Most parents understand instinctively how this works, making a big fuss of a child who does something of which they approve. The child quickly learns that this wins a lovely fuss and so comes running, 'Mummy, mummy, I got a gold star today!' in anticipation of the cuddle and delight that is their reward. As the association becomes stronger the gold star acquires some of the properties of the hug and delight: it makes us feel good. We start to want to get more gold stars and to work to achieve them. These conditioned reinforcers can be very powerful: we work to achieve them; they are motivating; their achievement is both a goal and, upon attainment, a reward.

Goal Setting

We talk a lot about *goal-setting* activity in organizations and perhaps don't pay enough attention to *goal-seeking* behaviour in people. There is no point in setting goals for someone unless that someone is motivated to seek that goal. We need to know, for each individual, what activates his or her goal-seeking behaviour. Most managers don't pay enough attention to any particular individual's learnt reward systems. If they did, they would be better at creating reward-rich environments for them. When a person is in what they perceive to be a reward-rich environment, they are likely to exhibit reward- or goal-seeking behaviour. This, I would argue, is the definition of the engaged employee. People are engaged because they are experiencing rewards. And because they are experiencing rewards, they are engaged.

We are just beginning to understand something of what constitutes a rewarding experience (as opposed to a rewarding outcome) for an indi-

vidual through studying the state of engagement and the state of flow. It is all a bit circular: when we are engaged we are finding something rewarding in some way; when we are finding something rewarding we are likely to be engaged in it. The pattern of goals, rewards and engagement is going to be different for everyone: a unique crystallization of their genetics, their experience and learning, their thought patterns and strategies, and the environment. All this means that using goal setting to enhance employee engagement and performance is not as clear-cut as it may seem. At the very least some types of goals have been shown to be more likely to elicit improved performance than others.

1) Approach goals

First – and these findings accord with the research we have just examined – there is a difference in the behavioural effects of avoidance goals and approach goals. An avoidance goal might be 'I don't want to be sacked', while an approach goal might be 'I'd like to be promoted'. Approach goals are associated with higher levels of striving and aspiration, with greater performance and mastery and with higher levels of wellbeing, while avoidance goals are associated with higher levels of depression and poor wellbeing (Grant and Spence, 2010), increased distress and anxiety, decreased levels of happiness, lower levels of satisfaction and poorer perceptions of health (Biswas-Diener and Dean, 2007). Appreciative Inquiry approaches to coaching and goal setting help individuals or organizations to avoid these adverse outcomes by helping them create and focus on approach goals.

2) Self-concordant goals

Self-concordant goals are also shown to increase the effectiveness of goal setting. Self-concordant goals are those congruent with an individual's developing interests and core values. The production of this book, for example, is a self-concordant goal for me as it chimes with my developing interest in writing, with my core values of affirmation and positivity and with my interest in the exploration and communication of ideas. That doesn't mean it's easy, but it does mean it's motivating. Self-concordant goals inspire a sense of ownership of the achievement of the goal. This leads people to try harder for longer and allows them to experience the glow of satisfaction of goal attainment. Goals set by others that are not concordant with the self, by contrast, often produce a sense of resentment, elicit minimal effort and offer little more than relief when completed.

3) Striving goals and mastery goals

In a similar vein, striving goals are more likely than aspirational goals to produce behaviour change. To strive is to pursue goals purposefully, while to aspire is more akin to wishing it were so. So I can aspire to be thinner but not do much about it, or I can strive to lose a few pounds by purposefully eating less, which (and I speak from experience here) takes much more mental energy. It also seems that mastery goals focused on increasing skill levels can sometimes serve us better than performance goals focused on an outcome (Grant and Spence, 2010). I find this with tennis, where focusing on shot-by-shot improvements (mastery) is much more rewarding for me than living or dying by winning (performance outcome). Finally, positivity helps people reach their goals as it is associated with optimism, perseverance and motivation.

Goal Setting and Environment Contingencies

Despite all that is known about how goals can aid engagement, wellbeing, enjoyment, performance and satisfaction, managers still frequently manage to use goal setting as a technique in a way that achieves all the opposite effects. This is because they don't understand well enough the relationship between environment, action and consequence on goal-seeking behaviour. Daniels explores this in some depth in his book *Bringing out the Best in People* (2000). To understand how some goal setting produces motivated behaviour while other goal setting produces disengaged behaviour, we need to understand something of the difference between positive and negative reinforcement and punishment.

If behaviour is being reinforced, it increases. If it is being punished, it decreases. The setting of goals is normally intended to increase or decrease some behaviour: production behaviour, selling behaviour or absence behaviour, for example. This matters not one whit. Whether goals achieve the desired increase or decrease in behaviour depends entirely on the contingencies around the goal. Intentionality is irrelevant. It is the consequences attendant on achieving the goal that are important in determining whether the goal works to increase or decrease the desired behaviour. There are four main sets of contingencies that affect behaviour (see Figure 3.1). Positive and negative reinforcement lead to an increase in behaviour. Positive and negative punishment lead to a decrease in behaviour. By definition, all of these work. However, positive reinforcement has different long-term effects on behaviour than negative reinforcement or punishment. Both of these latter contingencies are effectively coercive forms of behaviour control (Sidman, 2000).

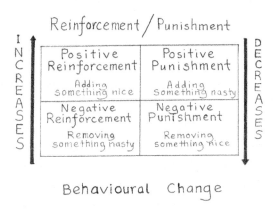

Figure 3.1   Reinforcement.

1) Coercive contingencies

At their simplest such coercive contingencies look like this: 'If you don't achieve your target, then you won't get a bonus'. 'If you don't come to training, then you can't be on the team' or 'If you are persistently late then you will face a disciplinary', these contingencies might work to reduce the incidence of target failure, missed training or lateness; however, it is equally likely that they will produce 'just enough' behaviour to avoid the punishment. So in the examples above we might see behaviour that could be characterized as: 'I will reach the target, just, and then I will stop working', 'I will attend the last training session before the match, but only if I think you have enough players available that you could carry out your threat', or 'I will be persistently late until I predict that you are on the verge of firing me. Then I'll be the model attendee until the threat of being fired has receded and we return to our usual pattern of you nagging and threatening me, and me ignoring you.'

We see this kind of minimal compliance at work all the time. People are present at work just enough to avoid being fired, they complete work just in time to miss being sanctioned, they do well enough to just reach the target and keep their job for the time being. Such behaviour indicates an environment that is long on coercive contingencies and short on positive reinforcement contingencies. In other words, there is a lot of possible punishment to be avoided, but little possible reward to be worked for. So the energy goes into working out how to do the minimum necessary to avoid the punishment.

Coercive behaviour control, over time, produces avoidance and escape behaviour. Coercive control is associated with activation of the behavioural inhibition system: people stick to what is known to be safe behaviour and actively work to avoid or escape potentially negative behavioural consequences. They are focused on not making mistakes, not getting it wrong, and the safest way to do that is to do as little as possible. People who extensively or solely use coercive methods of behaviour control become tainted by association as people to be avoided or escaped. This is the sad fate of too many managers who know no other way: much of their goal-setting behaviour is supported by coercive contingencies rather than by positively reinforcing contingencies.

What is shocking is how often these behaviour-reducing contingencies are set up unintentionally. For example, we frequently want people to use their budget wisely. Yet there is a common organizational contingency that

Supplement 3.7   Quick Ways of Spotting that Negative Reinforcement is in Operation

- The J Curve: performance shows a sharp rise just before a deadline, often with people scrambling to get it done.
- Negative talk: sometimes this is straightforward, sometimes it is more 'under the radar' talk of relentless pressure or insufficient time.
- Performance drops steeply after reaching the goal.
- There is no plan for positive reinforcement.
- If you remove a performance requirement, performance drops.

All of these features of a work environment suggest that work is being maintained by a set of negative reinforcers. It suggests compliance for fear of sanctions rather than commitment with hope of reward.

Adapted from Daniels (2000)

runs: 'If you save on your budget this year, I'll make it smaller next year' – something of a disincentive for achieving the goal of reducing spend. Another runs: 'We want you to sell lots. However, if you consistently exceed your sales target, we'll raise the bonus bar.' Not surprisingly, these contingencies have the effect of reducing the willingness of others to budget wisely or to exceed their sales targets enthusiastically. If you are not sure whether negative contingencies are in operation in your place of work, look at Supplement 3.7.

Considering all this, two strange and counterintuitive things become apparent about goal deadlines and goal attainment when supported by coercive contingencies. One is that deadlines give people permission to wait, while the other is that goal attainment gives them permission to stop. In other words, if all that is in it for me in achieving the goal is to avoid negative outcomes, then I will do the minimum possible as slowly or as late as possible to avoid those outcomes.

So goals are not automatically motivating, do not automatically achieve engaged behaviour or indeed raise performance. Goals operate within a set of contingencies that determine their effect. What goals do, or should do, is increase the opportunities for positive reinforcement, because it is the experience of positive reinforcement, contingent on particular goals, that can achieve all the amazing outcomes that we are told accompany goal setting. Positive reinforcement contingencies have different effects to coercive contingencies.

2) Positive contingencies

Positive reinforcement works to produce discretionary effort. It generates more behaviour than is minimally required. It encourages activation of approach behaviour – for example, exploration, creativity, innovation and learning. Positive reinforcement occurs when the consequence of a particular behaviour is pleasant, we might say rewarding. To increase or build up behaviour there needs to be an environment that produces small consistent rewards, contingent on the desired behaviour. To plan such a set of contingencies a manager needs to know what his or her people find rewarding, that is, what is a pleasant consequence for them? What is their equivalent of a gold star? This also means that the big goal needs to be broken down into lots of little goals, which can each, on attainment, be celebrated or rewarded. An inordinate number of managers find this very hard to grasp, believing instead that being paid is sufficient reward for all behaviour in itself. They often also struggle to understand how they can offer 'rewards' without extra budget. So how can someone build rewarding experiences into work without spending more money?

Imagine you are launching a new project. After some time and effort you have finally managed to get everyone connected to the project into the room. You could spend the first five minutes going on about how hard it has been to coordinate everyone (which most present will experience as a sort of 'telling off') and criticizing those who arrive a few minutes late for wasting the time of the others. Or you can spend the first five minutes congratulating everyone for turning up despite all the other calls on their time, thanking them for clearing this space and articulating what you are looking forward to about working with each of them or about having each of them on the project. By doing the latter, and by the way you conduct the rest of the meeting, you create a pleasant experience that is likely to be positively reinforcing. This means that next time you arrange a meeting it will be easier because of the good experience they had last time they attended: through positive reinforcement contingent on attendance, you are increasing the behaviour of attending your meeting.

Most people find rewarding, and therefore will work for, such things as social experiences, appreciation, having fun, feeling good, being recognized, being acknowledged, being thanked, being smiled at, the chance to be in the company of people they enjoy and, most importantly, a chance to use their strengths, experience flow and be engaged.

So, to summarize, goals are the antecedents for either reinforcement or punishment. In a work setting the purpose of goals is to increase the opportunities for positive reinforcement, as positive reinforcement drives motivation, goal seeking and attainment, and discretionary effort. This list looks remarkably like our earlier definition of employee engagement. This being the case, the work environment should be full of achievable and rewarded goals so that people have an unbroken sense of achievement and reward.

Some people, due to earlier experiences, have the ability to create their own environment full of goals and rewarding experiences and, as long as management doesn't inadvertently set up negative contingencies, they are essentially 'self-motivating'. Close examination would probably reveal that: they have found ways of doing their work that calls on their strengths; they set frequent mini-goals; they mark their mini-goal achievements in some personally rewarding way, perhaps by taking a five-minute break, making a phone call or by placing a tick on their 'to do' list; and they experience flow at work.

Many people do not know how to do this for themselves. They may well be reward-illiterate, meaning they are unfamiliar with common conditioned positive reinforcers: they live in a reward-impoverished environment. They are going to have to learn, at work, about goal achievement and positive reinforcement. They not only need lots of goals, they need goals that are easy to achieve and are celebrated when achieved. They need to learn to appreciate and respond to a whole new set of reinforcers, such as social approval, recognition, the satisfaction of a job well done or indeed, in too many cases, the experience of success. An environment that offers only a few challenging or stretching goals is highly demotivating for those who don't know how to structure their own goal and reinforcement path: they are stopped by feelings of hopelessness before they start. It is a skilled and sympathetic manager who can teach such unfortunate people how to become motivated by goals and success.

One of the things many people find rewarding about their work is its meaningfulness. Viewing work as having meaning is a healthy sign of engagement.

The Meaningfulness of Work

Stairs and Gilpin (2010) view engagement as a product of enjoyment, challenge and meaning, a definition which suggests that those who find their work meaningful are more likely to find it engaging. Our sense of the meaningfulness of our work is affected by the view we take of the purpose of our work. Research has found that people view work in one of three ways: as a job, a career or a calling (Wrzesniewski, 2003). When people view work as a job, they focus on its material benefits. Those with a career orientation work for the rewards that career advancement brings, such as greater self-esteem, increased power and higher social standing. And those with a calling orientation work primarily for the sense of fulfilment their work brings them. They believe their work helps make the world a better place, which is its own reward. These three orientations towards work are associated with the person, not the role. So someone working as a teacher may view his or her work as a job, a career or a calling. Each of these different perspectives is associated with different levels of engagement.

Blessed are the roughly one third of the working population who view their work as a calling. Having a sense of purpose in life and believing your work to be meaningful are both positively associated with authentic happiness and the satisfaction of a life well lived (Seligman, 2006). Meaningful work is also associated with many other good things, including greater work satisfaction, less work alcoholism, less work/life conflict, greater certainty and self-efficacy about career decisions, more intrinsic motivation and greater work satisfaction (Steger and Dik, 2010). A calling orientation is associated with high levels of work engagement. However, individuals who don't experience their work as a calling can also experience high levels of engagement. We look here at three sources of strategies for making work more engaging and meaningful: individual strategies, organizational strategies and leadership strategies.

Strategies for Increasing the Meaningfulness of Work

1) Individual

Fortunately, people have a strong drive to find meaning in their work. We seek always to make sense of the world, particularly in terms of 'who am I?' So, effectively we are programmed to find meaning in our work which contributes to our sense of our identity. We see this process in organizations. Imagine, for example, a group of people somewhere in an organization, maybe charged with some task incidental to the main purpose, who, to your surprise, act as if the salvation of the company is in their hands. They have imbued their work with great meaning, greater perhaps than that assigned to them by the rest of the organization who see them perhaps as 'only' managing the supply of stationery. Yet they have collectively formed a belief that, since managers are so incompetent in this area, it is only through their diligent action that the organization is saved from going under by the want of a timely staple. The ability to create such collective meaning in the face of organization indifference, or even ridicule, should be honoured rather more than it is as a very effective contribution towards greater employee engagement.

On a more individual level, some people approach the challenge of increasing their level of engagement at work in a more active way: they re-craft their job. For example, they may change the way they approach tasks to better suit their strengths. They may readjust the priorities of the job so they spend more time doing the parts they enjoy most. They may change the definition of the job so they get to interact with more or different people. They may even change the tasks that make up the job, discarding those they dislike and bringing in more of those that they do (Wrzesniewski, 2003). Such behaviour is often frowned on by managers who view it as unfair 'cherry-picking', yet it can be a very creative way of increasing engagement at work, as Clive Hutchinson's experience at Cougar Automation demonstrates in Supplement 3.8.

2) Organizational strategies

Activity at an organizational level also influences the possibilities of employee engagement. Organizations can work to create meaningful and engaging accounts of what they are about and what the organization's purpose might be beyond creating money for shareholders. A mission statement is not enough. This sense of greater purpose has to be evident in the way the company behaves. Additionally, they can help individuals within the organization understand exactly where they uniquely fit and what they contribute. The organization can recruit for engagement. They can use the appraisal system to identify and amplify the factors that enhance the chances of engagement, such as playing to strengths, receiving positive reinforcement and experiencing flow. They can make sure managers understand the impact they have on engagement and the crucial role they play.

3) Leadership strategies

The behaviour of the leader also affects levels of employee engagement. Leaders need to form relationships with others. They need to generate the

Supplement 3.8   Performance Management

At Cougar Automation we have completely changed our view of what is euphemistically called performance management. The traditional approach, which we used to use, typically involves systems of appraisals and one-to-ones where employees discuss their performance with their manager. Of course, most of the discussion inevitably ends up focusing on the problem areas, the things that aren't going as well as they might. And, as a result, all the actions that come out of the process, training or whatever, are aimed at the employee improving in these 'problem' areas.

Now, this kind of management action cuts completely across our belief in managing our people according to their strengths. In essence, traditional performance management seems to assume that the work is fixed and that people need to be changed to fit the needs of the work. The implication is that it is easier to change people than rearrange the work. But my experience is that it is very difficult to get people to improve at the things they do poorly. In fact, when I have tried in the past, not only has there been little improvement, but people just get dragged down by the constant focus on their problem areas. So, instead of changing people to fit the work, our strengths-based approach is to change the work to fit the people.

We do this in two main ways. First, we encourage people to rearrange the work with others so that they do more that plays to their strengths. We encourage people to discover their strengths and to tell their team mates and manager about their strengths and the things they love doing. Simple as this sounds, it quickly gets people to swap the bits of the job they do. And we find you don't need to swap much, as getting rid of one thing that drags you down and gaining one thing you love makes a tremendous difference. There may still be other things you don't like, but a small change in the ratio between work you love and work that drags you down really seems to make a big difference.

Secondly, we give people huge flexibility in how they do their work. It seems increasingly accepted in business that work should be standardized in the name of efficiency and quality. This is all very well in manufacturing where the aim is to produce thousands of identical products every day. But most of us work in service jobs, which are very different from manufacturing; service is all about handling the huge variety of needs that come from our customers every day. Customers are all different and even the needs of an individual customer change day by day. So, far from needing standardization, what we need is flexibility. We find that when we say to our people, 'find your own way to deliver what the customer wants', they work efficiently and deliver high quality. The result? We make money and the customer is happy. This seems to be because allowing our people flexibility lets them find the way of doing their job that works for them. They have more opportunities to play to their strengths, which results in improved efficiency and increased quality.

So, what we have learnt is that we get better results by changing the work to fit our people rather than trying to change our people to fit the work. Not only does this seem to give better financial results, but everyone is a lot happier. Not many people I meet seem to like appraisals.

Contributed by Clive Hutchinson

shared sense of purpose and mission referred to above and to involve the followers in the organization. Meaningfulness and engagement are enhanced by a mutuality of commitment between employer and employees. Leaders can ensure that it is psychologically safe for people to invest in their work, that they can expose aspects of themselves, and enthusiasm, aspiration and passion for their work, without fear of negative consequences. They can recruit for organizational fit as well as for abilities and experience. They can invest in training, empower employees, make sure the organizational rewards fit the work and communicate well. All these practices make a difference (Steger and Dik, 2010). In other words, all the thoughts, beliefs and practices advocated in this book are likely to increase employee engagement.

Summary

In this chapter we have looked at the phenomenon of employee engagement and examined what we know about how to enhance it. We know that helping employees identify, develop and use their strengths aids engagement. We know that goal setting used to increase the opportunity to receive positive reinforcement (rewards) increases engagement. And we know that goal setting done badly can work to decrease engagement. We know that experiencing flow at work is likely to be a good sign of engagement; and we know that believing one's work to be meaningful is also a healthy sign

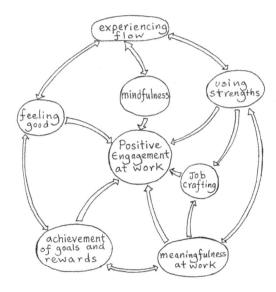

Positive engagement at work

Figure 3.2   Positive engagement at work.

of engagement. We also outlined some strategies to implement at the individual, organizational and leadership level that are likely to enhance the level of employee engagement. We also noted that while employee engagement brings benefits to the individual and the organization, employee disengagement is not neutral, but adversely affects both the individual and the organization. One might say there is a moral imperative to help people find meaning and engagement at work.

Psychometric measurement of strengths

A number of psychometric instruments exist for measuring personal strengths.

The VIA

This is Petersen and Seligman's original character strengths measure and can be accessed free of charge on www.authentichappiness.org.

Strengthscope
Developed by the Strengths Partnership, this is a versatile, work-based strengths measure which is supported by training and extensive supplementary materials (see www.Strengthscope.com).

Realise 2
This is the measure of evolutionary and adaptive strengths developed by the team at the Centre for Applied Positive Psychology, extensively supported with publications and website support (www.cappeu.com/realise2.htm).

Strengthsfinder
This is the Gallup measure of talents and strengths (www.strengthsfinder.com).

Recommended Reading

Strengths

Seligman, M. (2006) *Authentic Happiness*. London: Nicholas Brealey.
This is an easy read about character strengths and happiness and includes self-report measures on happiness, optimism style and character strengths.

Buckingham, M. and Coffman, C. (2001) *First Break All the Rules*. New York: Simon & Schuster.
This is the first, and for my money the best, of the Gallup strengths book series. It is a great read and clearly presents the results of their research into what makes a great manager.

Linley, A. (2008) *Average to A+: Realizing Strengths in Yourself and Others*. Coventry: CAPP Press.
An excellent, readable account of the psychological basis for strengths combined with pragmatic advice for identifying and getting the best from strengths, with lots of real-life examples used to illuminate points being made.

Goals and reinforcement

Sidman, M. (2001) *Coercion and its Fallout*. Boston, MA: Authors Cooperative.
If you want to understand more about the negative effects of coercive behaviour control, this is the book. Very informed, it is in parts highly readable and in others challengingly technical. This book demands some concentration.

Daniels, A. (2000) *Bringing out the Best in People: How to Apply the Astonishing Power of Positive Reinforcement.* New York: McGraw-Hill.
A readable and informative book about the technicalities of using goals and positive reinforcement to achieve motivation and high performance. Demands concentration.

Karen, P. (2002) *Don't Shoot the Dog.* Lydney: Ringpress.
I haven't referred to this book directly in the text, however I introduce it as a great, very readable paperback introduction to the whole field of behavioural contingencies and change. The author introduces all the main means of changing behaviour based on the four basic contingency patterns, and gives examples of using them in practice that range across work and family life.

4

Positive Communication and Decision-Making

Introduction

Communication and decision-making are key processes for most organizations; essential for success, they also contain the potential for failure. Communication is well known to be problematic. Decision-making is also frequently harder than it sounds. How can communication be improved?

Positive Psychology at Work: How Positive Leadership and Appreciative Inquiry Create Inspiring Organizations, First Edition. Sarah Lewis.
© 2011 Sarah Lewis. Published 2011 by John Wiley & Sons, Ltd.

How can we make good decisions? In this chapter we shall consider both as social and emotional processes, recognizing that this is not how they are usually viewed. From this perspective we shall learn about the role that emotion and connectivity plays in communication and performance. We shall examine the factors that affect decision-making, as well as the role of sense-making in organizational life.

Communication

Communication is often misunderstood as being a technical exercise. The challenge is to find the precise form of words that will create the same sense or image in the receiver's head as in the transmitter's head, the unspoken assumption being that if I hear exactly what you say, I will understand exactly what you mean. Within organizations whole departments are devoted to creating communication statements that can be launched into the organization to create a perfect and universal understanding of intent. Dictionaries offering definitions of the meanings for words lend support to the illusion of the possibility of perfect communication: if words have fixed meanings, then I have only to select the words with the correct meaning to convey my message.

From this perspective, the challenge of communication becomes that of getting the right words in the right order. By definition, a failure to understand what was intended by the message, and to change behaviour accordingly, is either a failure of comprehension on the receiver's part or a failure of composition on the sender's part. Within organizations people focus on 'getting the right message out there', the right message being that which will achieve buy-in and avoid resistance. Communication frequently becomes seen as an event rather than a process. As an event, it has a limited existence: a specific communication becomes a specific, time-limited event. When it's over it's finished: everyone heard, everyone knows, everyone understands. Except that it doesn't seem to work like that.

Senior managers and leaders are frequently astounded – and frustrated – to discover that large swathes of the organization are oblivious to plans, events and changes that they feel they have put considerable effort into communicating. 'But we communicated about this weeks ago. We talked about it at the annual meeting!' they cry in frustration. It is clear that they feel that their intense, focused communication 'initiative' should have been

"One container, as
ordered"

sufficient to have rendered further communication on the matter unnecessary. Therefore, they reason, if there is a breakdown in communication it owes more to the shortcomings of the audience than to the communicative skills of the leadership team. It is but a short hop, skip and a jump from here to labelling people as 'resistant to change'.

Understanding communication as a technical exercise in reasoning and semantics rarely results in unqualified communicative success even for very short and simple messages. Understanding communication in this simple transmit-and-receive, event-based way leads to a vicious circle of blame for communication failure, the main possibilities for explaining the problem being that either someone said it wrong or someone heard it wrong. For anything as complex as organizational change such communication is never going to deliver the hoped-for ease of transition. An alternative approach is to understand communication not as a technical challenge but as a social process.

Communication is fundamental to the ongoing challenge of social alignment. Social alignment can be understood as the complex process of creating sufficient shared meaning among people to facilitate things moving forward in a helpful and useful direction. Communication is seen as an ongoing process of negotiation of various perspectives, creating a constantly shifting reality. In this way communication can be understood as a social process that is crucial to the creation of this social alignment. It is crucial to the iterative, unending, unfolding process of coordinating ourselves with other people. This view of communication as an unending process of sense-making stands in sharp contrast to the common organizational view of it as a series of finite communication events.

Viewing communication more as a process of sense-making than of technical skill also affords a much more creative view of its possible effect. Considered as a social process, communication offers more than a chance to convey predetermined information; it offers an opportunity to create meaning. All communication takes place within a complex context of past history, individual experience, present setting and prior expectations, for example. Meaning created by any specific communication episode is formed within this bigger, ongoing context. To complicate matters further, communication is not purely about language, verbal or written. Our stance, posture, gaze, tone of voice, movements all add to the context within which the communication takes place, and so does the setting, what we are wearing, what just happened, what happens next. Communication becomes an unfolding dance. Recent research in positive psychology suggests that some dances are more productive than others, and that the productivity of the communication dance has a lot to do with the degree of connectivity between the dancers.

Connectivity

Connectivity is a concept that explains how group performance can be more than a sum of the parts. How well an interconnected group (e.g., a management group) is able to perform is not just about who is in the group, it also depends on the relations and interactions between members: if each individual's performance is dependent on the team as a whole being able to work together, then it doesn't matter how good any individual is on their own; if the group isn't working well together, the group performance will be poor. Connectivity is an important indicator of how well a system is functioning, how able it is to respond to changes and how well connected the elements of the system are to each other. Connectivity within groups is expressed through the number of nexi found in the conversation, nexi being strong and sustained patterns of interlocked behaviour between members which are indicative of a process of mutual influence. Sophisticated communication analysis is necessary to uncover these patterns. However, the ratio of positive to negative comments made within a group's communication pattern has been found to be a good proxy for a measurement of nexi. That is to say, such a ratio gives a good indication of the degree of connectivity in the group.

Losada and Heaphy (2004) were interested to discover the relationship between patterns of connectivity in management group conversations and their performance. They studied 60 top management teams having business-related meetings. Before they began their observations, they rank-ordered the teams by success on the basis of: profitability, 360-degree feedback on the team and customer satisfaction surveys. They divided the teams into three groups: 15 teams were ranked as high performing (they performed well on all three measures); 19 were classified as low performing (they performed poorly on all three measures); and 26 were classified as medium – effectively this group was 'the rest'. So now they had three conditions: high-performing groups, low-performing groups and medium-performing groups. They were interested to see if the patterns of communication in these three conditions differed in any way, so they observed a number of working team meetings for each team.

To measure any differences in patterns of communication they focused on three aspects of team conversations: the ratio of positive to negative comments; the ratio of inquiry (asking questions) to advocacy (stating positions); and self-directed comments (comments pertaining to the group) and other directed comments (comments pertaining to the wider world, such as customers). Positive comments were those that showed support, encouragement or appreciation, while negative comments were those that showed disapproval, sarcasm or cynicism. They then compared these measures across the three performance conditions. The data were analysed using complex, nonlinear dynamic analysis. This, combined with the fact that the measures took place across sequential times, meant that causal rather than purely correlational relationships could be established.

The results are striking. The single most important factor in predicting organizational performance, which was twice as powerful as any other factor, was the ratio of positive to negative comments. In the teams defined as high performing, the ratio was 5.6 positive comments to every negative comment; in the medium performing groups it was 1.8 positive comments to every negative comment; and in the low-performing groups it was three negative comments to every positive comment. The design of the study meant that the possibility that causality ran the other way, that poorly performing teams express more negative to positive comments as a consequence of doing badly, could be discounted. Instead, it can be asserted that the teams that conversed in a predominantly positive way did better.

Equally interesting, the top performing teams had pretty much a 1:1 ratio of inquiry to advocacy statements and the same balance of self- to other-oriented comments. In other words, they inquired into each other's positions and brought the wider world into their discussions and decision-making. The ratios of these two measures in medium-performing teams were slightly lower at two inquiries or other-oriented comments to three advocacy or self-oriented statements. The poor performing teams, however, were locked into another world, where the ratio was 20 (or more) to 1, i.e., they made 20 times as many advocacy or self-oriented comments as they did inquiries or other-oriented comments. As an aside, this finding certainly resonates with my experience with some poorly performing management teams where whole meetings can pass without a question being asked. Clearly, the high-performing teams had measurably different patterns of communication which contributed to their performance. And the most important difference was the prevalence of positive comments.

Dynamic Patterns of Communication

As mentioned earlier, this measurement of positive to negative comments is, in effect, a measure of connectivity. It is interesting to explore why the correspondence between positive comment ratios and connectivity is so close. The heart of the relationship seems to lie in the differing effects of positive and negative comments on conversational dynamics. A negative comment tends to have a shutting down effect. It discourages further connection among the group around any particular theme. While a positive response encourages an expansion of ideas, it seems to encourage people to stay connected and to explore a particular theme further. The atmosphere of a positive comment-oriented meeting also tends to be very different. In this research, it was found that the high-performing teams created and occupied an emotional space characterized by a sense of buoyancy and expansiveness. This expansive space opened up possibilities for action and creativity. Conversely, interactions in the low-performing team were characterized by a lack of mutual trust and support or enthusiasm. The emotional space was different and the interaction less generative. These different patterns of interaction, and the general atmosphere they create, can be classified as different dynamic patterns. Different patterns of dynamics are associated with different outcomes in terms of creativity and the coordination of action.

In the low-performing teams the pattern of interaction generated a fixed point dynamic. Essentially this means their interactions follow a more or less fixed pattern where little new is generated. Such conversations keep returning to the same point or conclusion. We might refer to the team as being 'stuck'. Medium-performing groups experience limited cycle dynamics. The possibilities their interactions generate and the form they take are more varied than the low-performing teams, but tend to oscillate between various ways of being. The team is unable to break out into new patterns of interaction or to create truly generative ways forward. The high-performing teams break out of these fixed or limited cycles of repeating patterns into a much more generative space, meaning they are able to generate new patterns and possibilities. Such groups are effectively much more creative.

If we accept the implications of this research, it suggests that how groups relate, how they interact, is fundamentally important to their performance. Being able to offer positive comments to others is not a nice-to-have, an optional extra when things are going well, it is an imperative necessity for high performance. Such positive patterns are not commonly observed. Instead, we have a widespread culture that suggests that effective leaders and managers are those who are not afraid to bawl someone out for poor performance. The idea that generosity, forgiveness, appreciation, encouragement and positive feedback are necessary to achieve high performance is still a fairly radical thought, especially when times are tough. This is not to say that negative comments don't have their place. It is known that above a ratio of about 30:1 positive to negative comments the group will become severely dysfunctional, lost in a cosy mutual love-in that cannot tolerate the slightest hint of criticism. However, this is not a danger most groups have to worry about. Fredrickson suggests that optimal performance is between 3:1 and 11:1 positive to negative comment ratios (Fredrickson and Losada, 2005). The term 'positivity' is generally used to refer to this set of dynamics; so we can talk about the degree of positivity in a team or organization meaning, at heart, the ratio of positive to negative comments and all that follows from that. Given this we might ask, how can an organization that has a culture of giving predominantly negative feedback in its communicative interactions generate more positive comments and develop more positive communication?

How to Build Positive Communication and Increase Performance

Cameron (2008a) describes organizations with positive communication patterns as those where affirmative and supportive language replaces negative and critical language. These are organizations that exhibit an 'abundance' of positive comments. Positive comments engender positive feelings and positive feelings enhance connectivity. This connectivity between people is the means by which resources flow and coordinated action takes place. In turn, it is this co-coordinated exchange that facilitates higher productivity and higher quality performance through the formation of social capital and the creation of synchronism. Synchronism generally refers to the keeping of time together. In organizational terms it refers to the presence of simultaneity and coordinated action. It describes the phenomena whereby people are able to act in synchronization with each other, to act in concert, without elaborate command and control mechanisms. One of the facilitating processes is probably the presence of high quality connections, which we discuss in more detail in Chapter 7. Figure 4.1 illustrates how these different features fit together. They explain the relationship between positive communication and high performance. It would seem that the circle could start with an increase in positive comments in the organization, a change that it should be within the power of the organization to make. Cameron (2008a) offers two pointers for how to start creating a culture of positive communication: offering positive leadership and creating positive self-images.

Leadership and Positive Communication

Cameron points out that supportive and positive communication needs to be modelled by leaders; it needs to be genuine, authentic and sincere. For many leaders this would necessitate a fundamental shift in their worldview.

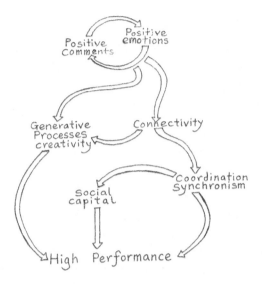

The relationship between positive communication and high performance

Figure 4.1   Positivity.

If as a leader your career success has been predicated on being able to spot the flaws, point out the shortcomings and name the problems, then shifting gear to a primary focus on spotting strengths, pointing out the achievements and naming successes is a challenging shift in focus. For many it means putting their much-prized critical evaluation skills to one side and developing instead their positivity generating skills. Such a shift necessitates the development of an appreciative ear and eye. It rests on working to draw the best out of people, not correcting their faults. This is not an easy shift for many to make, and we discuss what this means for leaders in Chapter 5. Meanwhile organizational processes can also be adapted to promote positive communication.

Best Self-Feedback

The other process Cameron offers is that of creating best self-feedback for people. Best self-feedback is a radical alternative to the common 360-degree feedback. The best self-feedback respondents don't assess the individual against a pre-set list of organizational competencies, but instead create pictures of the unique contribution of the individual to the organization and to the lives of those around him or her. Unlike 360-degree feedback which, in my experience, frequently elicits disappointment, embarrassment, confusion, frustration, anger and shame, and occasionally pleasant surprise, best self-feedback typically elicits pride, gratitude and aspiration. It is a positive organizational process.

The way it works is that a person asks 20 people (workmates, friends, family) to write three short anecdotes in answer to a positively phrased question such as 'When have you seen me making a special or important contribution and what distinctive strengths did I display?' or 'When have you been most proud to know me, to call yourself my friend?' So they write three stories about when they saw the person at their best. The person ends up with 60 short stories. The person analyses this positive information themselves. They draw out key themes that capture their best self-strengths and their unique contribution to create a best self-portrait. It is not easy to spot our own strengths, so this process can be a revelation to people as they begin to understand how and when they shine in the eyes of others. Alex Linley's account of his reflection of Mary's best self back to her shows the challenge of helping people recognize their strength at times (see Supplement 4.1). Since the stories are behaviourally based, it is eminently possible for the recipient to identify, amplify and magnify the behaviour that is valued by others. They can develop strategies for capitalizing on these strengths. There are other benefits too: see Supplement 4.2.

My experience has been that once people can truly own their strengths, they can truly own their weaknesses too. No longer are they caught in the trap of attempting to hide or disguise their weaknesses, or in the ceaseless quest to excel at everything. Instead, they can put their best energy where it brings most reward. They can volunteer for tasks and challenges that attract them because of their fit with their strengths, safe in the knowledge that such a task will bring out the best in them. Conversely, they can decline to volunteer for tasks that will test their weaknesses, fuelled by a vague notion that doing what they don't like and are no good at will, in some self-flagellation-informed way, be good for them. Perhaps the most important outcome is that people often experience an enhanced desire to live up to this positive image of themselves at their best. As people spend more time in their best self-mode, playing to their strengths, so more people will feel more positive about them, and the passing of positive comment

Supplement 4.1   Building Esteem in an Esteem Builder

Mary is a social care worker, someone who works to support social workers with their cases. She doesn't have a great academic background, and for that reason she often doubts her own worth and value but without any real reason for doing so, since she is brilliant at what she does. I know Mary because she is a friend of mine, and over the years I have had the opportunity to see her in many different situations. She's known me when I've been feeling down, and she's picked me up. She's been there when I've questioned myself and my own abilities, and she's helped me to believe. She's always seeing the positives in others, but often didn't see the positives in herself.

Over time, I saw this emerge as a pattern. Mary would help other people blossom, believing in them, supporting them, showing them the way. She always sees the best of what other people are capable of and then helps them to see that for themselves. Mary is a transformation agent: she helps people emerge into being the best that they can be. And in her line of work – social care and social work – that's an amazing quality to have. She works with people who need all the belief they can get, and she gives it to them: children who, by virtue of their parents' problems, would have been destined to a life of social exclusion themselves, but instead go on to get jobs, establish stable relationships and become productive members of society; babies who might be too young to remember, but who grow up with adoptive families who love them, rather than with natural families who can't or won't. The nature of much of Mary's work is about stopping bad things from happening, so it's not always easy to see the difference that she has made.

But for Mary, 'It's just what I do, there's nothing special about it.' I could see that with those beliefs she was stopping herself from believing and becoming who she could become – just the opposite of what she managed to do for her clients in transforming their lives Seeing this, I thought that it was time for the Esteem Builder (for that's the strength that people like Mary demonstrate) to see some building of self-esteem in her own life and identity.

One time when the famous phrase came up, I challenged it. 'What do you mean, there's nothing special about it? Look at the difference you made to Matthew. How many other people could have done that?' Matthew was angry and apparently unreachable. Repeatedly betrayed and let down by his parents and the other adults around him, he didn't trust anyone and didn't care. But over time, his resistance lessened and

Continued

Supplement 4.1   *Continued*

the messages from Mary started to get through. In the end, she'd helped him to stop going down a route of desperation, possibly even saving his life in the process. 'Who else could have done what you did?' I asked. 'Maybe you're right', Mary replied. 'Maybe there is something that's a bit different about what I do.'

With that, the seeds were sown and slowly but surely Mary started to recognize the remarkable ability that she has, to take that ability into herself, internalizing it as part of her own identity, the inner core of what and who she is. As she did so, not only did she change the way she thought about herself, she also changed the way she works with others. Now, she shares her experiences of how to help people believe in themselves. She also knows what to look for more specifically in terms of the results – when people believe in themselves and what they can do, she is able to show how they then go on to get their lives back in order, how they become more confident, more capable of dealing with life's ups and downs and, specifically in her remit, more able to provide a safe, secure and caring environment in which to bring up their children.

Knowing what she does well, Mary has grown in the confidence to do more of it – even going so far as to run CPD sessions for other social workers on how to build confidence in people. In these sessions, she helps others to develop their own skills as Esteem Builders. She teaches them to believe – in themselves and in others – by focusing on what they have done well and what works. In this way, the successes, however small, build into a different self-identity that provides the foundation for a better life going forward. The social work team believe in themselves more as a result, and they believe in their clients. That's a difference that ripples out, far and wide, to many: social workers believing in themselves more, helping them to find what is working with their clients and so to solve problems and improve life circumstances, all of which make a difference to children's lives. And it all started because an Esteem Builder started to believe in herself more.

Key elements of this case study have been
changed to protect anonymity.
Contributed by Alex Linley

Supplement 4.2   Benefits of Best Self-Feedback

- It is directly connected to behaviour that the person has displayed in the past, so it can be repeated and enhanced in the future.
- Almost always reveals strengths and abilities that wouldn't be found in a Strengthsfinder tool.
- People discover how they can add unique value in ways that are natural and effortless to them.
- People often develop strengthened relationships with their feedback givers.
- They experience a desire to reciprocate.
- There is an enhanced desire to live up to the positive best self-description.
- They start to reinterpret their own history as being more strengths-based.
- When it is practised in organizations, cohesion and mutual support are positively affected.

From Cameron (2008a)

---

will become both more likely and easier, in a virtuous circle. This emphasis on affirmative feedback doesn't mean that corrective feedback can be ignored. Rather it needs to be done in a positive way, as described in Supplement 4.3.

What is remarkable is that this positive spiral of increased positivity, increased connectivity and then improved performance can be sparked by attending to the nature of moment-to-moment conversations. The answer to improved communication doesn't lie in big organizational change programmes, but in a shift in the dominant understanding of what produces great performance and greater attention to how we respond to each other moment by moment. These opportunities arise all the time and many of these incidental conversations in organizations involve making decisions.

Decision-Making

In the same way that organizations often treat communication as an exercise in semantics, so they treat decision-making as an exercise in logic. Just as we have found that emotion plays a huge part in communication

---

Supplement 4.3   Giving Corrective Feedback in a Positive and Supportive Way

- Describe what happened, or what behaviour needs to change.
- Describe the consequences, or the reaction of the person, to the event or behaviour.
- Suggest alternative ways of behaving.
- Keep ideas about personality, or a dispute between alternative versions of what happened, out of the discussion.
- Be sincere in your desire to help.
- Stay problem rather than person focused.
- Be specific about the behaviour under discussion.
- Respect the other person's perspective. Don't get into arguments about whose perspective is right.
- Own what you are saying, in other words don't start with 'I've been asked to tell you ...'
- Make sure the things you are saying stay connected, local and specific to each other.
- Listen and respond to what the other person has to say in thoughtful, non-judgemental ways.

Behaving like this should strengthen and preserve the relationship.

---

patterns and consequently performance, so shall we find that emotion plays a huge part in decision-making and consequently in performance. Before we explore this, let's remind ourselves of the dominant model of good decision-making. Damasio (2005) summarized the prevalent model as 'the supposedly clear process of deriving logical consequences from assumed premises, the business of making reliable inferences, which, unencumbered by passion, allow us to choose the best possible option, leading to the best possible outcome, given the worst possible problem' (p. 167). Decision-making is thus characterized as essentially problem-solving and so is seen as an exercise in logic.

Note the belief inherent in the dominant model that decision-making is best unencumbered by passion or, shall we say, emotion. There is nothing to distinguish the attractiveness of one possible decision from another except our power of reason. In theory, then, there is an infinite number of possible decisions from which we can rationally select the best. It is as if the decision-making landscape is flat. In fact, the number of variables that we need to take into account – for example, the effects of all decisions all the way down the time line; the effects of all decisions on all key players and connected players; and the many possible criteria against which decisions can be evaluated (which must themselves be decided) – is limitless. The brain cannot accommodate this infinite number of possibilities; nor can the most sophisticated spreadsheet. It is clear that decision-making doesn't actually happen like this, as research in this area has demonstrated.

Damasio, who works with brain-damaged people, recounts an incident of decision-making that occurred when he was discussing with a patient when his next visit to the laboratory should be.

> I suggested two alternative dates, both in the coming month and just a few days apart from each other. The patient pulled out his appointment book and began consulting the calendar. The behaviour that ensued ... was remarkable. For the better part of half an hour, the patient enumerated reasons for and against each of the two dates: previous engagements, proximity to other engagements, possible meteorological conditions, virtually anything that one could reasonably think about concerning a simple date ... he was now walking us through a tiresome cost-benefit analysis, an endless outlining and fruitless comparison of options and possible consequences. It took enormous discipline to listen to all this without pounding the table ... but finally we did tell him, quietly, that he should come on the second of the alternative dates. ... He simply said 'that's fine then.' (p. 193)

This is an example of 'good decision-making practice' in operation. The man involved is working on a clear problem: which day to choose for his follow-up appointment. Then, having a clear idea of the problem, he went on to attempt to assess the two dates against a range of criteria. Only here the process got stuck. After half an hour he was no nearer to being able to make the decision. Also, nothing had kicked in to his awareness to allow him to say, in effect, 'this decision isn't worth this much effort, just make a decision'. The man exemplified good decision-making theory and got nowhere.

Damasio's work, both studying such people and conducting experiments, has made it clear to him that the missing element of the decision-making process in this case is any sense of internal feelings. He is careful to distinguish these internal feelings from externally-oriented emotions. Internal feelings are much slighter and not necessarily visible to other people or even to our own consciousness. He gives these internal feelings that are crucial to effective decision-making the technical name 'somatic markers'. Somatic markers are bodily sensations that convey information about the attractiveness or otherwise of various possibilities for future action. In the absence of these somatic markers the patient above had no way of distinguishing between the two choices. For him there was no inherent difference in attractiveness between the two options, no way of quickly distinguishing between the appropriateness of the two, or indeed of just 'making a choice'. In the absence of such shortcuts to decision-making he had to fall back on logic; and we can see how successful that was!

Emotions in Decision-Making

The moral of this story is that effective decision-making is not solely about 'pure logic'. In fact, it is impossible, in the domain of the personal and social, to make decisions solely on the basis of 'pure logic'. An emotional component is necessary for effective decision-making. Damasio's theory about how this works is that as we contemplate, even for a microsecond, various future scenarios in relation to the decision we are trying to make, a somatic marker accompanies such images. This feeling, be it so faint as to be undetectable in consciousness, is essentially a summation of all our previous experience or knowledge about that potential choice, expressed as a feeling. As we contemplate various scenarios, fleeting feelings of unease, excitement, keen anticipation, pleasure, distrust, anxiety, and so on, are activated. The unpleasant sensations act as danger signals, the pleasant ones as motivators: somatic markers act to create alarm bells of concern and beacons of incentive. They act as a biasing device. These feelings shape the decision-making landscape.

With somatic markers available the landscape is no longer flat; it contains peaks of attainable good and troughs of avoidable bad. Suddenly decision-making becomes a lot easier with potentially good decisions easier to spot and potentially bad decisions easier to avoid. Indeed, known bad decisions can be discounted. Much of this discounting of options, as indicated by somatic markers, takes place before the process of selection reaches consciousness, saving us from being overwhelmed by choice. Many times these somatic markers about different decisions are faint, even imperceptible, however I had a particular decision-making experience that brought their presence strongly into view, which might help illuminate the point.

As a child I loved to ride and I worked at the local riding school. Like many young girls I desperately wanted a pony. My father was a townie transported to the countryside by success. He knew nothing about keeping such animals. My pleas were met by a series of anxious questions. 'Where will we keep it? How much do they cost to keep? What happens if …?' and equally anxious statements: 'They're very big animals. It's a huge responsibility.' Not to mention the invidious: 'Are you sure? Is it really what you want? It's a very big step.' And so on. Suffice to say, I couldn't muster the necessary confidence and sangfroid to overcome all his fears. No pony for me and life moved on.

Picture the scene 25 years later. I have recently taken up riding again and am enjoying it in a whole new way. I decide I want to buy my own horse. This should be a moment of great delight; instead I feel as if I am making a decision that will bring the sky down on my head. The level of anxiety I experience trying to turn this decision into reality is huge. On the day I go to the yard to hand over the cheque I am shaking with fear. Every bone in my body is telling me I am making a huge mistake. I have had children and bought houses and never felt a sense of responsibility or fear like this. Clearly, this emotional response was disproportionate to the purchase. Rationally, I knew this was a simple decision that could easily be undone if it didn't work out, yet my body was telling me in no uncertain terms that

this was a highly loaded and potentially very dangerous decision. The clear somatic marker that made enacting this decision so hard (the actual purchase was my third attempt, I had backed out twice before) came from the past association of horse-buying and high anxiety. The somatic marker from the past offered information in a way that was almost impossible to ignore, despite its outdated and unhelpful nature.

From this discussion we can see that feelings are an important source of information in effective decision-making. Emotions from the past affect the degree of aversion and attraction of different possible options now. Indeed, they affect whether or not various options even surface into consciousness. Emotions and feelings affect our decision-making in other ways too. For example, one of the ways the 'dreaming' phase of the Appreciative Inquiry process works is by creating positive somatic markers that are associated with the image of a good future outcome. Such images and markers can draw us through the short-term difficulties or obstacles that it might be necessary to encounter or overcome on the way forward. Dreaming creates a beacon or incentive in the landscape of future possibilities.

Appreciative Inquiry is also concerned with the creation of positive emotion, recognizing positive emotion as a source of energy for change. Isen's (2005) and Fredrickson's (2005) work on positive emotions and positivity have illuminated the many beneficial effects of 'feeling good'. When we consider these we can see how they are likely to enhance good decision-making (Supplement 4.4). In essence, positivity enables people to respond flexibly and creatively when faced with challenges or complex situations. This is illustrated beautifully by Liz Martins' account of a short intervention with a children's mental health multi-agency team that was experiencing difficulties. Rather than following the usual route of examining the problems, the group celebrated its successes. This facilitated unexpectedly creative and rapid decision-making about what to do (see Supplement 4.5).

It is perhaps important to note that the benefits of feeling good are not because such feelings allow people to play down, ignore or distort negative information: it is not a Pollyanna effect. Rather, positive affect leads people to be able to consider many aspects of a situation simultaneously, make evaluations and to choose behaviours responsive to the situation and task demands. Their thought processes are simultaneously both more efficient and more thorough. People in a positive state of mind show less dichotomous thinking; they are better able to integrate their thoughts and ideas.

Supplement 4.4 The Benefits of Positive Emotion

People experiencing positive emotional states, for example content-ment, happiness, interest, joy, excitement, passion, playfulness, pride or optimism, are:

- More creative.
- Able to show improved negotiation processes and outcomes.
- More thorough in what they do.
- More open-minded.
- Able to display more flexible thinking and problem-solving.
- Able to show more generosity and social responsibility in interper-sonal interactions.
- More likely to do what they want to do.
- More likely to be socially responsible and helpful in what they do.
- More likely to enjoy what they are doing.
- More motivated to achieve goals.
- More open to new information.
- Able to think more clearly.
- Able to handle more complex information.
- Able to integrate, process and manipulate information more effectively.
- Able to show more social behaviour (e.g., helping, sociability, friend-liness and social responsibility).
- Likely to have reduced amounts of interpersonal conflict.
- More successful at problem-solving.
- More efficient and thorough in their decision-making.
- Able to consider many aspects of situations simultaneously.
- Able to switch attention from unsolvable to solvable problems.
- Less defensive.
- Able to evaluate risks and make good judgements.

Adapted from Isen (2005) and Fredrickson (2005)

They are less anchored to an initial hypothesis and are more willing to explore alternatives. This flexibility also helps people to switch their atten-tion from unsolvable to solvable tasks. It allows them to switch more fre-quently between a consideration of their own needs and the needs of others, or the needs of the present and the needs of the future. Feeling good

Supplement 4.5   Doing it Differently

Following difficulties, the future of a children's multi-agency primary mental health service was uncertain. I was approached as an independent consultant and suggested a strengths-based, whole-system approach – a one-day event, based on Appreciative Inquiry, for all stakeholders to develop the future direction. The senior strategic managers were more familiar with reviews where a consultant researched the problems and produced a report with recommendations, but accepted the proposal.

I invited two colleagues to work with me to facilitate the day. As we planned the event with a small 'design group' of stakeholder representatives, the 'appreciative' design met some resistance. Surely we need to talk about the problems the service faces? One senior manager was particularly unimpressed – 'I hate all this positive touchy-feely stuff'.

On the day the room layout, including small tables set out with colourful flowers and sweets, signalled that this was different from the usual consultation event. However, anxiety for some was high. The team manager arrived – 'I'm dreading this … a roomful of people telling us how crap we are.' The team members looked pale and even the senior manager opening the day was tight with anxiety.

After welcomes, we were quickly into appreciative interviews in pairs. 'Tell your partner a story of when this service was at its best, when it really made a difference to a child …' The room became a buzz of noise, people laughing, hands gesticulating. After sharing a few of the stories in the big group, we surfaced the themes and put them on the wall. The whole room looked and absorbed the strengths of the service and how it made a difference to children. The team members were relaxed and smiling now.

Then to sharing dreams of what else the service could also be. As people listened, they heard the challenges and what needed to be different. After lunch, we had three rounds of conversations based on the morning's themes. In a break, someone commented: 'People aren't avoiding the negatives, it's just different somehow.' The manager who hated 'touchy-feely stuff' told the room that her conversations had been 'fascinating and useful'.

Later, as individual action points were shared, it became evident that the collective wisdom suggested that the service should be reconfigured to sit within locality teams. Later that week this was confirmed by senior decision-makers.

Feedback suggested that the strengths-based approach had been crucial. It brought energy and lightness to the day. It allowed the team members to be 'valued' publicly so that, as someone noted, they 'walked out three foot taller than they arrived'. This honouring of the team seemed to free up the system to be able to consider alternatives.

Together people brought out what worked for children, explored how to create more of this and saw greater potential in a different service model. Involving the whole system gave understanding and ownership, and brought agreement, unlikely at the outset, among senior stakeholders.

The commissioning manager felt 'many months ahead' of where they would have been with a more traditional review process. He commented that it was tough for the team, but they felt part of the decision-making, understood the reasons for it and would be joining their new teams 'with their heads held high'.

Contributed by Liz Martins

allows us to be more flexible in our thinking, which in turn enables us to be more creative in our decision-making, wherever that decision-making may take place.

Micro-Decision-Making

In organizations a lot of emphasis is put on the big set-piece decision-making forums that are meetings. However, people make decisions together in many informal ways. Gittell (2003) has examined decision-making in informal contexts, asking what affects the effectiveness of the decisions made. Her research found that two distinguishing criteria are the presence, or absence, of high quality communication and high quality relationships. High quality communication is defined as communication that is frequent, timely and accurate. When high quality communication and relationships are present between people who are dependent on each other for work outcomes, the coordination around the work becomes much easier. Such relational coordination enhances localized, problem-focused decision-making that helps with work performance and productivity. She argues that organizations need to create opportunities for communication and relationships of this high quality to occur outside formal decision-making forums, to facilitate the effective coordination of work.

It might seem obvious that such relationships and the easy coordination they offer are beneficial to the smooth running of organizations. Unfortunately, in many organizations various factors prevent this process from happening naturally. For example, the organization might be spread geographically across different workshops or sites, while different parts of the process will almost certainly fall under different organizational functions. In addition, management might not recognize the value of this type of conversation, seeing it instead as time-wasting or work avoidance. Also managers frequently view themselves as the coordination agents and fail to appreciate the value that lower-level self-coordination can offer. In the face of these and other factors, many organizations can't rely on a continual flow of these types of micro-decision-making conversations where people who have the knowledge about the issue, and the abilities to solve it, are able to come together naturally. It may be necessary to create 'relational coordination' events where people from across a process can come together to facilitate improvement. The 'transformative collaboration' processes we examine in Chapter 8 offer a way to create such opportunities.

Other Factors that Enhance Decision-Making

1) Mindfulness

Positive psychology has developed considerable interest in the idea of mindfulness. Cultivating mindfulness, they have discovered, is good for us as individuals, resulting in greater competency, health, longevity, positive affect (feeling good), creativity, charisma and reduced burnout (Langer, 2005). Mindfulness is good for organizations too, as it enhances their ability to adapt and learn. When mindful we are alert to the possibility of change. This state of mind is helpful to effective decision-making. Given this, you might think that organizations would be vigilant in their mindfulness, yet most organizations introduce large chunks of mindless activity into organizational life. They set up repeatable routines that allow the organization to continue to function 'as if' nothing changes. This is an expression of the organizational quest for certainty and efficiency. While this mindless behaviour produces the benefits of efficient, streamlined procedure, it introduces the cost of a loss of adaptability.

When we come together to make a decision the temptation is to seek certainty and answers, and to be paralysed if it isn't immediately obvious how that can be achieved. We want to introduce a quick, fixed account of how things are so that we can make decisions from a clear position. In this context being mindful is about being able to exploit the potential of the uncertainty rather than to be paralysed by it. Later in this chapter we examine how we can do this by considering how ongoing sense-making might facilitate mindful action. If we are going to move from our 'automatic' way of solving a particular problem to a more mindful way, by definition, we are going to need to bring some creativity to the task.

2) Creativity

Creativity has traditionally been seen as an individual personality trait. And there is good evidence that people vary in their abilities to be creative. However, creativity can also be viewed as a state rather than a trait; in other words, we are all more creative on some occasions than others. What sorts of things make a difference? Our emotional state, as we have seen, seems to have an impact: we are more able to display creative thinking when we are feeling good. Atmosphere also seems a likely contender: creative people are known to be more childlike and playful, so creating a playful, relaxed atmosphere might release some latent creativity in the rest of us. It is also known that having both collaborative and competitive relationships with colleagues in the same field can trigger creative activity, suggesting that communities of practice might have a role to play in an organization looking to enhance its overall creativity. Greater creativity in individuals and groups can be encouraged, as Vanessa King's workshops demonstrate (see Supplement 4.6).

3) Wisdom

In the same way that some people are inherently more creative than others, so some people are inherently wiser than others (see Supplement 4.7). Wisdom can be defined as rich knowledge and experience in the matters of the human condition, sometimes called the pragmatics of life (Baltes, Gluck and Kunzmann, 2005). Wisdom operates through the development and operation of heuristics. Heuristics help us to reach solutions under conditions of limited resources. They are automatic processes for searching out and organizing information. For example, they guide how much and

Supplement 4.6   Seriously Creative – Building Strengths in Creative Thinking

Increasingly, employees across the whole organization are encouraged to come up with ideas to improve products, services or processes and to deal with complex problems, so developing creative thinking skills is key. Further, creativity can improve performance, engagement and job satisfaction.

The organization's culture and value it places on creativity or innovation are important, as are the support and receptivity of managers to new ideas. In addition, three further dimensions are needed for creativity at work: an understanding of how ideas happen, a 'toolkit' of creative thinking skills and the motivation to use them.

I run workshops designed to address employees' will, skill and belief that they can think creatively. Vitally, as most participants do not consider themselves to be creative, these workshops are grounded in the reality of their specific organization and/or team, and participants apply their learning to real issues during the workshop.

Participation in the workshops is voluntary. I have found that although many participants who choose to attend believe they were not inherently creative, they are 'attracted by the idea of the workshop' because 'it sounded interesting'.

To foster motivation, the early part of the workshop explores the organizational and personal benefits of developing creative thinking skills. Building on this, 'creative confidence' is facilitated in two ways: by helping individuals examine their limiting beliefs about creative abilities and then, through subsequent activities, enabling them to challenge and reframe these. Participants learn that ideas don't just happen. There is a process through which they are generated.

The workshop explores core creative techniques, covering divergent and convergent thinking, selected to have face validity for 'non-creative' functions. Care is taken to explain the rationale behind each activity. Participants explore these techniques, trying them out on real issues they have identified. This helps in taking their new skills back to the workplace and, further, participants feel a sense of progress on a topic they have been working on. Importantly, idea generation is followed by a look at the innovation process, showing the steps necessary to move from idea-generation to implementation.

The final part of the workshop examines personal creative habits and blocks to creative thinking. Participants are invited to share ideas for working around barriers and for establishing new habits.

These workshops have enabled participants to move from lacking in confidence to releasing energy and enjoyment of creativity in the work-place, the positive affect experienced serving to increase their ability to generate more ideas. One participant's comments were typical. She started the workshop sitting stiffly saying, 'I don't know why I signed up, I'm just not creative.' By the end she said, 'I can't believe I came up with so many good ideas.' Her manager later reported on the energy and enthusiasm she continued to display.

Contributed by Vanessa King

Supplement 4.7   The Qualities of Wise People

- They have exceptional knowledge about how wisdom is acquired. They understand something of the nature of human existence and they try to learn from their own mistakes.
- They have exceptional knowledge about how to use wisdom. They know when to give and when to withhold advice. They are people you would go to with a life problem.
- They have exceptional knowledge about the context of life. They understand that priorities change over a life-time. They know about the different conflicts possible between different life domains.
- They have an exceptional personality and high social functioning skills. They are good listeners and very humane.

Adapted from Baltes, Gluck and Kunzmann (2005)

which information is taken into account. Well-developed heuristics around a particular type of situation explain the difference between someone who gets to 'the nub of the matter' in three questions and someone who asks endless questions that don't seem to move things forward. The effective questions are the product of experience and reflection, and a well-developed set of heuristics.

The consideration of heuristics takes us back to the beginning of this discussion when we noticed how we are able to 'shortcut' through all the possible options in our decision-making thanks to the presence of somatic markers. In a similar vein, we can shortcut through all the possible assess-ments of any particular situation and the possible actions to take through the use of heuristics. Both of these processes are key to effective decision-making and allow us to make good decisions under imperfect conditions. We need to recognize better that our decision-making circumstances are always imperfect, and that our best defence against poor decision-making is recognizing the part that somatic markers and heuristics play in effective decision-making. This means we need to pay attention to them and have processes for monitoring how our decision-making is going. Some organizations have evolved processes that help them maintain excellent communication, and to continue to make decisions, under the most trying of conditions.

Moving from Decision-Making to Sense-Making

Weick and Sutcliffe (2007) studied the process of mistake avoidance and correction in inherently risk-heavy organizations. These are organizations where small mistakes can have fatal consequences, such as fire-fighting teams, aircraft carriers and surgical teams. They call these organizations, collectively, high reliability organizations. In these organizations, because of the infinite number of variables that affect outcome, mistakes and errors are pretty much bound to happen; they can't all be 'planned out' through tight systems and processes, although these play an important role. Considering these systems, the authors have developed an interesting notion of unexpected events acting as a ruthless 'audit' on the organization's capabilities. In other words, it is easy to be misled about the adaptability and capability of your organization when all is well; the true test is what happens when things unexpectedly go wrong. Such events tend to bring areas of unpreparedness and weakness into sharp view. In these 'high reliability' organizations things go wrong all the time, yet this 'going wrong' doesn't always result in an eventual mistake or error.

Pursuing this interest in how mistakes *don't* happen in such vulnerable organizations, Weick and Sutcliffe have discovered two very interesting strategies that these organizations use to enable them to keep acting in potentially paralysing situations. They note the general 'trial-and-error' nature of proceeding in non-standard situations where, although each event may share a common context such as fighting a fire, landing a plane or performing open heart surgery, each is also unique; and how these strategies allow the people involved to constantly review the appropriateness of the action being taken so that potential mistakes, or the beginnings

of mistaken action, are spotted early and consciously diverted away from or otherwise interrupted. For example, when landing a plane on a short runway on a moving target, variables such as wave effort, wind speed and direction, the position of the sun in sky and the skill and experience of the pilot are going to be different every time. In these situations constant assessment and correction have to be made, and it is not clear whether a particular action will result in success or error when that action is started. Actions that become mistakes don't start out that way: they are usually an attempt to put things back on track. The nature of the action becomes clearer as the action unfolds, hence the well-known expression 'It seemed like a good idea at the time'.

Organizations need to be able to spot when potentially good ideas are starting to reveal themselves, in a particular context, as potentially bad ideas. Research into teams of people who successful negotiate such fragile situations reveals a complexity of thought. For example, they are able to work with ambivalence. They manage to take risks and be cautious, to demonstrate intimacy and detachment, aggressiveness and surrender, repetition and improvization, intuition and deliberation, curiosity and timidity. There is a recognition that at different times each of these values may be the most valuable. Being ambivalent is more valuable, in these situations, than steering a steady middle course. I find this very interesting in the light of the frequent presentation of effective leaders as being those who brook no doubt or argument, and of good decisions needing to be made on firm ground. Weick's research shows that being able to preserve opposing actions within a system facilitates adaptability.

1) LCES

LCES stands for Lookouts, Communication links, Escape routes and Safety zones. It is derived from the study of effective fire-fighting in difficult situations, where the teams are working both to preserve life and to fight fires. Lookouts are separated from the action of active fire-fighting. Their role is to watch the big picture, to spot unusual fire behaviour, change of wind direction, and so on. Clearly, there must be a strong relationship of trust between the lookouts and those in the thick of it. Second, communication links are clear, everyone knows how it works. The group also identifies, and keeps re-identifying as things change: their escape routes, at least two, in the case of emergency; and the safety zone that is known to everyone, that they can retreat to assess the situation and communicate with each other. They regularly retreat to the safety zone to review the situation and to change escape route plans, communication processes, agreed safety zones and who keeps lookout, as necessary. These structures support effective ambivalent adaptive behaviour.

2) STICC

The review is a collective endeavour where the leader's sense-making and decision-making is transparent. Leaders ensure this by employing STICC: Situation, Task, Intent, Concerns and Calibration. The leader takes everyone through the following: This is what we're in (situation). Here's what I think we should do (task). Here's why we should do that (intent). Here's what we should keep our eye on because if that changes we're in a new situation (concerns). Now talk to me (calibration). The leader at this point is inviting calibration of his or her sense-making against everyone else's. It is interesting to consider the difference the adoption of these sense-making processes might have to other areas requiring high reliability that are subject to very uncertain and unpredictable conditions, such as child protection.

These are minimal structures that encourage wise and adaptive behaviour and so more positive outcomes. It cannot be over-emphasized that, within these helpful structures, the quality of relationships is paramount.

If people don't trust each other, if they don't attend to each other's contributions, if they don't dare contribute important information because of their rank, the structure will be less effective and will not deliver the goods. In addition, it helps when people truly understand the interrelatedness of their positions, when they see themselves as part of an interrelated, interdependent and interconnected system.

In their studies of high reliability organizations Weick and Sutcliffe found that they preferred the idea of sense-making to decision-making. As a fire-fighter says, 'if I make a decision it is a possession, I take pride in it, I tend to defend it and not listen to those who question it. If I make sense then this is more dynamic and I listen and I can change it. A decision is something you polish. Sense-making is a direction for the next period' (Weick, 2006, p. 59). Sense-making is an ongoing process of forming and evaluating hypotheses of what is happening and going to happen and adjusting behaviour in the light of the ongoing sense being made. Sense-making is open to evaluation by others who can see how the sense is being made and can contribute to help make better sense. Sense-making systems are also better attuned to picking up weak signals that might herald a big impact, because specific people can be assigned to attend to them. In this way the mindfulness of the system is enhanced. Decision-making by contrast is experienced as high risk. Making definite statements of 'how things are' and therefore 'what we need to do' can introduce an unwarranted sense of certainty. In such an environment weak signals can get ignored as not fitting the picture, and then little errors become big mistakes.

Summary

In this chapter we have examined the importance of positive emotions to both good communication and good decision-making. Research illuminating how high-risk organizations achieve high reliability helps us to understand the importance of ambivalence and sense-making over certainty and decision-making to ensure adaptive behaviour. These findings support our suggestion that the organization is more helpfully thought of as a complex adaptive system, with some built-in redundancy and diversity, than as an efficient machine if we want to ensure good communication and decision-making. We have also noticed how organizational structures, and mindsets, can mitigate against high quality, informal, fragmentary yet highly valuable coordinating communication and decision-making. We have noticed that compensatory action may have to be taken to ensure that good quality coordination and synchronism can be achieved across organizational processes.

Further Reading

Taleb, N. (2005) *Black Swans: The Impact of the Highly Improbable*. Harmondsworth: Penguin Books.
For those interested in the vexed question of how organizations might work to spot the unexpected, this is a great read, if at times tough going.

5

Positive Leadership and Change

Introduction

In this chapter we shall examine the nature of positive leadership and organizational change. Ideas of both authentic and positively deviant leadership offer positive models of how leaders and followers can have a mutually beneficial impact on each other. While Rowland and Higg's field research identifies the really effective leadership change behaviours, Cameron and Cooperrider offer new ways of thinking about strategic development that are better suited to positive and appreciative ways of understanding organizations. While examining these ideas, we shall

Positive Psychology at Work: How Positive Leadership and Appreciative Inquiry Create Inspiring Organizations, First Edition. Sarah Lewis.
© 2011 Sarah Lewis. Published 2011 by John Wiley & Sons, Ltd.

consider questions such as: Are leaders born or made? What is good leadership? How could a leader avoid triggering 'resistance to change' and how effective is top-down directive change?

Leadership

Authentic leadership

Avolio and colleagues (2010) began their engagement with this question by trying to establish whether good leaders are born or made. They undertook a comprehensive meta-analysis of existing research into leadership. They referred particularly to research on identical and fraternal twins studied over long periods of time. Using twins is a standard research method for trying to resolve nature versus nurture debates. Their summary of the analysis is that the emergence of people into leadership roles is due approximately two-thirds to life experience and one third to heritability. This suggests that life experiences are more important than innate abilities in achieving formal leadership positions: leaders are made.

Before conducting this research, Avolio and colleagues spent some time identifying what constituted the roots of good, positive or genuine leadership. To establish this they spent five years exploring the concept in discussion and by referring to historical accounts of what had been recognized as 'good' leadership. They found that leadership as a positive construct elicits such descriptors as genuine, reliable, trustworthy and real (Avolio and Luthans, 2006). This research led them to 'authentic leadership'. They conceived this authenticity as both owning one's personal experience and as acting in accord with one's true self. From their research, Avolio and colleagues define authentic leadership as being confident, hopeful, optimistic, resilient, transparent, moral or ethical, and future-oriented. Their initial ideas of authentic leadership suggest that the core components are relational transparency, internalized morality, adaptive self-reflection and balanced processing. Before looking at each of these facets of authentic leadership, we note the importance of the idea of 'root' leadership features.

One of their conclusions was that such authentic leadership was a root function, while style of leadership was a surface function. So, good leadership could be expressed through a number of leadership styles: transformative, charismatic, visionary, directive or participatory. This observation immediately releases us from the dilemma of having to decide which style of leadership is most effective. It also helps us to recognize that any style can embody leadership that is morally exemplary or morally repugnant; the difference lies in the leaders' root or core, what we might call their morality or values.

For example, it is known that effective cult leaders are often very charismatic. To take but one example: David Koresh. He was the leader of the Branch Davidians, a religious sect that, under Koresh's leadership, practised polygamy and child abuse, among other abuses. Many members died in 1993 following an assault on their premises in Waco, Texas, by the American Bureau of Alcohol, Tobacco and Firearms. The Branch Davidians literally followed David to their deaths. By the accounts of the survivors, some of whom still held allegiance to him, he was a very powerful and charismatic leader. However, he would not fit Avolio's definition of an authentic leader, because at root he was not a morally good man. Accordingly, Avolio and colleagues were able to dismiss these different 'types' or 'styles' as indicators of 'good' leadership and focused on identifying the essence of good leadership, however it might be enacted. They discovered there were four key facets to authentic leadership, the first of which is relational transparency.

Relational transparency
Relational transparency is about being transparent in your relationships, not pretending to be something you are not. However, this is a more delicate and subtle observation than it might at first appear. For relational transparency is not about letting it all hang out, nor is it about being yourself, warts and all. Goffee and Jones (2006) summarized their learning about what makes good leadership, based again on an extensive study of all that had gone before, as 'be yourself, more, with skill'. They emphasized that the most important words in this pithy doctrine were 'with skill'. Ann Shacklady-Smith's account of her journey from an emphasis on 'stepping out of her comfort zone' to a realization of her greater effectiveness when working with her strengths illuminates the contrast between the traditional challenge of working on your weaknesses and the positive leadership challenge of working with your strengths (see Supplement 5.1).

Relational transparency is about appropriate, thoughtful, intentional and wise self-disclosure and self-management, not kneejerk unmediated responses. The leader gains trust through self-disclosure, which includes openly sharing information and the expression of genuine thoughts and feelings, while working to minimize displays of unhelpful, destabilizing or inappropriate emotions. A key distinguishing skill is self-awareness.

Supplement 5.1   Leading from *Within* the Comfort Zone

For several decades I have been steadfastly pursuing the mantra of 'stepping out of my comfort zone', pushing through the discomfort of anxiety, fear and sometimes trauma associated with doing particular professional work tasks and projects. This Yerkes-inspired (1907) concept is based on the idea that anxiety improves performance until a certain level of arousal has been reached, beyond which performance deteriorates. Google 'comfort zone' and you will discover the term has entered popular discourse on topics from self-improvement to skincare. I feel, however, the concept is too widely applied, particularly when viewed from the perspective of positive psychology and the more current thinking around strengths-based development (Seligman, 2006).

When I consider my own 'out of comfort zone experiences' there is a common pattern – a feeling of dread, discomfort, dis-ease which lurks in the mind and body hindering positive thoughts, undermining self-confidence and enjoyment of the work involved. Nor, on reflection, did I achieve much pleasure once the various projects were completed. Rather, I felt relief until the slow build-up of anxiety descended in recognition of the next trauma-filled activity that was on my to-do list. On closer analysis I realized that the source of the discomfort was often in doing work that was in some way at odds with my values and beliefs.

In contrast, I notice that having brought Appreciative Inquiry principles to the centre of my work and my *being* in the world, quite the opposite is true. When I reflect on my 'peak' challenging work experiences I recall *'feeling confident', being 'in the flow', 'feeling at ease with the world', 'at peace', 'work develops with ease' and 'offers a sense of wonder and sheer enjoyment', 'with unimagined positive outcomes'.* I am in fact *'in my comfort zone'.*

The contrast between how I feel about leading and working from within or outside my comfort zone is remarkable. Why would I choose to be anywhere but in my comfort zone? I explored these issues in dialogue with other facilitators. It seemed that the issue I was pondering had a lot to do with being authentic, being true to who you are, and is a leadership approach whose time has come (Jaworski, 1998). Helping leaders of change to realize their authentic selves offers a more fruitful way of working with the emergent changes of our times (Wheatley, 2007): in Appreciative Inquiry terms, focusing on extending their strengths.

A wise friend told me: 'When you are doing what you are called to do, using all of your unique talents and gifts you are in the flow, life is easy' (Mulhern, 2010).

> Thinking about the current economic challenge we all face I relish the prospect of leading change from within my comfort zone and helping others to do likewise. In my experience this is the authentic way to help deliver wellbeing and fairness for all and that when this happens life can be easy.
>
> Contributed by Ann Shacklady-Smith

Self-aware leaders understand their strengths and weaknesses and the effect of both of these on others. One of the things self-aware leaders are aware of, and guided by, is their sense of morality, the second of the four facets of authentic leadership.

Internal morality

Authentic leaders have an internal reference point for their morality, a sense of right and wrong, as some might say, a moral compass. The importance to organizational health of leaders able to maintain a virtuous approach to working with others even during tough times is becoming ever more apparent. This was demonstrated in some fascinating research undertaken by Gittell, Cameron and Lim (2006) on the effects on the aircraft industry of the assault on the World Trade Center in 2001.

An immediate consequence of this tragedy was that all planes were grounded immediately after the event. A longer-term consequence was that many people lost their faith in air travel and switched to road or rail. The effect for the airlines was that traffic instantly dropped below the level necessary for profitability, from 97% occupancy to nearer 80%, and their share price dropped. Gittell was interested in different airline responses to this challenge and the effect of those responses on recovery. Airlines took immediate action, slashing staff numbers, on average by 16%, cutting flights, on average by 20%, and introducing new working practices.

However, there were variations within this overall action: one of the 10 airlines studied cut their staff by 24%, while two made no layoffs at all. Of those that did lay off staff, some did with a distinct lack of good faith: they invoked *force majeure* or 'act of God' exemption clauses which allowed them to make workers redundant without regard to any severance pay due. They enthusiastically seized the opportunity to push through unpopular changes to working practices. This unethical strategy unleashed a costly union court action, and the airline's leadership had to be replaced early in

2002, at least partly in response to a loss of credibility with employees. Some airlines still laid people off but with an expressed reluctance, and they honoured severance and lay-off agreements, even though to do so caused them to make late payments to bond holders, so it clearly caused them financial pain.

At the other extreme a few airlines chose to absorb the shock and the cost, at least in the short term, and worked to find other solutions. As others cut their routes, they benefited by maintaining a presence and indeed expanding their services. This was only possible because they took the counterintuitive decision not to lay off staff. The virtuous action came first. You might think that the quickest recovery would accrue to the airlines that took the quickest and most draconian measures to return to profitability. You would be wrong. Gittell's analysis shows that the airlines that suffered the least fall to their share price, and whose share price recovered most quickly, were those that made every effort to keep their people despite haemorrhaging money. They also were the quickest to return to profitability.

The recovery of the stock price was significantly and negatively related to the extent of the layoffs at the time of the crisis, the strength of the relationship averaging -0.688 for the three-year period 2001–4. The researchers are clear that the mediating factor between response and recovery is the effect on relational reserves, noting that: 'layoffs deplete relational reserves, and relational reserves allow firms to bounce back from crises, maintain desirable functions, and adjust positively to unexpected aberrations' (Gittell *et al.*, 2006, p. 17). While relational reserves are key to organizational resilience and recovery, they are in turn related to financial reserves. Having enough cash and sufficiently low debt to allow the firm to finance longer-term expenses is key to being able to sustain virtuous behaviour in difficult times.

Once again we find that a little slack in the system, in this case financial slack, something that is regarded by the markets as inefficiency (all that money lying around, doing nothing!), becomes a real asset when things suddenly change. The organization that did best in this study, Southwest Airlines, has a long-standing policy of maintaining a rate of optimal rather than maximal growth. This allows it to maintain very high cash reserves, a policy that pays dividends when an unexpected disaster strikes. Southwest airline leaders didn't know what this research reveals, namely that virtuous housekeeping supports the ability to behave honourably towards those who toil for you, which in turn maintains and builds relational reserves such as morale and goodwill, which enhance organizational resilience and bounce-back, which, in turn, facilitate rapid recovery. They were guided more by their internal moral compass and were able to use that to drown out the clamour of 'common-sense' or 'business theory' edicts about how they should run their business. We might call this a demonstration of authentic leadership. Sometimes it seems as if such leaders are in a minority, as we contemplate the rise of the psychopathic leader.

Psychopathic Leaders

An interesting sideline of research into the psychology of leadership has been into how people with severe personality disorders, as well as out and out psychopaths, make it into key leadership positions, and they do. People with disorders of narcissism (excessive self-regard), psychopathic personalities (inability to empathize, lack of morality), paranoia (everyone is against me/us, trust no one) and schizoid tendencies (delusions of grandeur) all make it into positions of power. These disorders are associated with seriously deleterious or unpleasant organizational behaviour. In the worst cases the excesses they display once in positions of power bring organizations to their knees. It has been suggested by one eminent leadership researcher, Malcolm Higgs (2009), that Lee Iacocca at Chrysler, Jean-Marie Messier at Vivendi and Dick Faulds at Lehman Brothers all displayed strong signs of a personality disorder as they indulged in reckless behaviour which damaged the companies they led.

One might wonder how such people were recruited to positions of power in the first place. The answer is partly that organizations, while recruiting for desirable attributes, inadvertently recruit for psychopathic tendencies. As Babiak and Hare (2006) point out, a charming demeanour and grandiose talk can be mistaken for charismatic leadership and self-confidence, while an ability to con and manipulate is also an ability to persuade and influence – both very attractive attributes to people looking for top leaders. Even psychopaths' general inability to establish and work towards long-term strategic goals (they have a more opportunistic tendency) does not handicap them. Instead, when required to show 'vision' and 'strategic thinking' they are able to talk with conviction, delivering a compelling social experience that creates an illusion of visions of the future but which, on analysis, actually contains very little of substance. Psychopaths also share with the greatest leaders an ability to take risks, which can be mistaken for

" It's only a bit of snow "

high-energy action orientation, or courage; only their risk-taking stems from impulsiveness and thrill-seeking rather than from careful, cold calculation. Their impulsivity and ability constantly to switch focus can be mistaken for a much desired ability to multitask. Their inability to feel much emotion or to empathize with others can be mistaken for executive talents such as being able to make hard decisions, keep their emotions in check or remain cool under fire. In short, psychopathic and other personality disorder tendencies are not that easy to spot, especially given our tendency to see what we want. Babiak and Hare suggest that organizations are especially likely to recruit such a person when the organization is vulnerable, confused and uncertain, and someone offers a compelling and authoritative display of strong leadership. See Supplement 5.2 for hints on how to spot, and prevent, potential trouble.

One of the things these disorders share is a distorted, self-oriented moral compass. Or rather, their moral compass is set to 'me'. Authentic leaders are able to balance other people's needs against their own and against some idea of inherently good or ethical behaviour. Thus they are aware that the most expedient way forward may not be acceptable. Authentic leaders, unlike psychopathic leaders, have no choice but to behave ethically; it is a moral imperative. When they are forced to behave against their principles, with their backs against the wall, it causes them personal anguish. Organizations need to learn how better to distinguish authentic leadership

Supplement 5.2   Spotting Trouble in your Midst

Someone ...

- who is all things to all people
- about whom people hold deeply divided opinions (seen as a saving angel by some and a dangerous devil by others)
- who wields disproportionate power to status
- who can skilfully play individuals, telling them what they want to hear
- who has an uncanny ability to make bad things, things that don't work and people in their way disappear (Teflon man/woman)
- who lies and cheats with impunity in the service of some greater goal, and
- who demonstrates loyalty only to self

... just might be displaying strong psychopathic tendencies. As they advance up the organization and external control and non-deferential feedback lessens, the bigger the mess they can create.

How can you lessen the likelihood of this happening to your organization?

- Be brave enough to let go of the problem people early.
- Select for optimal not maximal qualities.
- Do proper biographical tracking history on your top appointments.
- Beware of trading off weaknesses for some great strength.
- Use 360-degree feedback and listen to what those of no current 'use' to the person have to say. The once seduced, now discarded, may have a less enamoured view of the charmer.
- Use Hogan's Dark Side psychometric to assess your leader's potential excesses.
- Give leaders a stable deputy and make sure they have adequate power to influence, control and veto leadership action, i.e. make sure they don't gain absolute power!
- Offer support to help self-management such as coaches, mentors, therapists.

from psychopathic leadership. It sounds like it ought to be easy but clearly it isn't. The third facet of authentic leadership is adaptive self-reflection.

Adaptive self-reflection
Adaptive self-reflection refers to a process of reflecting on your own behaviour in such a way that you learn something useful about yourself. It is characterized by being non-judgemental, curious, having a learning orientation and by patterns of thinking that are open and positive. It stands in contrast to what is known as maladaptive self-reflection. This less useful kind of reflection, familiar to us all I'm sure, is self-judgemental and obsessive. It is characterized by going over a mistake or error again and again, trying to work out how you could have done it. Such maladaptive reflection is characterized by feelings of guilt and blame. It achieves little except a temporary loss of any of the positive qualities the person could bring to bear on the situation as they become immersed in their efforts to recast the past.

Adaptive self-reflection, in contrast, enhances leaders' abilities to respond to new circumstances. Useful, adaptive reflection is characterized by mindfulness (a concept we explore in more detail in Chapter 8) and responsiveness. Professor Michael West's account of how he incorporates mindfulness into his daily life as a leader clearly shows how it can aid authentic leadership (see Supplement 5.3). Such reflection is directed towards learning rather than blaming, is oriented to the future rather than the past and is processing for information rather than to assign blame. A period of such reflection is usually triggered by a particular event, perhaps one that held a surprise. Effective leaders often have a lifetime history of utilizing such events to trigger this type of reflection. Events that trigger effective learning

---

Supplement 5.3   Mindfulness as a Path to Wise Leadership

What does mindfulness mean in practice? Kabat Zinn offers the following illustrative exercise. Take a raisin and feel it in your hand; look at it closely and study it; explore how it feels – its texture, hardness or softness, shape; smell it deeply and discover all the nuances of its scent; place the raisin in your mouth and be aware of the sensations of movement as you do this; taste it – savouring the unfolding of the taste in your mouth; swallow it and experience the sensations associated with that. Such a sharp floodlight cast on one experience gives you a sense of what mindfulness means. It is this sense of mindfulness that I endeavour to bring to my work as a leader at Aston Business School. I find mindfulness helps in all aspects.

By being mindful I find I am present in interactions with those I lead and less likely to fail to detect important signals, messages and emotions. I am also tuned in more to my own motivations (to get the meeting over quickly, the desire to be liked) and therefore to make wiser choices. Being mindful also alerts me to my own moods and feelings – fatigue or irritation which can hamper effective interactions or decision-making. It also makes it more likely I can choose positive emotions (and decide to be supportive rather than resentful). Mindfulness also helps me to be aware of the reactions and needs of others and to manage meetings more effectively by picking up on the tenor, temperature or energy levels of meetings. And I think it helps me to judge the effects of my behaviour on those I lead – to be more aware of the impact of my behaviour as a leader and adjust accordingly. I also find mindfulness helps me maintain a focus on priorities – mindfulness acts as an anchor ensuring I don't drift away on too many currents of immediate demands or distractions. Most importantly, it helps me to adhere to value-driven behaviour – mindfulness is a route to the fundamental. It therefore reminds me to focus on what it is my colleagues and I are trying to achieve: advancing understanding of economies, organizations, wellbeing at work and of businesses in order to promote social good.

For instance, I was recently in a meeting trying to resolve a conflict between two members of staff that had become bogged down in issues of status, defended positions and tense interactions. I felt stuck and frustrated as we went back and forth without making any progress and with an increasing weariness. Mindfulness helped me feel that stuck position. That mindfulness then reminded me to revert to core values – in this case that we must provide students with an inspirational, life-transforming educational experience. That provided a clear direction for both parties in the conflict and appealed to values that transcended their entrenched positions. Both parties had to give ground, but they could do this more easily in the context of serving a higher purpose. Such moments of mindfulness serve me again and again as a leader and make the task even more of a privilege and pleasure.

Williams, Teasdale Segal and Kabat-Zinn (2007) *The Mindful Way through Depression*. New York: Guilford Press, p. 47.

Contributed by Michael West

include things like working in a different culture, changing job or career, reading, working with people with very different views and initiating a new project. Effective leadership training often seeks to create such 'trigger events' to help people develop the complexity of their understanding of themselves, their task and their context. The Metafari and Metasaga leadership journeys devised by Leif Josefsson, and Kate Coutts with Lesley Wilson respectively, work by creating opportunities for just this kind of adaptive self-reflection (see Supplements 5.4 and 5.5). The most effective leaders develop an ability to recognize and use such events as they occur. They are, as Avolio would describe it, constantly in a state of 'developmental readiness'. They know how to learn from life.

Supplement 5.4   The Metafari Story

How old are you, Rafael?

You cannot ask that question in that way to a Maasai. With your ways of thinking I am around 40 years. But we don't count years. I am a younger elder, a retired warrior.

It took us another three hours to explore the idea of age. I got a lesson around how our assumptions form what we take for granted.

Zacharias, as we sit here around the termite mound, tell us about what we see. Why do you ask me such a question? You probably know more than I do. But coming to think about it, I have often wondered about how so small creatures can create so large things together. What about their leadership and organization?

Zacharias, the local Maasai leader had noted that there were lots of creatures visiting the mound even though they did not belong there. Zacharias pointed.

Sometimes we think of ourselves as those little black ants. We go the city, pick up something of use, like the mobile phone, and return home again.

Rafael had been sitting by the waterhole for a full day. As we talked in the evening, he was amazed.

The waterhole brings all animals big, small, the powerful and the graceful to the same place with one purpose, to find the necessity in all living being – water. As we watched the different types of animals each at a time I noticed that no one is claiming full time presence and monopoly of the resource. I saw cooperation, not competition. If I, a Maasai, who has lived in the bush for all my life can learn from this journey, what could it not mean for a leader coming from your part of the world?

The Metafari project started out as a conversation around a website in Sweden. We talked about how to present the websites to the target groups. What could it be like?

Maybe it should be like a waterhole? This initiated a vivid discussion about the waterhole.

What is a waterhole? What happens around the waterhole? Who comes to the waterhole? What are the elements of a well functioning waterhole?

The questions created wonderful conversations and ideas about other exciting metaphors. The coral reef. A termite mound. The tidal landscape.

Would it be possible to arrange Metaphor Safari? I dreamed. Through different connections the Metafari became a reality in Tanzania. Through Ruth Nesje, the founder of Tanga International Conference Center, I got in touch with Rafael ole Monoo, who has become my friend and partner in this project.

Metafari is about inspiring the mind to decode the meaning that can be derived from every event, be it cosmic, living world creations of animals and plants, or geographical like wind movement, seasonal temperature, as it unfolds from what happens before our own eyes.

From the dawn of morning there is the eternally amazing turn of night into day, a moment always inspiring to body and mind as the transformation takes place. It can make us be part of the amazing creation by whoever founded it.

The Metafari is an odyssey of discovery decoding the meaning behind events of nature that could have wider meaning on issues that surround our social, professional and even religious life.

The Meta-journey can of course take place anywhere, anytime. Kate Coutts, founder of Metasaga expresses it gracefully:

Discover yourself in the world around you.

Contributed by Leif Josefsson

Adaptive self-reflection can be triggered by helping people to reflect on what went right, so enabling learning about success. Karena Gomez's account of how helping the leadership team of a large IT change project reflect on past successes raised energy, created ownership and reduced external supports costs, is an excellent example of the power of reflecting on, and learning from, success (see Supplement 5.6). This is easily as

Supplement 5.5   The Personal Journey of Leadership Development: Metasaga

Metasaga is a journey through the culture, heritage and physical landscape. It allows leaders at all levels to engage in deep self-reflection by exploring their environment. It utilizes a strengths-based, whole-system approach to evaluate how they operate as leaders and the performance of the organization they lead. It makes them reframe their thinking using metaphor, narrative, tradition and artefacts found in their physical environment. It combines the business techniques of non-directive coaching, dialogue and Appreciative Inquiry with the traditional storytelling. One participant referred to it as a 'philosophical treasure hunt'.

Metasaga grew from the work of Leif Jossefsson (Metafari) in Tanzania. It began as an individual coaching tool, but quickly developed into a group activity. The first group Metasaga took place in Unst, Shetland in June 2008 for senior leaders from the Education Department. It has now spread out into other public sectors and private business across the country.

So how does it work?

The Metasaga is created in the local environment, preferably the home area of the participants, but this is not essential. A route or trail is identified containing five or six stops. Each stop centres on a significant feature in the landscape. We take the feature and utilize it as a metaphor or trigger to consider the values or themes it suggests.

The next step is to discover the questions that arise from the exploration of both the place and the metaphor. The guide suggests a few questions, and members of the group are also encouraged to develop their own questions, thus increasing their ownership of the learning experience. Participants do not share their answers with the group as a whole, but are encouraged to enter dialogue in ones or twos.

A task is often set around the theme, which encourages experiential learning Often a piece of music is shared that captures the learning experience discovered at the stop.

Each stop should build on the previous and develop reflection in a number of areas related to personal and professional development. The idea is to allow deep thinking and reflection at an individual level while providing an opportunity for collective responses to be shared if appropriate. Individuals are encouraged to journal their experiences.

Orkney have created a medley of Metasagas covering six regions. These Metasagas, created by pupils, allow the individual to explore their own development through the rich tapestry of the Orkney landscape.

Metasaga is about sowing seeds of thought, about giving people space to think. People have found their own answers to their own questions on Metasaga. Barbara realized her acting position in an organization was not for her and she withdrew from the permanent post interview. Jane, on the train journey home after her second Metasaga, began to write poetry, something that had been locked away for years. Susan reclaimed a holiday spot that contained difficult memories after creating a Metasaga around the place.

Leading it you have to trust that what is happening internally is right for each individual. It is their journey. The metaphors and questions allow them to journey deeper. Many of the decisions, the answers, are never shared. Much of the feedback talks of the power and the simplicity, not the detail.

The more rooted I am in my location, the more I extend myself to other places, so as to become a citizen of the world.

(Paulo Freire)

Contributed by Kate Coutts and Lesley Wilson

important as learning from our mistakes. It is, of course, important to learn from mistakes, but counter-intuitively we are able to do that better when we are not consumed by feeling bad. Authentic leaders display an ability to process life experiences and opportunities in a way that is free from undue bias. Undue bias refers to both the interfering effects of excesses of emotion and to the distorting lens of the personality disorders mentioned earlier. The ability to escape the grasp of these makes for the fourth key element of authentic leadership: balanced processing.

Balanced processing

Balanced processing is described as a form of information-processing that is less susceptible to denials, distortions and exaggerations. It describes an ideal whereby a leader objectively analyses all relevant information before coming to a decision. From our discussion in Chapter 4, we know that the implied ideal of complete objectivity in decision-making is unattainable, indeed undesirable, so we take it that what is referred to here is the ability to have some awareness of the distortions and exaggerations that our emotional responses bring to our decision-making and to use the information they bring wisely. Implicit in the phrase is the ability to balance the needs of self and others; the present and future; managers and staff; head office and the localities; and all the other complexities of any particular context

Supplement 5.6   Leaders Use Appreciative Inquiry to Prepare for a Change Management Challenge

For three months in the winter of 2008, I worked within an Organization Change project in a bank in Saudi Arabia, as part of an external consulting team. The aim of the project was to improve the working relationship between the business areas and the IT function; there were several areas of focus, including organization design, governance of projects and programmes, prioritization and finally the change management stream.

Alongside creating a traditional change management plan, I used an Appreciative Inquiry interview with each of the eight directors, including the CEO, asking about their previous positive experiences of implementing change. The leaders got caught up in telling stories of previous success, and the interviews nearly all overran! There was a selection of rich stories to draw on, for example, there was a previous project implementing ITIL (a best practice methodology for IT management), which had many of the same challenges as this current work; also there was a business continuity project which came up in several of the stories told. The themes from the stories were about 'people seeing that when they say something, someone is listening', 'collaboration', 'taking the fear away from change, seeing it as positive'. I had explained at the start of each interview that the stories would be used to populate some of the activity within the change plan and to weave into the communications about the programme. The programme manager had been very sceptical about the interviews, as had my other colleagues, and there was a feeling that focusing on stories of success ignored the reality of the current situation. There had previously been a lot of comment that the senior leaders within the IT function were not bought into the change and that they 'did not want to change'.

After the interviews, there was a noticeable increase in the level of interest of the senior leaders in the project, and for the second phase internal change managers were appointed, rather than relying on adding resource to the external consulting team. Reflecting on the process of the AI interviews, I was given the opportunity to meet the leaders in this way because the programme manager thought that 'it wouldn't make things worse'. The process was almost seen as an indulgence within the programme. What became clear from the interviews themselves was the amount of energy unlocked by the stories told. The leaders began to see how they could influence the changes and how similar some of the challenges were to work they had previously been involved in. The most significant change was their desire to put internal resource onto the programme, and to take ownership of the changes themselves as a department.

Contributed by Karena Gomez

in which a decision needs to be made. As we saw in Chapter 4 positivity is an asset when it comes to making effective decisions in complex social environments, and so it proves in leadership. Positivity is found to be strongly associated with authentic leadership.

Authentic leaders are generally positive about who they are and what they can achieve through others. They focus attention on exhibiting positive behaviours day in and day out. They demonstrate an expressed belief that everyone has something to contribute to the project. They are aware of their strengths and see one of their challenges as being to identify their colleagues' strengths and to help them develop them. They are equally aware of their own weaknesses or vulnerabilities and discuss these with colleagues, so making themselves open to question. In this way they turn their vulnerabilities into strengths, since such disclosure encourages reciprocal behaviour from others. They balance the need to achieve the task and to develop others.

It has been found that leaders able to demonstrate these positive behaviours promote higher follower satisfaction and commitment (Luthans *et al.*, 2006). Interestingly, authentic leaders achieve this influence not through coercion or their powers of persuasion so much as inspiring by example. Both Cameron and Fredrickson's work suggest that the process that supports this relationship between observing virtuous or positive behaviour and exhibiting more of it oneself is one of contagion. In other words, authentic leadership is catching.

Authentic leaders create authentic followers. Such followers display parallel qualities to their leaders. Together, leaders and followers can generate an engaged, highly positive, ethical organizational climate. This is exactly the process that Cameron found in his research on flourishing organizations. As the level of authenticity and positivity in the organization grows, leaders and followers become able to develop each other. One of the ways they do this is by becoming ever clearer about each other's strengths. However, there are particular challenges associated with helping leaders to recognize their strengths.

1) Strengths leadership

Increasingly, it is being recognized that the best leaders don't work to become perfect. Rather, they focus on honing their strengths and finding others to make up their limitations. It has been identified that no one defining set of strengths exists for effective leaders; rather, effective leaders know how to use their strengths to enhance their leadership (George and Sims, 2007). Just knowing your strengths is not enough: Clifton and Nelson studied how long it takes talented individuals to arrive at world-class performance and found it to be between 10 and 17 years (1992, p. 63). It is clear there are no shortcuts to becoming an excellent leader, however knowing your strengths clearly helps. Kaplan and Kaiser (2010), however, found that leaders don't know their own strengths, which also means they are often unaware of the 'fatal flaws' that accompany their strengths. Fatal flaws can at worst be another source of leadership derailment, while at best they weaken and undermine leadership performance.

Fatal flaws are those characteristics that can become career-damaging, or at the very least have a significant impact on performance. They can arise out of over played strengths. Morris and Garrett (2010) point out that many leaders, due to childhood deprivations, are out to prove something. It is this unconscious combination of inner uncertainty and lack of confidence, with exceptional strengths of which they are unaware, that can lead to a consistent overplaying of the strength to compensate for an inaccurately perceived vulnerability, which in turn can result in recurring unhelpful behaviour: the fatal flaws.

While the pattern of insecurity and strength may take many forms, we can recognize a not uncommon script that goes as follows: 'I never succeeded at school; I know I'm stupid and only got to this position by luck, therefore I must constantly demonstrate evidence of intellect or they'll find me out.' Fuelled by this fear, overwhelming intellect is used remorselessly to prove minor points, as well as more beneficially to develop impressive strategy. People around the leader become scarred by their leader's inability to let small points go, to overlook minor errors, indeed to be at all forgiving of those who do not share their incisive analytical ability. Such a scenario is not uncommon for people who failed at school, but who go on to become self-made leaders. The sense of self-doubt and inadequacy imbued by years of academic failure and embarrassment can leave very deep scars. Long after they have seemingly proved their ability to succeed in a different context they are still haunted by fear of ridicule, humiliation and failure.

Such leaders do not need to be made more aware of their faults; they need to become more aware of their strengths. Through understanding their strengths better they will be able to mitigate their unintended effects. Unfortunately, two things work against leaders getting this feedback in the normal course of events. First, they don't get affirmation of their strengths because it is assumed they know how good they are at certain things. Secondly, they discount any positive feedback they do receive. The scenario of an individual's lack of awareness of their own strengths, and of other people's assumption that since it is so glaringly obvious they must know, is so commonly encountered as to be a cliché. In fact, in general, people are unaware of the nature of any exceptional strengths and consistently underestimate such strengths (Kruger and Dunning, 1999).

Anyone who has ever given 360°-feedback will have come across situations where the individual has scored themselves average on some competency, while others have consistently, and across all groups, scored them highly. This is a clue to an unowned strength. A denial of exceptional talent is not necessarily down to false modesty or winning humility, it can be due to a genuine lack of awareness and appreciation of what makes them special and different from their contemporaries. Among other things this lack of appreciation of their strengths makes it hard for them to understand why others don't have the same abilities. They assume others must have the same strength but are simply too lazy or stupid to use it. This is not a great state of affairs.

Most leaders learn to adjust to the rarefied atmosphere of positions of power and recognize the distorting effects it has on the flow of negative and positive information. Therefore, they become very suspicious of positive feedback and discount it as invalid or exaggerated, and as being offered only as a sop to their ego. Kaplan and Kaiser (2010) found that some leaders act 'as if only negative feedback will nourish them' (p. 110). Altogether this can produce a situation where leaders underrate themselves in comparison to their co-workers; do not know their strengths and are resistant to hearing about them; do not know their fatal flaws; and assume other people are as capable in their areas of strength as they are. It is not hard to see the problems this can cause: leaders constantly out to prove themselves; unable to capitalize on their strengths because they don't know them; unconsciously overplaying strengths so they become fatal flaws; and permanently puzzled and dismayed by the poor performance of those around them.

Kaplan and Kaiser suggest that what is needed here is corrective mirroring, by which they mean not only a mirroring of how the leader is doing at present in their role (i.e., situational mirroring), but also self-image correcting. Corrective mirroring works to correct misperceptions arising from the past: if someone has grown up believing they are deficient in some area, they need plenty of positive feedback with lots of examples to be able to make a suitable shift in self-perception. Kaplan and Kaiser suggest that the process of providing this feedback is aided by the presence of an affirmative relationship that the leader trusts. It needs to be someone who is seen as a creditworthy source of feedback, with no axe to grind or palm to grease. In organizations it is often someone outside the line relationship who is best able to offer such corrective feedback, for example, a colleague, a mentor or a coach. Alternatively, leaders can become more aware of their strengths through a combination of adaptive self-reflection and storytelling, combined with visualization and attentive listening, as illustrated by James Butcher's account of his work with a leadership team (see Supplement 5.7). Positively deviant leaders, as observed by

---

Supplement 5.7   Leaders at Their Best

This exercise blends methods from Appreciative Inquiry and solution-focused approaches to help leaders clarify their distinctive strengths.

People come on leadership development programmes for all sorts of reasons, but often with a feeling there's something missing from their leadership practice (and perhaps with some feedback to tell them so). But what about the distinctive strengths they bring to leadership, the qualities that make them the leader they are?

We ask people to think about a time when they have been at their best as a leader. It could be a large public event or a passing moment in a corridor, something recent or something remembered from years ago. In pairs, people tell their story as vividly as they can. What happened? What did they do and say – and just as importantly, not do and not say – that made this an example of successful leadership? What were they thinking and feeling? How did the other person respond? What makes this example of their leadership so significant? What are they particularly proud of?

As one person tells their story, the other listens and notices the strengths they hear, to report back at the end – often we take our own qualities for granted.

Brought together again, the group is invited to close their eyes for a visualization, to imagine a day, next week. Overnight a miracle occurs: on this day they are able to be at their best, with all their strengths fully at their disposal. They imagine waking and starting to notice that today, things are different. We go through the day from those first moments, then preparing for the day ahead, to arriving at work, all the activities of the day, the journey home and the moments before sleep. What's different about this particular day that tells them that something has happened, that today they are able to be their best selves?

Back in pairs, people help each other to create a leadership proposition that crystallizes who they are at their best, drawing on themes from the stories they told and the visualization of their ideal day. These leadership propositions are shared with the rest of the group, then each person plans ways to realize that best version of themselves more fully and consistently.

Reproduced by permission of James Butcher

Cameron and colleagues, specialize in ensuring that all are aware of their strengths.

2) Positively deviant leadership

Positively deviant leaders demonstrate an affirmative bias in their leadership and emphasize people and organizational strengths (see Clive Hutchinson's account in Supplement 5.8 of such practice at Cougar). Wooten and Cameron (2010) have identified such leadership as being key to the success of flourishing organizations. Positively deviant leaders focus on what goes right, what is life-giving, what is experienced as good, what is inspiring. As mentioned in Chapter 4, this isn't to say that they ignore the converse; rather, their primary emphasis is on elevating and boosting what is positive in the people and the organization. Such leaders value outcomes such as interpersonal flourishing, meaningful work, virtuous behaviour, positive emotions and energizing networks. Joep C. de Jong's meditative reflection on the nature of appreciative leadership shows how such leadership adds value by positively deviating from the standard idea of knowledge as data to one of knowledge as a much more holistic spiritual wisdom (see Supplement 5.9).

Supplement 5.8   Leadership in a Strengths-Based Organization

As a strengths-based organization our view is that the role of leaders or managers is to help people to excel. To do this they need to help their people play to their strengths, clarify outcomes, set people free to do the work their way, support their people and create a culture of openness. As we started to clarify that this was what we wanted from leaders and managers, we started to ask ourselves what strengths are needed for these roles. What strengths are needed to be an effective leader or manager?

In answering that question we realized there was a problem. Like most companies the people we chose to become managers were those that were best at doing their current (non-managerial) job. Also, the people we selected were probably good at standing out from the crowd. They were usually ambitious, competitive individuals focused on their own success. Now there is nothing wrong with these traits in themselves but we recognized they probably weren't the strengths needed to be a good manager of people.

As we discussed what strengths we did want, we came up with things like having a focus on others, having the ability to see what makes different people tick, having empathy, being naturally trusting, having self-confidence and getting a kick out of seeing other people develop. Now, we saw that this list was nothing like the list of strengths our selection processes actually selected for. As a result, we have made some radical changes to how we appoint leaders and managers. In short, we put the selection in the hands of our own people. We reasoned that if you were going to be a great leader you needed committed and enthusiastic followers. What better way to get this than to ask the followers to select their own leaders? At a stroke, we got rid of the problem of selecting the wrong people as leaders. Given a choice, people don't seem to choose people to lead them who are ambitious, competitive and self-focused. Instead, they pick people who inspire them, help them to succeed and sort out problems for them. As a result, the nature of leadership is gradually changing at Cougar Automation. It is very much a change for the better.

Reproduced by permission of Clive Hutchinson

Supplement 5.9   Appreciative Leadership

In my journey to become an appreciative leader, I have come across two ideas that resonate for me:

1. The notion that there is such a thing as the added value chain in leadership; and
2. The idea that the primary task of leadership in the future will be to assure the balance between the clock of our external world and our own internal clock

Regarding the first notion, the basic idea is that there is a value chain that may have specific value for the leaders of tomorrow. This value chain starts with the assumption that all we have at the beginning of the value chain are data, meaning the raw data we have – 'a', 'b', 'c', etc., or '1', '2', '3', etc. When we add value to data the data become 'information' (simply stated, words and figures). When in turn we add value to information we get 'knowledge' – for example, the words used in sentences providing us with instructions. Today, in most Western societies, knowledge is considered a source of power, owned by individuals, institutions or organizations. It is here that a major shift may be expected, the notion that 'shared knowledge will become a source of well-being to the community'. And when value is added to that type of shared knowledge we move into the realm of 'wisdom', where we see a growing interest for the realm of connecting-sharing and co-creating. It is here that we see a strong emphasis on the ability to show genuine empathy for those we are working with. And then a final

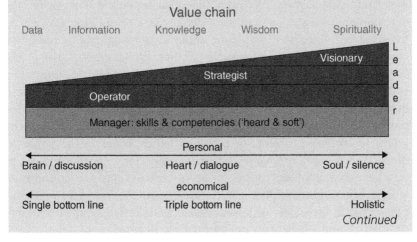

Continued

Supplement 5.9 *Continued*

is set when we add value to wisdom and enter the space of spirituality or wholeness in business. It is here that we start to call leaders 'appreciative leaders' or more commonly 'authentic leaders'. The main characteristic that we use to identify leaders in this space is whether or not they can be regarded as authentic. Another element is their ability to take a truly holistic perspective of their actions, often beyond the 'triple bottom line' perspective. Parallel to the value chain we see a wider use of our abilities and of our interests. Developing from a single, bottom-line fixation, driven from our brains and discussions around who is right or wrong, to a holistic understanding of what we are doing to ourselves, to our planet, driven by a deep understanding of what it is we are about. Something we can only discover when we let go of what is right and what is wrong, a discovery that takes place in the silence of our souls.

I can foresee that we shall enter an era where leaders may play a major role in understanding the holistic nature of whatever it is we do, maybe a provocative idea, however fitting the unconventional thoughts and ideas required for the appreciative leader of the twenty-first century.

Contributed by Joep C. de Jong

Organizational Change

Let's turn now to the question of change: how is it best led or managed? The traditional answer has been that change should stem from the development of a strategy, and that strategy is 'a central, integrated plan for achieving objectives that define approaches for managing resources, customers, competition, and growth' (Wooten and Cameron, 2010, p. 53). From this generic definition we might note the words 'central', 'integrated' and 'plan'. At its heart it contains the metaphor of the organization as a machine. Lewis *et al.* (2007) explore this metaphor and its meaning for organizational change in depth, suggesting that it facilitates a belief in the power of naming problems to produce change; belief in the power of instruction to achieve change; belief that emotions are problematic in organizational life; belief in the power of criticism and fear to motivate change; belief in the split between the leaders and the rest of the organization; belief in the power of separating elements to reduce organizational complexity; and a belief in a right answer to the problem of design.

From these beliefs about the nature of organization there follows a set of assumptions about the role of leaders in change, as articulated by Stacey (1996), for example, that leaders can successfully choose the adaptive shape of their organization *before* the environment has changed. This suggests a highly desirable omniscience and that change is a linear process and that organizations tend towards stable states. From these assumptions, it follows that change is relatively straightforward, should be driven from the top and can be uniformly implemented according to a detailed change plan. Rowland and Higgs (2008) were interested why, if this was the case, 70% of change efforts are estimated to fail, and so set out to discover what leaders actually do in times of organizational change, and how different leadership behaviours might correlate with different change outcomes.

Initially, they undertook a review of the literature to establish a theoretical base for their analysis. They then conducted narrative, case-study research with leaders. They asked 50 leaders from 19 organizations to tell them about their experiences of introducing change. They collected 110 stories (Higgs and Rowland, 2005), which they were able to plot against the four distinct approaches to change they had identified in the literature (see Supplement 5.10). In other words, any story they recorded in their research tended to be more predominantly related to one of these quadrants than another.

The two axes in Supplement 5.10 refer to how change is viewed and to how achieving change is approached. Change can be viewed as a predictable phenomenon, seen as straightforward, easily managed and linear, or as a complex phenomenon, one that is non-controllable and non-linear. On the other axis change can be viewed as something that needs to done in the same way everywhere, one means to one end, or as something that might be done differently in different areas of the business: different means to achieve the same end. Analysing the stories that fell within each quadrant to identify some of their common and distinguishing features, they suggest each quadrant can be named as a different approach to change.

Approaches to Change

1) The directive approach to change

The directive approach to change is predicated on a belief that change is essentially straightforward and predictable. This approach asserts that change can be achieved uniformly across the organization by giving clear

Supplement 5.10   Higgs model

Uniform approach

	Directive Change	Master Change	
Change as a predictable phenomenon	"I can manage change"	"I trust my people to solve things with us"	**Change as a complex phenomenon**
	Self-Assembly Change	Emergent Change	
	"Launch enough initiatives and something will stick"	"I can only create the conditions for change to happen"	

Disseminated and differentiated approach

Reprinted with permission from M. Higgs (2010) Change and its Leadership: The Role of Positive Emotions. In A. Linley, S. Harrington and N. Garcea (Eds.) *Oxford Handbook of Positive Psychology and Work*. Oxford: Oxford University Press. Also, by permission of Oxford University Press, Inc (www.oup.com)

direction on what needs to be done. It is a top-down approach, where people are given prescribed steps to follow. Key messages are sent out from the centre to be 'cascaded' through the organization. Change is often delivered through a series of projects. People are expected to get on with it, and those who don't are seen as problematic. There is likely to be much conversation about getting buy-in and overcoming resistance. This approach is likely to be very familiar to you as it is far and away the most common approach. It is also, as we shall see, one of the least successful.

2) The self-assembly approach to change

The self-assembly approach is similar to the directive approach, except that there is more flexibility for local areas to decide *how* they implement the change. The centre sets direction, while detail and accountability are left to the local managers. Essentially, this is the 'toolkit of change' approach. The centre designs and sends out what it considers to be useful tools (pro-formas, training kits, etc.) for local managers to use at their discretion. Usually a support system is made available to help managers implement these various approaches. Both the directive and self-assembly approaches are based on a belief that everything can be seen, analysed, designed, planned, managed and predicted from the top. So there is no need to involve others in the design. Their job is just to implement.

3) The master approach to change

On the other side of the figure we have the approaches that recognize change as a complex phenomenon. The master approach to change believes in a central approach to achieving change, but recognizes that people need to be equipped with some skills to see change through. A message about what needs to be done is set from the top and there is a common plan, consistent language and agreed projects to support the change. People are invited to help with the design of the change within a centrally set direction. Leadership and coordination across the organization are recognized to be important, so people are equipped with 'leading change skills' and networks are created to aid cross-organization coordination.

4) The emergent approach to change

Finally, we have the emergent approach to change. This approach can be characterized, perhaps unkindly, as making it up as you go along and is certainly often experienced like that. Within an overall purpose (e.g., to become more profitable or to find new markets), the direction of the change is adjusted as people make sense of what is needed to achieve the desired direction. Such an approach requires a willingness to set off on the journey of change, knowing neither the exact path to take nor the final destination. The leader who takes such an approach sets a few general rules to guide what individuals do, typically around desired outcomes and core values. People are then free to start acting: getting on with things as they see fit. In this way change is likely to start in a small way and build from the ground up. At different times the organizational attention is focused on different things – areas of priority and importance shift. Coordination and coherence are achieved through networks of conversation and information exchange, both formal and informal. The role of the leader is that of creating the conditions for change, rather than designing or directing the change.

Now, the $64 million question is, how effective are these different approaches? And are different approaches more successful with different types of change? To start to answer these questions Higgs and Rowland had to classify 'types' of change, so they could correlate them with the approaches to change, against success. They did this along the dimensions of complexity, scope, magnitude, timescale, source, history of change and driver for change. Complexity refers to whether the change is about changing a few things or many things; scope refers to how many people in the organization will be affected; while magnitude is a function of complexity and scope. So low complexity and low scope equal low magnitude, while high complexity and high scope equal high magnitude. Source refers to whether the perceived need for change is externally or internally driven. History refers to how familiar the organization is with change and driver is about whether it is one person's initiative or a team-driven initiative. All the stories were classified against these dimensions. Rowland and Higgs went back to the participants and asked them to rate the success of each change initiative on a scale of 1–5. So with a classification of the approach to change, a classification of the change itself and a measure of success, an analysis could now be conducted to find out which approach was most successful in which change situation. This is what they found.

Here is the big news. In none of the change contexts did the directive or self-assembly approach to change have a positive relationship to success. Indeed, Rowland and Higgs state quite categorically that one should 'avoid toolkit "self-assembly" change in any scenario' (p. 44). This finding was a shock to the participants. The only situation where these approaches had a *neutral* impact was when the change was low in magnitude and was driven by an internal change source, in other words, when it was a small local change, initiated by the leader within their domain of control. With this minor exception, we can boldly say in the light of this research that these approaches do not work! On the other hand, the master and emergent change approaches were positively correlated with success in all types of change. It seems the feature they have in common, recognizing the complexity of change, is the defining feature of greater success.

Their other exciting finding was that for high magnitude change, that is change high in scope and complexity, by far the most successful approach was the emergent approach. This result also came as something of a surprise to the participants, since in their accounts the emergent approach was

CHARGE !

most frequently cast as the outcome of the failure of a directive approach. Rowland and Higgs state that 'the emergent change approach was the most correlated to success – statistically an extremely large amount of the variation in change success (more than a third) for high magnitude change' (p. 42). And high magnitude change projects are undoubtedly the ones that people are thinking of when they talk about organizational change, suggesting that the emergent approach to change is, in essence, the most successful approach to organizational change. However, while people recognize high magnitude change, they don't necessarily recognize an emergent approach to change.

Higgs and Rowland found that while they were able to identify which projects fitted into the emergent category, 'emergent' wasn't necessarily a label the change leaders used to describe this way of doing change. Instead, they were likely to have described the change as being messy and iterative, or as having to make it up as they went along. Higgs and Rowland's observation is that the emergent approach to change is often an evolution of a more planned approach to change that hasn't delivered the goods: 'from the interviews, it was apparent that the emergent approach occurred in the context of a change framework that was more planned and structured. It is feasible from this data to propose that the emergent approach describes how change actually happens as opposed to how change is articulated' (p. 132). This is a crucial finding, as it suggests that how we characteristically talk about organizational change is positively misleading. The large group approaches to change we look at in Chapter 8 offer the beginnings of a way to work in an effective way with emergent change.

Leadership Change Behaviour

Having established the different approaches to change and their relationship to success, Rowland and Higgs moved on to consider the different behaviours exhibited by leaders, and how these were or were not associated with the different approaches to change. Via a factor analysis, they identified three key 'styles' of change leadership behaviour evident in the stories: shaping, framing and creating capacity.

1) Shaping change

Someone who uses shaping behaviour likes to be the mover and shaker of change. They set the pace, expecting others to follow. They can be very expressive and persuasive. In another context Higgs refers to this as 'hero leadership' (2009): the change comes solely from the leader's activity, energy and inspiration.

2) Framing change

Here the leader works with others to create vision and direction, they share an overall plan of what needs to be done and the leader gives others the space to do what they need within the business goals. Someone exhibiting these behaviours is seeking to change *how* things are done as well as *what* is done.

3) Creating capacity

The behaviour associated with this approach is that of developing the skills of others so the whole organization becomes involved in creating the change. Leaders who work this way are likely to provide coaching and support.

These different behaviour styles correlated well with the different approaches to change: shaping behaviours are strongly associated with a directive approach, framing behaviours with a master approach, and creating capacity behaviours with an emergent approach, although each change approach was likely to contain elements of each of the three categories of behaviour. Shaping behaviour had a negative impact on change success in all the contexts examined, while framing and creating capacity behaviours were positively related to change in most contexts.

Before we move on to explore more of Higgs and Rowland's work, I want to emphasize the value of this research in offering a necessary corrective to prevailing views of leadership and change. Their work has given us a language and taxonomy for talking about change leadership that is about behaviour, not personality traits or mystical leadership abilities. It provides evidence with which to confront those wedded to hero leadership, and to support those inching towards facilitating emergent change. Directive, 'just tell them' leadership, it is clear, is inappropriate and unhelpful and is indeed a positive hindrance to large-scale organizational change, such as culture change. And yet organizations find it hard to let go of this illusion of leadership control.

Effective Leadership Behaviour

What does the effective leader do in situations of large-scale change if they aren't directing and shaping? Rowland and Higgs found that leaders who demonstrated a strong combination of framing and creating capacity behaviours appeared to be particularly successful in most change scenarios. So next they examined these in more detail, conducting a further study with 60 leaders from over 30 organizations and garnering over 100 change stories (Rowland and Higgs, 2008). Analysis of these data revealed four distinct sets of leadership change practice and behaviour. They called these 'changing leadership' behaviours attractor behaviours, edge and tension behaviours, container behaviours and movement or transforming space behaviours. The most successful change leaders were able to enact all these behaviours at different times in different contexts, as appropriate.

1) Attractor behaviour

Attractor behaviour creates a magnetic pull in the organization towards the change. Leaders displaying this behaviour generate a shared spirit, facilitating the creation of connected stories and releasing energy for the change. Immediately, we can see what Appreciative Inquiry has to offer as it is all about creating a magnetic pull towards a desirable future. The co-creation of dreams of the future, the positive energy and the co-created stories about the organization are all effectively attractor behaviours. Attractor behaviour also encompasses creating emotional attachments and connections among people and across the organization. Being able to see patterns and themes within an organization and connecting them to the wider change is also part of the attractor behaviour pattern. This helps everyone 'make sense' between what is going on in his or her world and the wider story of change. This connection of the parts with the whole, and with each other, is exactly what the various 'whole-system change' methodologies such as Open Space, World Café and Appreciative Inquiry facilitate so effectively. The creation of synchronism, where people can act in harmony, is at the heart of these methods and this 'attractor' behaviour set. While the leader is working to create this socially connected central force for change, they can't let things get too cosy; they also need to create and manage edge and tension.

2) Edge and tension

Almost as a counterbalance to the optimistic harmony and positive energy created by attractor behaviour, edge and tension behaviour keeps people focused on the hard decisions that have to be made. It's about ensuring that bad news isn't ignored, that negative feedback (e.g., from customers or staff) is not discounted or trivialized. The leadership behaviour might involve spotting and questioning unquestioned assumptions, or it might be about setting high aspirations and objectives. Rowland and Higgs are clear that this demanding environment is combined with an emphasis on spotting and using talent and strengths. Attractor and edge and tension behaviour are an expression of system ambiguity. On some occasions the need will be to create harmony and high positive energy through attractor behaviour, while at other times the most effective thing will be to hold people in difficult situations until they figure out a different way to move forward. Clearly, such challenging behaviour can be performed more or less skilfully. Poorly done, it risks engendering resentment and creating rifts, and undermining rather than complementing attractor behaviour. Creating a pull towards the change and managing difficult realities is not sufficient; the leader also needs to create some certainty, some safety within all the potential confusion. Rowland and Higgs call this 'creating a container' behaviour.

3) Creating a container

This aspect of effective leadership behaviour is really about creating confidence, while embracing uncertainty. The leader needs to be able to remain calm and exude confidence in the organization's ability to find a way through, even when it is unclear what that way may be. They need to create some certainty among all the uncertainty. They do this through their clarity of expectation. They make performance expectations and values and behaviour clear: people know what they need to achieve and the ethical frame within which they might go about it. Leaders in this mode also create safe spaces to have hard conversations. It becomes possible to say the unsayable, to question the sacred. This aspect of effective leadership behaviour demands that they demonstrate resilience, hope, optimism and self-efficacy: it is a call on their psychological capabilities and on their relational transparency.

4) Transforming space

Finally, Rowland and Higgs identified transforming space behaviour. This behaviour is focused on what I would call creating change in the moment. It is about micro-opportunities and moment-to-moment decisions that, by the choices made, show the new way. When in this mode leaders effectively slow down the meeting or the interaction so that hidden assumptions can be unearthed, or the learning that has just taken place can be identified and named. They create new spaces, or transform existing ones, to facilitate new encounters and conversations. At its heart this is about promoting what we would now call very mindful behaviour. It is about paying close attention in the moment and about being very aware of where attention is, and isn't, focused. It is about interrupting established, unthinking behavioural and conversational sequences to create something different.

All the behaviours listed above were correlated with successful change, and the most successful change was correlated with the use of all four behaviours. Rowland and Higgs (2008) found that these behaviours, together, accounted for around half the variance in success of change in all change contexts, while shaping behaviours continued to be negatively related to change success. At different times on the change journey, and in different contexts, each of these four behaviours will be the most appropriate. In general terms it can be seen that these behaviours encompass ideas of whole-system change, positivity, system ambivalence and social capital.

Taken together they can be seen as an enactment and endorsement of an understanding of the organization as a complex adaptive system.

Developing Strategy

Bringing all this together, this research into leadership and successful change suggests that change is best approached as an emergent phenomenon, and that skilled leadership behaviour is authentic, positive and able to maintain and work with system ambiguity. This suggests that strategy also needs to be viewed somewhat differently. Wooten and Cameron suggest we should start to see strategy as 'a set of processes that enables collective resourcefulness and generative dynamics that lead to positive states or outcomes' (2010, p. 54). Collective resourcefulness refers to the manner in which organizational members work together to develop and implement strategy through policies and practices, while generative dynamics refers to organizational activities that create, develop, transform, multiply and leverage its resources and capabilities. The development of new capabilities makes it possible for the organization to respond to changing environments with value-adding strategies. Cameron has built on this work with his development of the competing values framework to help leaders with their strategic challenges (see Supplement 5.11).

1) Competing values framework

This framework can be seen as an expression of the ambiguity inherent in complex adaptive systems. It illuminates the predominant strategies available to organizations as they seek to resolve the ambiguity. Each quadrant offers feasible organizational and leadership strategies. No particular one is right or correct, but each offers something different. As the demands of, or on, the organization change, its predominant strategy may need to change. So any strategy is only a temporary resolution of the ambiguities inherent in a complex adaptive system. Organizational strategy can be seen as offering a series of temporary positions of certainty in inherently ambiguous situations. And while most organizations adopt one or more of these quadrants as their dominant patterns of organizational strengths, effective organizations need to be able to respond adaptively to changing situations. A key point is that each of these broad, strategic positions can be enacted in such a way as to encourage positively deviant behaviour. Cameron is not

Supplement 5.11   Values frame

Long-term change			Individuality flexibility			New change
	Culture Type:	CLAN		**Culture Type:**	ADHOCRACY	
	Orientation:	COLLABORATE		**Orientation:**	CREATE	
	Leader Type:	Facilitator		**Leader Type:**	Innovator	
		Mentor			Entrepreneur	
		Teambuilder			Visionary	
	Value Drivers:	Commitment		**Value Drivers:**	Innovative outputs	
		Communication			Transformation	
		Development			Agility	
	Theory of	Human development		**Theory of**	Innovativeness, vision	
Internal Maintenance	**Effectiveness:**	and high commitment produce effectiveness		**Effectiveness:**	and constant change produce effectiveness	External Positioning
	Culture Type:	HIERARCHY		**Culture Type:**	MARKET	
	Orientation:	CONTROL		**Orientation:**	COMPETE	
	Leader Type:	Coordinator		**Leader Type:**	Hard-driver	
		Monitor			Competitor	
		Organizer			Producer	
	Value Drivers:	Efficiency		**Value Drivers:**	Market share	
		Timeliness			Goal achievement	
		Consistency & Uniformity			Profitability	
	Theory of	Control and efficiency		**Theory of**	Aggressively competing	
	Effectiveness:	with capable processes produce effectiveness		**Effectiveness:**	and customer focus produce effectiveness	
Incremental change			Stability control			Fast change

Reprinted with permission from L. Wooten and K. Cameron (2010) Enablers of a Positive Strategy: Positively Deviant Leadership. In A. Linley, S. Harrington and N. Garcea (Eds.) *Oxford Handbook of Positive Psychology and Work*. Oxford: Oxford University Press. Also, by permission of Oxford University Press, Inc (www.oup.com)

alone starting to think about strategy differently in the light of changing views of organizations. Cooperrider and colleagues have devised an appreciative approach to strategy development.

2) SOAR

Stravos, Cooperrider and Kelley's (2003) approach is built on Appreciative Inquiry principles. In contrast to the common strategic development tool of SWOT, which encourages organizations to look at Strengths, Weakness, Opportunities and Threats, they suggest SOAR. This stands for Strengths, Opportunities, Aspirations and Results. This model and practice of strategic development replaces the traditional linear process of assessment, planning and implementation with a process of simultaneous inquiry and development. SOAR is enacted in a participatory way, based on AI principles using AI practices.

By working in this way, everyone contributes to the development of the articulation of existing strengths, everyone helps identify market opportunities, all are engaged in creating visions of the future and all are focused on devising ways of measuring results. In this way strategy is co-constructed throughout the process of inquiry and the challenge of achieving results is integrated into the inquiry from the beginning. A process of inquiring, imagining, innovating and inspiring replaces the process of assessment, planning, implementation and control. Because of the nature of change accessed by appreciative approaches, the strategy comes to life as it is being developed: there is no time-lag between the initial stages of investigation and planning and later implementation. Strategic development becomes a vibrant, engaging whole-system process that produces positive change while it is happening as well as in the future. The process is built around four key questions: What are our greatest assets? What are the best possible market opportunities? What is the preferred future? What are the measureable results?

Summary

In this chapter we have considered the vexed questions of what good leadership is and how best to lead organizational change. It seems that good leadership resides in a basic moral goodness and authenticity, which, while more natural to some than others, can to some extent be developed. We have learnt that we must watch out for counterfeit authenticity. It seems that understanding strengths as well as weaknesses is a key aspect of good leadership, and that such self-awareness can facilitate the development of good followers, able to hold the leader to account. We have also learnt that it is not only *who* a leader is that is important in terms of his or her effectiveness, but also *what* they do. Some approaches to change are more effective than others with emergent change being the most effective. And there are four key behaviours that effective leaders demonstrate during large, emergent change situations. We noticed that much of the current literature on leadership, organizational change and strategy reflects a mistaken understanding of the nature of large organizations and that leaders in the field, such as Cameron and Cooperrider, are offering useful alternatives. Finally, we noted that large group change methodologies offer excellent guidance about how to offer positive leadership through emergent change.

Further Reading

Dark side leadership

Babiak, P. and Hare, R. (2007) *Snakes in Suits: When Psychopaths Go to Work*. New York: HarperCollins.
This is a chatty, gossipy introduction to the dark side of leadership.

Furham, A. (2010) *The Elephant in the Boardroom*. Basingstoke: Palgrave Macmillan.
Covers similar ground within a more academic and formal framework.

Effective change

Rowland, R. and Higgs, M. (2008) *Sustaining Change: Leadership That Works*. New York: Jossey-Bass.
This is a very readable account of their research, illuminating their findings with extended case-studies from their research

Lewis, S. Passmore, J. and Cantore, S. (2007) *Appreciative Inquiry for Change Management: Using AI to Facilitate Organizational Development*. London: Kogan Page.
In this practical text, my colleagues and I explain the different conceptualizations of organization that underpin directive and emergent change. It could be a useful addition to Rowland and Higgs if you want more background in this area, with some guidance about how to go about working for change in a more emergent way.

Effective leadership

Cameron, K. (2008) *Positive Leadership*. San Francisco: Berrett-Koehler.
Short, practical, readable and inexpensive.

6

Positive Sustainable Growth

a tightening of the
available talent pool

Introduction

Is sustainable growth possible? Can one actually do more with less? In this chapter we shall examine how the capacity and capability of people and organizations can be increased in sustainable ways. We shall discover how a focus on developing individual capability can act to increase

Positive Psychology at Work: How Positive Leadership and Appreciative Inquiry
Create Inspiring Organizations, First Edition. Sarah Lewis.
© 2011 Sarah Lewis. Published 2011 by John Wiley & Sons, Ltd.

organizational capacity. First, though, we need to note that the legacy of Frederick Taylor, an engineer who became one of the first management gurus, still looms large. From his initial thinking and writing about organizations we have inherited a tendency to consider them as no more than machines with human components. A common piece of advice when considering things mechanical is 'if it ain't broke don't fix it', and this is still the mindset of many managers and leaders, who hesitate to meddle with their organization in the absence of any evidence of a problem. This means that improvements are only ever seeded from an awareness of deficit rather than from a desire for abundance. Yet as Cameron's work (discussed in Chapter 2) illuminated, abundance is a source of competitive advantage. If we start to think of the organization more as a living system and less as a machine, we begin to open our minds to the idea of growing more from what we have, rather than needing to import more 'bits of kit' to grow.

Positive psychology focuses on cultivating human growth by going beyond fixing problems to creating positive states of flourishing. Traditionally, development and training within organizations focused on providing a mixture of 'must know' training (e.g., health and safety or technical knowledge) and 'need to know' input (e.g., management development or media training). Essentially, this approach concentrates on putting 'stuff' into people. An exception is some of the more advanced leadership development which makes some effort to help people increase their understanding of what is already there by focusing on their personality for example or their established skills. What positive psychology offers is some new ideas about how to help people become more productive at work, such as the idea that people can be helped to develop their skill at entering particular psychological states that help them at work, states that increase their capability and capacity.

Psychological states are essentially particular moods or feelings. They are changeable and transient, in contrast to psychological traits, which are permanent and stable, and constitute personality. Given that much developmental effort has been devoted to helping people understand their own personalities, perhaps we should first remind ourselves what personality is and why it offers so little potential for sustainable growth.

Personality can broadly be understood as the idea that people differ in their patterns of relatively stable traits. The five key traits are: how outgoing, how responsive to emotions, how agreeable, how conscientious and how open people are to new experiences. Personality theory suggests that these different patterns influence the ways people behave and that they help

Miss Pettigrew found presenting the annual report a challenge

distinguish people one from another. In other words, in similar circumstances people have a strong tendency to behave in different ways according to their personality.

The psychological traits that make up personality, born of a combination of genetics and experience, are thought to be more or less fixed by adulthood. So while people can learn different behaviours, it's pretty hard to change their underlying personality traits, so some behaviours will always be easier than others. This suggests that it's hard for someone to improve their performance in an area that plays against their 'natural' inclinations. Shy, anxious people who avoid the limelight rarely become confident public speakers or presenters. Of course, there are exceptions to every rule. However, this understanding of the difficulty of working against natural inclination is the basis of the strengths movement. It also explains why, while understanding how your personality is different from others' is helpful to working with other people, it doesn't necessarily help you individually become any more effective.

Psychological *states*, on the other hand, are transient human phenomena: they come and go. So, for example, we are happy or sad, interested or bored, for limited periods: our emotional moods and states are changeable. The interesting thing about states is that they can be induced or developed. The ability to induce a helpful psychological state can come under the control of the individual. Various psychotherapies and development methods, such as neuro-linguistic-programming, have utilized this ability, helping people to induce beneficial psychological states at will. However, the idea has not been applied systematically to the workplace. Work by Luthans, Youssef and Avolio (2007) suggests that psychological states that relate positively to performance might be a fruitful area for workplace investment. Some of the questions this line of exploration raises are: Is it possible to help people self-induce psychological states that enhance their performance? Can the organization work to induce these psychological states in individuals? Is it ethical to do so?

Psychological Capital

Luthans and his colleagues scoured the psychological literature to identify positive psychological states that could be measured, developed and managed to improve performance for the individual and the organization. They were looking for states that were life-enhancing and quantifiable. They found four key contenders: self-efficacy (confidence), hope, optimism and resilience. They dubbed these collectively as an individual's psychological capital (PsyCap). They haven't ruled out finding more psychological states that fit their criteria. Research suggests that PsyCap, the combined factor of the four separate capacities, is a better predictor of performance, satisfaction and absenteeism than the individual component capacities (Youssef and Luthans, 2010). In other words, taken together, these four capabilities add up to more than the sum of their parts: both separately and together they increase an individual's capacity. (For a formal definition see Supplement 6.1.)

PsyCap has been found to relate to desirable organizational performance in a number of important ways. For example, measures of PsyCap have been found to predict performance, satisfaction and absenteeism and be related to organizational commitment and an intention to remain in the organization (Youssef and Luthans, 2010). The development of PsyCap adds value to organizational assets such as financial capital, human capital (defined as knowledge) and social capital (networks). Clearly, for this capability to be demonstrated at work other contextual features need to be in place. These features are identified in Luthans and colleagues' extended model (see Supplement 6.2), which recognizes that PsyCap doesn't exist as a stand-alone predictor of organizational behaviour. Rather, it is one

Supplement 6.1 Definition of PsyCap

Technically PsyCap is defined as:
  an individual's positive psychological state of development that is characterised by: (1) having confidence (self efficacy) to take on and put in the necessary effort to succeed at challenging tasks; (2) making a positive attribution (optimism) about succeeding now and in the future; (3) preserving towards goals and, when necessary, redirecting paths to goals (hope) in order to succeed; and (4) when beset by problems and adversity, sustaining and bouncing back and even beyond (resilience) to attain success.

(Luthans *et al.*, 2007, p. 3)

element of a complex organizational psychological map for an individual. Its value is in identifying another point of influence for improving people's performance at work.

The extended model suggests that individuals with high PsyCap measures have the confidence to take on the task, possess the sustaining belief that they will succeed, can access the motivation to keep going when things get tough or find other ways around problems; and, when the occasional disappointment inevitably occurs, are able to quickly bounce back, recharged and motivated once more. The promise of psychological capital is that all the people in an organization can develop a greater ability to access these attributes, given the right development.

Equally importantly, each of the four individual capabilities that make up PsyCap are associated with good life experiences and outcomes for individuals, suggesting that helping people who didn't have the opportunity to develop these capabilities earlier in life is a morally justifiable endeavour. It can be seen as a virtuous behaviour, appropriate to a positive and virtuous organization. Of the four capabilities, self-efficacy has the most developed research profile.

1) Self-efficacy

Self-efficacy was originally conceptualized and defined by Bandura and Walters (1963). It is primarily about confidence, that feeling of quietly and fundamentally knowing that for all the surface anxiety around a task you are capable of doing it. Feelings of self-efficacy are highly correlated with

Supplement 6.2 PsyCap

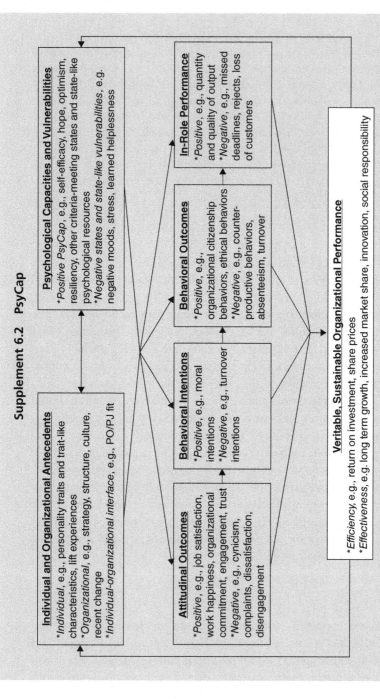

Individual and Organizational Antecedents
*Individual, e.g., personality traits and trait-like characteristics, lift experiences
*Organizational, e.g., strategy, structure, culture, recent change
*Individual-organizational interface, e.g., PO/PJ fit

Psychological Capacities and Vulnerabilities
*Positive PsyCap, e.g., self-efficacy, hope, optimism, resiliency, other criteria-meeting states and state-like psychological resources
*Negative states and state-like vulnerabilities, e.g. negative moods, stress, learned helplessness

In-Role Performance
*Positive, e.g., quantity and quality of output
*Negative, e.g., missed deadlines, rejects, loss of customers

Behavioral Outcomes
*Positive, e.g., organizational citizenship behaviors, ethical behaviors
*Negative, e.g., counter-productive behaviors, absenteeism, turnover

Behavioral Intentions
*Positive, e.g., moral intentions
*Negative, e.g., turnover intentions

Attitudinal Outcomes
*Positive, e.g., job satisfaction, work happiness, organizational commitment, engagement, trust
*Negative, e.g., cynicism, complaints, dissatisfaction, disengagement

Veritable, Sustainable Organizational Performance
*Efficiency, e.g., return on investment, share prices
*Effectiveness, e.g., long term growth, increased market share, innovation, social responsibility

Reprinted with permission from C. Youssef and F. Luthans (2010) An Integrated Model of Psychological Capital in the Workplace. In A. Linley, S. Harrington and N. Garcea (Eds.) *Oxford Handbook of Positive Psychology and Work*. Oxford: Oxford University Press. Also, by permission of Oxford University Press, Inc (www.oup.com)

performance. Self-efficacious people are exciting to manage because they welcome new challenges that stretch their experience base. People who have generally high levels of self-efficacy have five characteristics: they set high goals for themselves and self-select for difficult tasks; they welcome and thrive on challenge; they are highly self-motivated; they invest the necessary effort to accomplish their goals; and when faced with obstacles, they persevere (Luthans *et al.*, 2007).

An important limitation that distinguishes self-efficacy from a general 'confident personality' is that it is domain-specific: in some areas of our lives we exhibit great self-efficacy, in others very little. It depends on our experience in that domain. Yet it has also been established that self-efficacy can be present in generalized domains: for example, I may experience self-efficacy generally within the workplace, but not around DIY activities at home. How, then, might self-efficacy in work-related areas be enhanced? There are a number of factors that are known to contribute to the development of self-efficacy: mastery experiences, social modelling, social persuasion and arousal, each of which is explained below. Of these the most powerful is mastery.

Mastery

Self-efficacy is developed from experience, particularly the experience of mastering an action, an art, a body of knowledge or a technique, for instance. As parents we instinctively work to ensure children experience self-efficacy in specific domains by ordering a series of mastery experiences for them in a progressive manner. For example, first we encourage our children to pick up a pencil and make marks. Then we build a series of challenges that they can master with a little effort. 'Can you make a line? Can you make the ends join up? Can you make it bigger, smaller? Can you draw a picture?' and so on until the child can make the controlled fine motor movements of specific shapes we call drawing and which are the basis for writing. To be able to write, they have to master many skills along the way. Mastery experiences breed self-belief. The more we can arrange for people at work to participate in mastery experiences, the greater the chances of them developing a stronger sense of self-efficacy. Such people are more willing to have a go at something that will stretch them a little. A virtuous circle develops of experimentation at the boundaries of ability, mastery, improved performance and then further experimentation at the new boundaries of abilities. In this way capability and capacity grow. Alastair's account of Naomi's development in Supplement 6.3 illustrates this.

Supplement 6.3   The Space to Fail

This is a true story from inner-city teaching in deprived areas and the growth of self-efficacy and self-esteem.

The following account is of 15-year-old girl Naomi, who came from a very violent, abusive and male-dominated family.

The assignment was a 12-week challenge to perform a shortened version of *Macbeth*. Naomi had difficulty reading let alone performing a Shakespeare play. On learning of the task she exclaimed *'Sir; no way, I can't do that.'* The following steps are how Naomi's self-efficacy and self-esteem increased.

We began by watching multiple versions and discussing the story until it became tedious. We then went to see an operatic production, which the pupils did not enjoy. Their frustration began to build, then turned into smouldering motivation – they could do it better. Then they began to rehearse and, unsurprisingly failed. They forgot their lines, giggled and began to make their own individual mark on the play. Slowly, we began to relate it to their world and, for Naomi, this resonated with the violence, greed and power in her own life. She learned that she would play Lady Macbeth; again, she exclaimed that she couldn't do it. She then went with her class to the Birmingham School of Acting where they worked with final-year degree students. Naomi performed a monologue. It wouldn't have got a good grade and she failed; however, she received feedback from one of the senior lecturers, Andy Potter, exclaiming how impressed he was with her efforts. She beamed and bashfully looked at the ground. She then chose to take the role very seriously. A few weeks later Naomi performed the role of Lady Macbeth for her exam. She gained a Merit (B) in her BTEC exam. She had been expected to fail and had succeeded far beyond both her and my expectations.

I argue that talent itself whilst it can't be ignored, deserves little merit. Very little effort is invested in a talent. It is very often the knowledge and investment of effort and time that creates the skill.

Have we found ourselves teaching to compete rather than cooperate? To think narrowly rather than broadly? To be frightened of uncertainty and the risk of error that accompanies it? Why not take the risk, create the space to fail and ultimately succeed?

Contributed by Alastair Arnott

Vicarious modelling and learning

Another way we can improve our sense of self-efficacy is by observing others like ourselves who are succeeding in circumstances similar to ours. When I was younger and first learning to drive I was overwhelmed by trying simultaneously to manage three foot pedals, a gear lever, mirrors and lights while avoiding other moving objects on the road. It seemed like I might never succeed. I took heart from the observation that millions of others had learnt to master the skill of driving. Essentially I thought, 'If all those other people can do it, then it must be possible that I can too.' I successfully increased my sense of self-efficacy in the face of uncertainty and fear of failure by watching others succeed.

When I see someone not so dissimilar to me who is doing slightly better than me, it helps foster the belief in me that I can aim a little higher. This means that mentoring by peers or immediate superiors is likely to be more effective than having a remote 'expert' or 'someone from Head Office' teach

or train. If someone too dissimilar from us tries to share their stories of success with us, they may be discounted as interesting, but irrelevant (see Ewa Francis's account of a positive approach to developing effective mentors in Supplement 6.4). Another approach to developing self-efficacy is by the use of imagination. By encouraging a person to imagine self-succeeding in a future situation we are encouraging them to develop pictures of their

---

Supplement 6.4   A Positive Mentoring Programme

I was invited by a fast-moving consumer goods company to help them with their existing Mentoring Programme which has been taking place there for two years. Our aim was to develop specific skills for mentors and mentees and to define and plan how the best practice mentoring programme could be used in a more effective way both locally and globally. The participants were directors and senior managers. When thinking about how to work with them the key question I asked myself was: *'How can I generate knowledge of the system and find out the learning needs, not by focusing on gaps but by building on the existing expertise with the groups? How can I co-create positive engagement and programme ownership?'* I decided to use the AI process during two, three-hour sessions.

Discovery: Participants in pairs shared stories using the questions: *What is the best part of your role as a mentor? Describe time when you have found being a mentor really exciting?* Initially, they seemed surprised with this approach. However, before we reached the stage of their dream, they were smiling and there was much energy in the room.

Dream: Here, collectively, we explored their hopes for mentoring by posing questions: *What three wishes do you have for your relationship from now on? What three wishes do you have for mentoring in your organization?* By this stage they could not stop talking and much data was emerging.

We progressed to the **Design** and, as a group, we explored 'what should be' and created a set of statements that listed the qualities they most desired for their organization and mentoring relationships. Questions we asked were: *Out of all things we have identified above, what will move us forward to a better future? What do you have the most energy about?* The second question helped us to prioritize our intentions quickly.

During the **Destiny** stage we discussed the execution of our personal and organizational commitments as a way forward. Questions were:

What changes are needed to ensure that the above ideas, vision, will become reality? What is the role you could undertake to ensure that the above will become a fact?

The positive outcomes from this micro-intervention

We have co-created 'movement' of energy, ideas and a commitment to organizational change which made sense to senior managers. They articulated how they want to lead mentoring in their organization and what they want to change. Vital added extra value was that the directors defined the role they wanted to play in this change process. Additional results were clarification of the purpose and outcomes of the scheme; the role of mentors and mentees; shaping the process.

We generated knowledge which reshaped the project and served as the foundation for change overall and as a platform for evaluation. As a result of using AI, we have co-created value and a platform from which we were able to move to the next stage of implementing sustainable change.

Contributed by Ewa Francis

possible future selves. This is part of the power of the dream stage in Appreciative Inquiry: as people imagine themselves succeeding in a more positive future, so they develop greater faith in the possibility of it happening and in their ability to make it happen. Other people's faith in our abilities is also important.

Social persuasion

Very importantly, other people's expressed belief in us can affect our belief in ourselves. If someone, especially someone we know, trust and respect, expresses belief in our ability to do something, then our belief in our ability increases and we may be willing to try it. Sometimes an expressed belief by someone else that we can do something is all we need to tip us over the point of hesitancy, moving us from 'maybe' to 'I will'. The final factor that makes a difference to our feelings of efficacy is our state of wellbeing and excitement.

Physiological and psychological arousal

While not as powerful as the other factors that affect self-efficacy, levels of arousal have some effect. When we are feeling good we are more confident.

When we feel good we are more able to invest energy to achieve something than when we are feeling low or flat. Similarly physical health makes a difference. When we feel ill, run down, tired or bloated, things can seem beyond our ability. Sometimes we call this morale. When morale is low, even though the same people have the same skills and knowledge as before, performance drops. Morale-boosting increases the likelihood of performance revival. An important component of morale is hope; it is also one of the four key processes in PsyCap.

2) Hope

Hope as a psychological construct encompasses both willpower and way-finding. That is to say, hope is exhibited as both a desire to achieve something *and* as an ability to find a way (Synder, 2000). Hope is a cognitive state, a state of mind, a way of thinking. It is also an ability to plan. Together these can create an upward spiral of hope whereby the willpower motivates the search for new paths and the success of forging new pathways increases determination to keep going.

A brief aside: my son and a couple of his friends arranged to take our open rowing boat with its outboard motor on a weekend camping trip on the river. Various delays meant it was dark by the time they were loading the boat ready to depart. The final job was to put petrol in the outboard motor. The cap to the petrol tank is designed to dangle by the side, out of the way, while this operation is performed. My son confidently unscrewed the cap and let it go to turn his attention to the delicate balancing act of positioning the petrol can over the small petrol tank entrance. The cap sank slowly and irretrievably into the murky, oily, deep waters of the channel. Something had unexpectedly broken.

There followed a long row out of Oxford, past all the houses, to find a place to camp. Eventually pitching camp in the dark, they settled down for the night. In the morning they faced the challenge of getting a cover for the engine, or the more physically challenge of rowing. The rowing option did not appeal. Mulling things over one of them started to wonder if the plastic ring connector that had held their six-pack of beer might stretch round the petrol tank hole. Then, if they could find something plastic to cover the hole … You know what, it might just work. A plastic bag with a small air hole, held in place by the indestructible plastic of a six-pack holder, saw them through the rest of the trip. Travis's finest hour, as this was described to me, was born of a mixture of determination to finish the trip by motor and an ability to consider different ways to achieve the desired outcome: hope in action.

There is a well-established relationship between hope and performance in most areas of life, including academic performance, athletic achievement, physical and mental health and coping beliefs and skills. Being hopeful is good for you. Less work has been done on the relationship between hope and work performance, but early work suggests a positive relationship between employee hope and organizational profitability (Adams *et al.*, 2002). Managers and leaders can play a role in encouraging hopeful behaviour: using goal setting appropriately; helping to make sure the resources necessary for success are available; modelling and reinforcing hopeful behaviour; putting people where they can perform best; providing training or development experiences that are hands-on, participative and empowering; and encouraging contingency planning. Hope is a transient state and, like the other capabilities that make up PsyCap, can be developed through specific activities.

Goal setting has long been known to aid performance if undertaken appropriately (Lewis, 2008). Goals have most impact when set by the individual who is expected to deliver them, or jointly with their teammates or manager. Goals developed in this way are more likely to trigger both the willpower and the pathways elements of hope than when someone else sets the goal. This happens more often than might be expected. It is not uncommon for me to find myself having a conversation with someone about their goals where the answer to the question 'Where did that figure come from?' is 'I have no idea, I think they just plucked it from thin air'. This kind of goal setting, indeed this kind of conversation, does not inspire hope.

Hope can also be triggered by well-targeted stretch goals. Such goals, potentially achievable yet requiring some investment of effort, can stimulate excitement and exploration. Unfortunately, goal setting has often been done very badly, with stretch goals seen as an excuse to demand the impossible. So, to conjure up a sense of how stretch goals work when they inspire hope, you may need to step outside the workplace to remember the last time you set yourself a stretch goal that triggered strong feelings of hopefulness. Perhaps you have done bits and pieces of self-assembly DIY, but now you were planning to go for a whole kitchen. You probably found yourself, in idle moments, working out how things might fit together, or the sequence in which you would need to do them, or how to maintain maximum functionality during the build. This is pathway planning. At the same time you might be visualizing how great it will look and how much more convenient to your needs it will be, in ways that encourage you to stick at solving the many challenges such an undertaking poses, helping you maintain the drive and determination to keep going. In this way the one feeds the other. A first cousin of hope is optimism. And optimism is the third key capability that makes up PsyCap.

3) Optimism

If self-efficacy is a state of self-belief and hope is a state of mind, then optimism is a state of explanation. How we explain things to ourselves reflects the degree to which we are pessimistic or optimistic. Optimism is an explanatory style that attributes positive events to personal, permanent and pervasive causes, and interprets negative events in terms of external, temporary and situation-specific factors (Seligman, 2006b). This means that in an optimistic state I might attribute the great feedback from one of my events to my excellent facilitation skills, while attributing the less successful feedback of another event to the effect on everyone of the ceiling falling down. If I was in a more pessimistic state of mind, I might reverse these attributions, attributing the successful event to the fact that it was an easy group and the less successful event to my poor facilitation skills. Note how the different accounts of what happened are solely about my attribution of cause. In both scenarios the facts of the case are the same: good feedback/non-collapsed ceiling; poor feedback/collapsed ceiling.

Having a generally optimistic outlook has been shown to relate positively to many desirable outcomes: physical and mental health, effective coping with difficult situations, recovery from illness and addiction, and life satisfaction. It is also positively correlated with workplace performance. However, optimism is a powerful and potentially dangerous state. Being overly optimistic about positive outcomes or refusing to accept factors beyond one's control can lead people to take unnecessary risks and to be unable to heed warnings of impending danger or failure. Luthans and colleagues talk about realistic, flexible optimism, distinguishing this state from the harmful 'positive thinking' that Ehrenreich (2009) identifies. They suggest that optimism can be induced when someone's pessimism is not serving a useful purpose.

4) Resilience

The fourth PsyCap capability is resilience. Resilience is the ability to rebound from setbacks, to recover the ability to function effectively. But not only this, it implies an ability to bounce back stronger and more resourceful. This idea is captured in the term post-traumatic growth, the lesser-known counterpart of post-traumatic stress. Resilient people are adaptable. Resilience is developed through repeated exposure to gradually increasing difficulties from which people learn in a productive way. People over-protected as children often have little opportunity to develop resilience, while those thrown in at the deep end too often may develop fearfulness. Resilience is developed through experience and by the accumulation of assets and strategies. It's never too late to start developing greater resilience and there are a number of ways of doing so.

Asset-focused strategies
This approach to developing resilience is about building up both a person's actual resourcefulness *and* their self-perception of their resourcefulness. For these accumulated resources to be effective people have to appreciate that they have them: unacknowledged resources tend to remain unutilized. The kind of things we are thinking of as resources include: skills, knowledge, experience, wisdom, thinking tools, networks and emotional awareness. Appreciative Inquiry discovery interviews are a great way to enhance people's awareness of their existing resourcefulness. Many organizational programmes are geared towards increasing people's resourcefulness: training, mentors, development programmes, projects and job rotation are examples. These techniques for developing resourcefulness are generally well understood in organizations, although the connection with increased resilience is not always overt or transparent. Wendy Campbell offers a very personal account of how she came to understand the importance of resilience to leadership (see Supplement 6.5).

Risk-focused strategies
This refers to the development and implementation of active management to reduce the risk of failure, or to improve the speed and effectiveness of recovery from failure. Such strategies often develop from experience, an outcome of post-traumatic growth. For example, in the early 1980s many in employment had only really experienced boom times: being made redundant during the round of 'downsizing' that took place during the recession was a terrible and traumatic shock. Yet a few years later it was noticeable that some people had become quite resilient to the repeated redundancy they were experiencing.

It seemed they had developed a tried-and-tested plan they could quickly put into action when redundancy once again threatened which enhanced

Supplement 6.5   Appreciative Inquiry and Resilience

My journey with Appreciative Inquiry began in the [southern hemisphere] spring of 1998. A colleague and I were chatting, me telling him that I was completely restructuring my business following a severe illness. I had to make it something that could still make a difference as well as allow me to work in my then-limited capacity.

He suggested that I look at a new process of change, Appreciative Inquiry. He gave me the contact details for Liz Mellish, who was introducing the process to Australia.

I contacted Liz's office, and bought *The Thin Book of Appreciative Inquiry*. Over the next few weeks I delved into it, very much enjoying the freedom of thought and direction this new approach allowed.

Also through Liz I joined the global Appreciative Inquiry internet group and that began a couple of years of enjoying the deep appreciation that each group member had for each other and for everyone they dealt with. Compared to all other groups I had previously belonged to this was such a meaningful and deeply satisfying space.

From that group I learned about a training course on the process in Bath, England in October 1999. For months I vacillated between commitment to flying half-way around the world to attend and not having the courage to make this my first journey without my husband. But I continued to enjoy the internet group and in the end the urge to go overcame my lack of courage.

So, in early October 1999, I said goodbye to my husband and our teenage children, boarded the plane and set off from Perth.

On the afternoon of 12 October I arrived at Eagle House with my bags, ready to settle into my room and be ready for the training to begin the following morning. The gradual arrival of the other participants during the afternoon settled my fears. They came from several different countries, but were alike in their friendly and accepting – dare I say appreciative – greetings to the rest of us.

The next morning I got up early to go for a short walk. This is always my way of making sure I am ready to be fully present for whatever the day brings. Soon after 9 am I was seated in the sunny drawing room of Eagle House with about 20 people.

Over the next three days, Frank Barrett, Marsha George and Adrian McLean taught us deeply about Appreciative Inquiry. We learned from how they treated each other, from how they treated us and from how we then treated each other. I had never before been listened to with such respect and depth as during those three days. And in response I opened up to a part of myself for the first time as someone who cared profoundly for everyone in the room and for all the living creatures with whom we share this planet.

As I flew home, reflecting on the change that Appreciative Inquiry had gifted to my life, I winced when I remembered yet again that last morning in Bath. One of our fellow participants came down late to breakfast. He looked extremely upset. Someone asked him what was the matter and he burst into tears and said that his wife had contacted him that morning to tell him she was leaving him.

It's funny how we pull away from these raw emotions. However, my time with this group and this amazing process had brought me in touch with my strength, my resilience. So I stepped forward and hugged him tight, ignoring the urge to pull away and leave him alone. I held him until his sobs eased, then stepped back. Then others came forward with kind words and hugs.

He decided to leave instead of staying for the last day's training. When he left, his head held high and his shoulders set, he went with our best wishes.

Sitting in the plane I blushed at my audacity. But at the same time I knew that, now that I had touched my resilience for the very first time, I would always step forward to do what needed to be done for the best interests of my fellow travellers.

And that became the basis for the Resilient Leadership Programme™, a programme for community change leaders, which is at last ready to come to market.

All this thanks to this amazing process that we call Appreciative Inquiry.

Contributed by Wendy Campbell

their chances of securing a new position. In essence they developed risk-focused strategies both to speed their recovery from the trauma of being made redundant and to reduce the chances of short-term redundancy turning into long-term unemployment. These strategies might include: assiduously cultivating networks both when in work and when out of work; maintaining an industry profile; enthusiastically embracing any CV-enhancing opportunities that arose while employed (or unemployed); framing a positive account of their past; and using the techniques outlined above to help maintain an optimistic outlook (i.e., to retain hope). Very importantly, they learnt how to tell the story of their repeated misfortune in a way that didn't detract from their attractiveness as a candidate: focusing on what they had achieved while employed; being clear that bad things happen to good people; emphasizing what they had done and what they could do. These were all active strategies to reduce the risk of extended unemployment and to increase resilience during a period of a repeating cycle of employment and redundancy.

Process-focused strategies

This term refers to a different facet of resilience, one that enhances the use of the asset base. Process-focused strategies refer to the ability to pull together assets and risk reduction strategies when facing a challenging or threatening situation. It refers to skills that aid a good assessment of the whole situation, such as the ability to assess and regulate your own mental or physical state. It refers to the ability to keep your head, and keep thinking, in the face of a challenging situation.

For example, if a meeting gets bogged down and drags on, we can suggest taking a break so that people can have time out from the issue, refresh themselves, raise their mood and make themselves physically comfortable. When they return their ability to sustain effort in the face of challenge is likely to have been enhanced. Even within the meeting, if we recognize the prevailing mood is becoming an obstacle to creative thinking and that people are getting locked into the difficulties and impossibility of the situation, we might introduce humour to lighten the mood and release people from an unproductive gloom.

Incidentally, black or 'gallows' humour is very important as a resilience process. Speaking as a former social worker in residential child protection I can confirm that at times, as they say, if you didn't laugh you'd cry (or worse). Times can be very grim and sometimes in the bleaker moments an inappropriate joke is the key to allowing people to start functioning again. Such humour is always expressed in private, in-group situations, away from clients or other audiences, as a group resilience process. It doesn't travel. Out of context it appears inappropriate and insensitive. It isn't. It's an effective group self-regulation process, necessary to allow people to pick themselves up and carry on. Its purpose is not to express deep-felt feelings. Quite the opposite. Its purpose is to increase resilience by bringing about a mood change.

Many good workers are not very aware of their own processes and so are less able to self-regulate. They don't recognize the effects of fatigue or the impact of something that happened outside work. They don't appreciate

" We might introduce humour
to lighten the mood and to
release people from unproductive gloom "

that these seemingly unrelated events are having an effect on their ability
to stay creative, resourceful and focused. Sometimes it falls to someone else
to help them recognize that they are not at their best and need to manage
the situation actively. I remember working as a coach with someone who
was experiencing trauma in his home life. One of the most helpful things
I did was to assist him identify the priorities he needed to attend to *now* to
ensure he still had a job when the trauma eased and where he could go easy
on himself. We also identified who at work could be trusted to be sympathetic and helpful, what they might be told and who might react adversely
to any sign of 'weaknesses' and so had to be very actively managed. It
worked out well. He found a way forward in his home life and was able to
reapply himself to work with some vigour. Increasing people's self-awareness
and hence their ability to self-regulate is likely to enhance resilience and
reduce the risks of burn-out, breakdown, ill-health, despair and other non-
resilient reactions to difficulties.

PsyCap pulls these different positive states together in a way that helps leaders, learning and development specialists and human resources specialists focus on developmental activity that will increase the capability of individuals and the workforce as a whole. This offers a welcome corrective to the current emphasis in much leadership and management development of being aware of one's own and others' personality. A shift away from undevelopable traits to developable states as a source of performance improvement offers a potentially rich seam for development activity. Supplement 6.6 summarizes the learning and development experiences that help to build PsyCap. Supplement 6.7 is an account of creating increased organized resilience through PsyCap-informed intervention.

Appreciative Inquiry

Appreciative Inquiry offers a way to increase the capacity and capability of an organization without adding more 'kit'. It is a way of approaching organizational growth that resonates strongly with the principles and practices of positive psychology. In addition, it is one of the few approaches to change that recognizes the organization as a living human system. In order to engage with Appreciative Inquiry one needs to engage with what is for many people a whole new set of ideas about where the roots of organizational change lie. Key notions here include: that inquiry creates reality, focus, direction and growth; that organizations have a positive core which is a key asset for positive growth; that positive emotions are a source of organizational energy and growth; that a growth in relational connectedness leads to increases in community spirit and understanding; that growth and change can happen in non-linear dynamic ways; and that the self-organizing ability of organizations is a basis for sustainable growth.

These ideas stand in opposition to the common views on growth: that it is necessary to solve some problem or deficit; that organization is at its core very difficult and problematic; that investigation changes nothing, only planned intervention does that; that people have to be directed and organized to achieve change; that negative emotions (fear, anger) are the best source of energy for organizational change; that change is a planned linear process; and that it is individual people who have to change. It is increasingly being recognized that it is our adherence to this understanding that results in organizational change frequently being experienced as unsustainable. There are two key reasons for this. First, the traditional

Supplement 6.6   Building Psychological Capital

Developing self-efficacy

1. Arrange carefully sequenced master experiences. Avoid dropping people in at the deep end unless you know they will succeed.
2. Provide good, appropriate modelling.
3. Be encouraging: express confidence in their ability to succeed.
4. Make sure people look after themselves.

Encouraging hope

5. Use goal setting carefully, attentively and effectively. Involve people in setting their goals.
6. Positively reinforce tenacious, hopeful behavior: the input not the outcome.
7. Use involving, participatory and empowering ways of working, such as genuine delegation, group decision-making or large group change processes.

Developing optimism

8. Counteract pessimism by encouraging self-forgiveness; refocus them on the present; help them spot opportunities.

Developing resilience

9. Provide asset accumulating experiences.
10. Help people learn from setbacks so they experience post-traumatic growth.
11. Help people become more aware of how their mental and physical states affect their resilience and how to manage that for best outcomes.

Based on Luthans *et al.* (2007)

methods of change tend to put a huge strain on a few people: the effort is unsustainable. And second, any change in behaviour that is induced by fear or to escape any other negative consequence is liable to lapse once the threat is removed; maintaining the pressure necessary to sustain the change is also unsustainable. Appreciative Inquiry offers organizations a way to achieve

Supplement 6.7   Managing Change in Troubling Times

The context

Imagine if your business was contingent on one government organization for over 80% of your revenue. Now imagine that this government
organization was going to change 75% of your business, but they
weren't going to tell you when or how this was going to happen. How
would you react? With panic? Anger? Frustration? Well, this was exactly
the situation for Northern Lights Canada, a medium-sized human services company in Toronto. This uncertainty lasted 18 months and caused
tension, emotional outbursts and the potential for increased turnover
as people sought greater security elsewhere. Northern Lights engaged
us early on to create a training programme that would improve employee
engagement during this period of extreme change.

The interventions

We designed a workshop that would improve employee engagement
by allowing participants to focus on strengths, solutions and Appreciative
Inquiry. Prior to the workshop the staff completed the StrengthsFinder
2.0 online strengths assessment to explore what strengths they could
leverage in the face of adversity. Next, the workshop engaged participants in exercises that focused the group on solutions as opposed to
worrying about the problems being created by this major change. This
improved hope and optimism in the future.

Finally, we led the group through two Ds of Appreciative Inquiry:
Discover and Dream. After listening to stories of how they had overcome challenges in the past, employees were reminded that they had
successfully implemented major changes before and had even been
triumphant in the past. The visions of the future allowed the group to
bond and dream about what was possible. Participants left the workshop filled with positive emotion and greater energy to move forward
in a productive way. Comments from participants included: *'This was
very helpful and energizing. It couldn't have come at a better time for
our office that is under so much stress and uncertainty.' 'The visual on
the walls of everyone's strengths made me realize how strong our team
is and how to draw on those strengths to make things happen.'* These
and many more comments like them testify to the energizing nature
of building self-efficacy and positive emotions throughout the
workshop.

The impact

Five months after delivering the workshops, we discovered that the elements that the participants found most useful during the change were StrengthsFinder (with 75% of respondents reporting that this information was 'very useful' or 'extremely useful'), Appreciative Inquiry (with 62.5% of participants reporting this to be 'very useful' or 'extremely useful') and a specific solutions-focused exercise (with 49.9% of participants reporting this to be 'very useful' or 'extremely useful').

This positive psychology ladder of skills – strengths, Appreciative Inquiry and solutions-focused coaching – led to an upward spiral of greater productivity and wellbeing at Northern Lights. Senior staff confirmed that team leaders who were reticent about preparing their employees for the change before the workshop made a dramatic shift after the workshop. We believe that this was due to the combination of positive psychology theories presented in their specific order. By focusing on the employees' strengths we were building positive emotion and self-efficacy. Then we were giving them tools for analysing what they had control over and what they could do about it. Finally, we used AI to leverage those strengths and give them hope for the future. Adrianne Haight, Employment Services Coordinator, said:

> We have made it a focus to remind people of the great strengths that we were able to identify in your workshops ... In a time when we could be driven by anxiety and fears, we are staying true to our culture and values, and we are driving change from those elements of who we are...The announcements from (the government) came on January 20th. ...only a few short weeks after you and Shannon wrapped up your tour of positivity with us ... I can't imagine doing this now without going through that process first.

It was a grounding and foundation in positive psychology that was passed on to us, and we were happy to be the messengers.

Contributed by Shannon Polly and Louisa Jewell

sustainable change, by working *with* innate human processes rather than against them.

One of the difficulties of trying to explain Appreciative Inquiry as an approach and a practice is that it can sound hopelessly optimistic about people, and blithely oblivious to the realities of organizational life. To those who are steeped in a world of problems, difficulties, recalcitrant people, resistance to change, redundancy threats and deadlines it can sound charmingly naïve. People for whom the story of organizational change is one of difficulty and strife can dismiss any account of Appreciative Inquiry being successful as being due to some local factor: 'Well it's different in public sector organizations' or 'Yes, but they weren't engineers'. They can also find it hard to conceive of its applications to their workplace: 'You can't ask our accountants to dream. You'll get laughed out of court.'

My colleagues and I explore ways of working with these challenges extensively in *Appreciative Inquiry for Change Management* (Lewis *et al.*, 2007), written explicitly to help people with these kinds of challenges to appreciative practice. If you are interested in these ideas, but can't get how they work, the best way forward is to find a way to be present at an appreciatively informed event or to attend one of the network meetings for AI practitioners now running in many countries (see www.networkplace.eu for links to different country networks) where you will experience appreciative ways of working in action.

The alternative is to take a deep breath and have a go. The process is incredibly robust, because the human tendencies on which it's based are potentially present in all human relationships, they just need triggering or releasing. As the facilitator, leader or manager you don't have to generate lots of energy or make things happen. Instead, you create an environment where good things can emerge. Much of the knowledge in positive psychology offers an explanation as to how Appreciative Inquiry actually works. We shall call on this to elucidate the practice as we explain it, working to tie what sometimes sounds like a mystical process to some research-based knowledge.

In broad terms Appreciative Inquiry is about helping organizations discover and coalesces around their positive core in a way that creates aspirations and energy for a positive future. The positive core is the strengths and resources of the organization and the people and processes within it. These are exposed through the seemingly tangential approach of asking people to give accounts, or tell stories, of when things have gone right or been at their best. The inquiry aspect is based on the observation that an inquiry into a system is an intervention in that system: to inquire is to intervene. (See Nick Moore's account for a clear illustration of the power of questions to change things in Supplement 6.8.) The appreciation aspect is based on the idea that most organizations want more of the good things in their organization and fewer of the bad. They usually try to achieve this

Supplement 6.8   Improving Performance

I was working as an Interim Manager in an authority. One of the teams I was responsible for was the Referral and Assessment Team – the intake team dealing with initial contacts and referrals. The team had not been meeting its government target in time for the completion of its assessments. This was particularly true of Initial Assessments which needed to be completed within seven working days.

This had become a particular issue for government regulators. Finance was linked to a considerable improvement. Despite senior management pushing this issue with the team, there had been no significant improvement when I took up my post.

The team manager was absent on sick leave. Following discussion with the assistant team managers I attended the team meeting and asked the following discovery questions:

1. Tell a story about when you completed an Initial Assessment or another very time-limited piece of work within timescale and to a particularly high quality:
   • What happened?
   • How did you do this?
   • What did others do to help?
   • What other factors were present that helped this to happen?
   • What did you do particularly well?
   • What made that situation special so that it stands out from the rest?
2. What are the things about the way the team works currently that you value? What must we keep doing?
3. Thinking about the future, you have three wishes:
   • What do you want more of?
   • What do you want less of?
   • What do you think we could be doing differently?

The team held discussions in pairs and then fed back the key points of their partner's stories. The session went well. Afterwards the assistant team managers fed back that staff liked the approach. There was a good discussion about what needed to go in and what didn't, which I could see that some staff found helpful.

Continued

Supplement 6.8   *Continued*

I had seen this as an initial set of questions that I would develop during my time there. Although we did do more work on assessments on the quality of them I never had to return to the subject of timeliness as the completion rate rose after the meeting and soon met the target and stayed above it.

Contributed by Nick Moore

---

by focusing on getting rid of the bad things. We call this problem-solving. Appreciative Inquiry suggests that instead of working to eliminate what we don't want, we can change the balance by growing more of what we do want. This has the dual effect of changing the ratio of good (achievements) to bad (problem) things in the organization and of reducing the relevance, power and impact of the bad things. Rather than being solved, problems often dissolve as the focus of the organization switches to strengths, resources and achievements.

Appreciative Inquiry taps into the ability of the mind to link information and emotion. As one aspect of an experience is retrieved, related information becomes available from other parts of the brain. A good question activates these brain processes, while story-telling, with its inherent information-coding properties, permits a mass of information to be accessed and conveyed in a manner conducive to human processing and understanding. Stories are easy for us to process and decode. By asking about good times and achievements, about successes, sources of pride and heightened moments of wellbeing, the emotions associated with those stories become present in the moment. Positive emotional states bring a whole host of good things with them as the research of Isen, Fredrickson, Losada and Heaphy has demonstrated (see Chapter 4). Most importantly, they contribute to the development of a sense of community. This increased sense of community, or relatedness, within the organization is another key process that produces change.

When people share their stories of good things a number of things happen. There is often a rise in the level of hopefulness in the room. As people reconnect with the best of the past, they begin to develop greater optimism and hope for the future. In this way Appreciative Inquiry taps into and develops the PsyCap of the organization: it builds a community sense of self-efficacy, hope, optimism and resilience. People within the organization start to feel more connected, more hopeful and more capable.

The increasing sense of community is a key change process. As we saw in Losada and Heaphy's research in Chapter 4, connectivity is an organizational process that allows conjoint action. With Appreciative Inquiry, change now starts to be a community movement rather than a management-driven initiative. As the relationship network becomes denser and richer two important things happen. First, people start to identify with the community and community goals, which allows for the transcending of self-interest. Second, there is an increase in social capital, which allows for the faster flow of information, better use of resources, greater trust, better communication and increased responsiveness.

You will have noticed how Appreciative Inquiry focuses on strengths and resources. Throughout this text we have considered the beneficial individual and organizational effects of identifying and working with strengths. The same applies here. As the organization becomes aware of its strengths, it can utilize them more effectively to achieve its goals, rendering its weaknesses irrelevant. It can put its energies into focusing on its strengths.

With the discovery of the previously unarticulated positive core of the organization, and with the growth of hope in an increasingly connected system, comes a sense of possibility. The 'dream' phase of Appreciative Inquiry moves people to focus on this sense of hope and possibility for the future. For both the discovery and the dream phases of Appreciative Inquiry mindfulness is accessed. The organization is asked to attend to specific aspects of organizational life and to be mindful about how these come about: to look for the small things that make the difference between the best and the nearly best. The whole process recognizes the organization as a complex adaptive system, where individuals both create and are influenced by a larger context. This leads to non-linear change as the organization reconfigures itself.

More recently, some of the organizations David Cooperrider has been working with in this way over a longer time have noticed and experienced a transformation effect on their organization's day-to-day culture. Instead of Appreciative Inquiry being a methodology that is brought in from time to time to address different issues, they are becoming organizations of appreciation and inquiry, reaping the sustainable benefits brought by this way of being and working. Cooperrider suggests that this process of organizational transformation follows three phases as the organization becomes an inquiry, relational and strengths-based organization.

Supplement 6.9   Positive Profusion

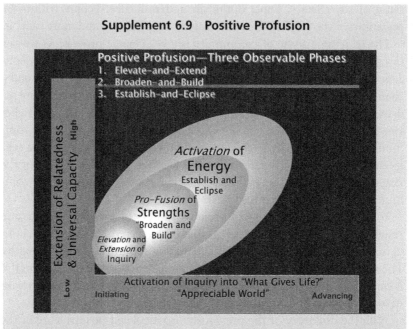

Reprinted with permission from D. Cooperrider (2009) The Discovery And Design Of Positive Institutions Via Appreciative Inquiry. Paper presented at, World Congress Of The International Positive Psychology Association. June 2009. Philadelphia, PA. Reprinted with permission from D. Cooperrider and M. Avital (Eds.) (2004) *Constructive Discourse And Human Organizations: Advances In Appreciative Inquiry*, Vol. 1. Oxford, UK: JAI Press.

Positive Profusion Theory of Growth of the Positive Organization

Cooperrider identifies three related phases of development central to the achievement of positive profusion (Cooperrider, 2009). In the first phase there is an emphasis on the power of Appreciative Inquiry, which is elevated as a process above other forms of organizational change. This might be reflected by the introduction of some of the processes mentioned in this book: the idea of starting meetings with an inquiry into recent achievements; of inquiring into successes in performance appraisals; of replacing 360-degree requests with 'best self-stories', for example. The power, value and contribution of such inquiry are recognized and become part of the organizational life or culture. Simultaneously, the effect is to increase the sense of connection and relationship within the organization.

The effect of this collective shift is threefold. First, as new positive-focus activities take up more organizational space, negative or deficit-focused processes take up less: there is a displacement effect. Second, by the same token the increase in positive emotion or affect leaves less room for negative emotions or feelings. Third, the increase in positive emotion means that the sense of relatedness, or community, increases, which in turn means that the organization becomes more developed. Overall, the greater positive emotion in the system means that the organization is spending more time building its resource base, or resilience, and less time solving problems.

One of the things that happen as organizations incorporate these positive and sustainable ways of achieving development and growth into their way of being is that they start to extend them across the organizational boundaries. They start working with clients, customers, partners or suppliers in a different way. In conversations oriented towards appreciation and inquiry, the unique strengths and resources of others become part of the extended system's awareness and web of connection. It makes it much more likely that the relational coordination, high quality connections and positive energy networks we talk about in Chapter 7 will be present. When they are, they bring huge benefit to everyone. Relationships across the organization increasingly develop within a climate of safety, inclusion and respect.

In the second phase of this positive profusion development process, Cooperrider suggests that as individuals are able to spend more time using their strengths in the organization, so the virtuous development circle of broaden-and-build, identified by Fredrickson and Branigan (2005), comes into play. The organization becomes stronger, more resourceful and more creative, exhibits more positivity and generally enters a virtuous circle of exercising strengths, experiencing positive emotions and developing greater resourcefulness. Clearly, all this is capability-building. Simultaneously, through the increased level of connection and dialogue, yet more possibilities for the future are created. As people work together collectively there is a merging of resources and a growth in confidence. The whole becomes greater than the sum of its parts. Here we see sustainable growth in capability and capacity.

In the third phase there comes a point where the organization develops new ways of being, with strengths at its heart. In a quantum leap, the organization becomes something other than what it was. By now the utilization of strengths is working to eclipse weaknesses. They become less visible, less relevant. The organization has moved away from a fixation on weaknesses, problems and failures to an elevating focus on strengths, successes and achievements. In this way the organization becomes the embodiment of the leader's quest, as articulated by Peter Drucker to David Cooperrider: 'The task of leadership is to create an alignment of strengths ... making a system's weaknesses irrelevant' (Cooperrider, 2009).

Cooperrider's exciting models offer a conceptual understanding of how psychological and social capital can come together in an organizational development framework. By putting Appreciative Inquiry processes at the heart of organizational life, and by incorporating into them the emerging positive psychology approaches to recognizing and building strengths, the organization can create conditions that will lead to sustainable growth in capacity and capability.

The Three-Circle Strengths Revolution

As we can see in Supplement 6.10, Cooperrider suggests that there are three aspects to developing strengths-based increases in organizational capability (Cooperrider, 2008).

First, strengths become elevated within organizations. By this he means that a recognition, appreciation and utilization of the strengths of the individuals and the organization becomes a habitual way of behaving, so that such behaviour becomes the first rather than the last resource for growth. Second, people work with their strengths together with others in a way that creates additional capability in the organization. For this to happen people need to know the strengths of others and how to combine them with their own to produce good outcomes. Third, the organization expands its focus to include the wider world.

Cooperrider is unashamedly aspirational in his belief that commercial organizations can do good in the world. He suggests that as the highest human strengths (courage, wisdom, love of humanity, creativity and entre-preneurship) are refracted into the world, so they will have a positive and beneficial impact at world or societal level. He believes that these ways of working can change the world, taking the idea of sustainable growth to a global scale. We have talked about sustainability here without touching on the ultimate sustainability of life on our planet. Many of our biggest organizations are beginning to work out how they can be profitable in a planet-focused, sustainable way. Cooperrider suggests that we are on the verge of a strengths revolution which will increase the likelihood of a sustainable

Supplement 6.10 3 Circles

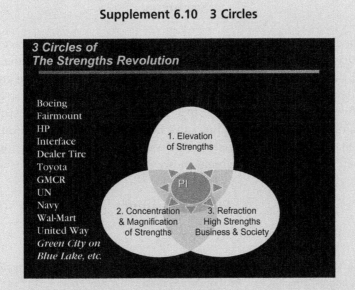

Reprinted with permission from D. Cooperrider (2009) The Discovery And Design Of Positive Institutions Via Appreciative Inquiry. Paper presented at, World Congress Of The International Positive Psychology Association. June 2009. Philadelphia, PA. Reprinted with permission from D. Cooperrider and M. Avital (Eds.) (2004) *Constructive Discourse And Human Organizations: Advances In Appreciative Inquiry*, Vol. 1. Oxford, UK: JAI Press.

future for all. In this way business becomes an agent of benefit, helping to build sustainable world societies.

In many ways his vision of what organizations can be is evocative of the organizations Cameron identified as flourishing (see Chapter 2). These organizations, with their abundance bridge, are able to release people for volunteer work, support local projects, invest in green ways of working, etc. Cooperrider's work suggests that an organizational focus on Appreciative Inquiry into strengths is a path for growing such abundance. He identifies these organizations as creating sustainable value (Laszlo, 2008). Sustainable value creates value for shareholders and all society's stakeholders, including the environment and the community. It stands in contrast to our previous understanding of the creation of value that is being shown to be unsustainable.

Summary

In this chapter we have considered how positive psychology and Appreciative Inquiry offer an answer to the organizational challenges of doing more with less by creating an ethical and sustainable path for organizational growth and development. In doing this we have examined the PsyCap construct of positive psychological traits open to development, and Cooperrider's model explaining how adopting Appreciative Inquiry as a way of organizational life enables transformational growth and development, facilitating the growth of flourishing and abundant organizations and societies.

Further Reading

PsyCap

Luthans, F., Youssef, C. and Avolio, B. (2007) *Psychological Capital: Developing the Human Competitive Edge*. London: Oxford University Press.
This book, by the construct's authors, gives a full explanation of the development of their ideas and the early work that has been done to demonstrate its effectiveness in boosting productivity.

Appreciative Inquiry: Latest developments

Advances in Appreciative Inquiry series.
This expensive series of edited texts contains all the current and most up-to-date thinking. Alternatively, the *Appreciative Inquiry Practitioner*, an online, bi-monthly publication, is an excellent high-value source of current developments in Appreciative Inquiry. www.aipractitioner.com

The European Appreciative Inquiry network or Begeistring Community is an online meeting place for Europe and beyond. www.networkplace.eu

7

Positive Relationships at Work

For some years I have worked with a plastics manufacturer. The manufacturing operation operates a 24-hour day shift system, while the commercial and managerial function works a normal 40-hour week. This means there are times when the site is alive with managers, and other times – evenings and weekends – when management support is very thin on the ground. One of the many fascinating things about working with this organization was how much more smoothly the workers thought things went when the managers weren't present and they could make their own decisions and organize their work. By their account they got a lot more done, with a whole lot less stress.

Management saw things slightly differently. It seemed to them that, left to their own devices, the workers organized things to suit themselves and not to management instructions. Undoubtedly, both accounts were true. In the absence of managers managing things, workers effectively self-organized. The quality of this self-organization varied considerably. On some occasions quotas would be filled, the product shifted through, the yard cleared, the goods stockpiled and the site kept basically tidy. At other times there would be a lack of coordination between the various parts of the process, resulting in bottlenecks, goods being dumped in strange places and quotas not being fulfilled.

When I started to ask about how it worked when it worked well, it very quickly became apparent that it was down to personal relationships that extended across functional lines. People who had at one time worked together, who knew and liked each other, could negotiate across these organizational boundaries to make things happen. They could get together in a responsive, proactive way to solve issues or prevent minor problems turning into major disruptions. In the absence of these relationships, people felt their responsibility

Positive Psychology at Work: How Positive Leadership and Appreciative Inquiry Create Inspiring Organizations, First Edition. Sarah Lewis.
© 2011 Sarah Lewis. Published 2011 by John Wiley & Sons, Ltd.

stopped at the edge of their function: once the goods went through the door to the next function, what happened was no longer their responsibility. With a good set of relationships people could, and did, negotiate up and down the line to manage, and vary, the rate of production to one that the system could cope with. In the absence of such communication, goods simply piled through the door to add to the chaos, or people sat on their hands waiting for goods to arrive.

Introduction

What are good working relationships? How do they add value to an organization? What is positive team working? What characterizes positive work relationships? In this chapter we shall look at what characterizes positive team working and how organizations manage to foster a sense of community and connection in more transient working conditions. We shall look at how investing in the generation of positive working relationships helps increase organizational capability and capacity in a sustainable way.

Positive relationships not only feel good, they are good for us at a deep and fundamental level. The presence of good quality, positive relationships affects us at a physiological level in a way that reduces our vulnerability to stress and enhances our general health and wellbeing. They have this impact through their effects on our hormonal, cardiovascular and immune systems. Positive relationships aid recovery from illness and correlate with increased longevity. Through the action of oxytocin, the 'bonding' hormone associated with the most intimate aspects of life such as childbirth, breastfeeding and orgasm, positive relationships are associated with substantial increases in trust. Through their effect on the immune system, they offer protection against some respiratory infections. They also offer protection against some prostate diseases (Cameron, 2008a).

Positive relationships also have good effects for us at work, being linked to increased career mobility, access to mentoring and other organizational resources, power and influence, and the creation of social capital. In positive relationships we can express and handle a much broader range of emotions, we are more resilient and better able to bounce back from difficulties. We have a stronger self-identity and are likely to make more accurate self-assessments. Positive relationships are associated with higher levels of energy, more learning and cooperation, better resource utilization,

cost reductions and time-saving (Cameron, 2008a). Being in positive relationships, at work and elsewhere, is fundamentally good for us as individuals and for organizations.

One fascinating revelation in this area is that the direction of benefit is
not as expected. It had long been assumed that the benefits of being in
positive relationships accrued for the individual from the receiving of good
things – love, compassion and caring from others. Somewhat to researchers'
surprise, it turns out that it's the *giving* of good things that confers the
beneficial effects. It is the demonstration of altruism, compassion, forgiveness and kindness, for example, which enables a positive relationship to

have the maximum impact on an individual's wellbeing and performance. It is truly good to give. Many organizations try to promote positive working relationships by forming people into reasonable-sized workgroups where they stand a chance of getting to know each other. Sometimes these workgroups are teams.

Positive Team Working

1) Teams processes

Teams, and team working, are very popular in organizational development. Senge (1993) identified teams as the key unit where learning takes place in organizations. Many scholars and authors have noted the human desire to form social groups and how teams at work can fulfil this need, while others have extolled the productivity benefits that come from people bringing different skills and roles together in a coordinated way to achieve some purpose. Many organizations are built around the team as a core, recurring unit. At their best, teams produce synchronized, collaborative, enhanced output.

However, assembling some people and telling them to get on with something does not necessarily produce a team, even if they are called one and their manager is known as a team leader. Teams are groups that are interdependent, bound together by their reliance on each other. In 1995, Baumeister and Leavy identified that positive team relationships are more likely to arise when: people have frequent interactions with the same few people; those relationships are free from chronic interpersonal conflict; there is concern for the wellbeing of all members; and the team is stable and likely to continue to work together. We might note that this last condition is one that is increasingly under threat as workplaces continually reconfigure themselves to adapt to change. In their efforts to adapt, they may well increase the proportion of their workforce on temporary contracts.

Richardson and West (2010) have pulled together some of the key research findings to identify how the basic ingredients of a good team (the inputs) are converted into excellent performance (the output). To stand a chance of being effective, they found that a team needs to: have an inspiring team task; be able to value and use the diversity within the team; ensure clear and evolving roles for all members; and develop positive team relationships. Positive team relationships are enhanced by the development of

team attachment. This in turn is encouraged by working closely and intensely together, achieving some early team wins, appreciating each other's efforts, valuing closeness and interdependence and receiving shared reward for the team outputs. So, an effective team is a good mix of people who get on well with each other and understand what they are there to do. They also need confidence, trust and support to do it.

Team psychological capital

The collective confidence of the team, the belief that together they can organize and action the things necessary to achieve good outcomes, is very important to the development of good relationships. This confidence can be seen as an expression of the team PsyCap. As with individuals, this measure of capability is fostered by increasing skills and by developing team self-efficacy, optimism, hope and resilience. Positive team relationships grow when people feel good together. Many team-building and development interventions are designed to increase the team's self-knowledge and self-efficacy. Trust is also an important component of positive team relationships.

Trust

People start to trust each other when they know what they can expect from each other and when they feel well regarded by each other. Trust tends to grow when people, who are reliant on each other's efforts, work together successfully and cooperate. As we have discussed elsewhere, trust is highly valuable to organizational endeavour, saving time, money and wear-and-tear on the system. In a trusting team people can afford to be vulnerable, in the knowledge that any mistakes they make will be dealt with generously and considerately. This allows people to be bolder and braver in their actions: they are more able to take the risk of being creative and innovative. This allows the team's capabilities to expand, as the team enters a virtuous circle of experimenting, learning, growing in confidence and ability, succeeding at more challenging tasks, taking on more challenging tasks, and so round again. This is a further example of sustainable growth, where the capacity and capability of the organization increase in a sustainable way.

Supportive leadership

Also important to positive team working is supportive leadership. Cameron's work gives us an idea of what such supportive, positive, relationship-enhancing leadership might look like in practice. He suggests that leaders can enhance positive relationships by starting meetings or discussions by talking about what is going well, emphasizing success. Such a leader might also role-model positive energy in the way they interact with the team. Positive leaders embrace much of the thinking in this book, for example, they encourage change by highlighting positive images of what is desired rather than dwelling on negative images of the worst possible outcomes (Cameron, 2008a).

Richardson and West found that together these team processes (psychological capacity, trust, supportive leadership and social support) create excellent team performance, such as heightened team achievement, team members' wellbeing, organizational altruism, inter-team cooperation and innovation. Teams that work like this can be considered to be functioning in a healthy way. It seems that essentially we do know what makes effective and positive team working more likely; it's making it happen that's the challenge. The puzzle is how some teams manage to create and mix all the ingredients identified by Richardson and West into a healthy functioning team while others, with the same initial ingredients of team diversity and a common goal, get stuck in dysfunctional patterns of behaviour. Ancona and Isaacs (2009), who have been exploring how team conversation and interaction dynamics influence performance, throw some very interesting light on this question.

2) Team interactions

Their suggestion is that contributions in a team, particularly in team discussions, can be simplified into four basic acts: move, follow, oppose and bystand. Each act is distinct, has a place in positive team dynamics and can be expressed by any team member. *Move* acts are those that suggest action in a certain direction. For example: 'I think we should consider cutting our prices at this difficult time.' They create energy, direction and momentum. However, until someone responds, they are just left open. Once someone produces a *follow* act, such as 'Great idea, I've been thinking much the same myself', the circle is closed. The power of the circle closing can be tremendous. Those involved in this quick '*move, follow*' sequence frequently believe that the decision is now made and so are ready to move on to another topic, oblivious to that fact that the eight other people round the table have given no indication of their position. A facilitation colleague of mine, Steve Brooks, from whom I have learnt much, used to refer to this group dynamic as the golden handshake. It is particularly strong if it occurs regularly between powerful people (e.g., leader and deputy), when it can have the effect of closing down further discussion.

As I write I am thinking of team leaders I've met who manage the golden handshake on their own. They propose an idea and then happily agree with themselves that this is definitely the way forward. At this point the slightly more enlightened become aware of the eight other faces around the table and ask them what they think. A number of things can happen next. A healthy team will overlook their leader's *faux pas* and act as if the question is still open. Another team will all just *follow*, so that the idea isn't examined or tested, while a group with reservations that they can't quite work out how to express remains silent. Leaders often misread silence as agreement and so remain in their closed, golden circle.

However, in a well-functioning team the original idea proposed in the *move* might be strengthened by an *oppose* act. In our example, in response to the proposed action – raising prices – someone might say, 'I don't think we should start competing on price! I don't think we should adjust prices, there's a real danger we'll just become an "us too" product.' This might lead to an expansion of the original idea to accommodate this consideration, or an alternative *move* might be proposed. Either way the original idea is tested and possibly further developed by an *oppose* move. Needless to say this contribution is not always appreciated at the time, which is one of the reasons people may choose not to voice their *oppose* feelings.

The *bystand* act (which is not the same as being neutral or absent from the group) plays a similar role, bringing in information that the group needs but does not yet have. In this instance such a *bystand* act might be to say, 'It sounds good, but I know Co-company did it last year and they are bitterly regretting it now, it didn't improve sales at all and they've lost a good bit of their margin.' Again, this contribution could cause the group to refine their decision. The *bystand* act brings perspective and insight to the situation, inviting the team to become more reflective. So we can see that when these acts interact well, ideas get proposed, explored, strengthened, developed, agreed or replaced by something better in a way that adds to group performance.

This all looks great on paper, but it is rarely how it feels in the heat of debate. What often happens as the temperature rises is that the impact of someone's words and their intention become muddled. For example, a *move* might be expressed as 'I don't know what's the matter with you all. It's obvious: we have no choice but to raise prices. It's a no-brainer', while the *follow* becomes, 'Absolutely, let's just make a bloody decision'; the *oppose* sounds like, 'What? Now you want to change the strategy! I'm just wasting my time here' and the *bystand* move becomes, 'For goodness' sake, do we want to go bust like Co-company!' While the intention of each contribution remains the same – to move things on – the poor expression means that the intention is drowned out by the noise of frustration, exasperation, sarcasm, insult, etc. and the other people in the group, being human, react to the noise not the intent.

The *oppose* move is particularly vulnerable to being wrongly attributed to negative intentions. At its best it acts to protect something important (in our example a long-term strategy), to perfect an idea by illuminating some defects in it or to ensure the integrity of the idea by testing it. However, it is often experienced as being obstructive or deflating. It is not only poor expression that can cause this team dynamic to get muddled. Stuck sequences, an absence of one of the acts from the team's repertoire or a cultural prohibition on the expression of anything deemed 'negative' can reduce the effectiveness of this team dynamic. In a healthy team, while muddles and breakdowns occur, the team itself corrects them.

Any team member can make corrections to the dynamic. So a *move, move, move* sequence where one idea follows another and none gets attended to can be interrupted by any of the other acts. A *move, follow, follow, follow* sequence can be strengthened by *oppose* and *bystand* acts before it becomes an ill-considered done deal. While *move, oppose, move, oppose* patterns can be helped by some *bystand* observation. Meanwhile poorly expressed *oppose* or *bystand* acts can be helped by someone listening to the hidden positive intent of the contribution behind the negative impact, and bringing that more into the open. Typical ways of doing this are saying 'There could be something in what you are saying' or by creating an invitation for the person to expand on their point. Given such space, they often are able to calm down and choose their words more carefully.

In a positive, healthy team there is usually a good match between the impact and intent of contributions, while mismatches are noted and corrected. There is a balance between the four acts. When teams are functioning well these different acts serve to create divergent thinking, repair any team process breakdowns and create new behaviour in the light of changed contexts. Positive teams, able to create and maintain a flexible balance of these core discussion acts, tend to: make sure all acts are enabled and balanced; reinforce *bystand* and *oppose* acts as these are the ones that are most open to misinterpretation or to be absent; and work to create flexibility in the sequencing and expression of the acts. Together, they create a dynamic pattern that is generative: together, the team can generate better quality ideas and execution than they could individually. The team becomes greater than the sum of its parts.

3) Team strengths

In addition to the contributions to positive team working we have discussed – team PsyCap, team trust, supportive leadership and team acts – the research suggests that knowing and understanding each others' strengths have a huge impact. Connelly (2002) found that per person productivity in teams at an automotive warehouse increased by 6–9% in the year that a strengths-based intervention was used. This result stood in contrast to the previous three years where the improvement had been almost zero. Effective teams are those that align functions with strengths. Alex Linley (2008) has been exploring how teams can use the unique strengths of each person in a combined way to enhance joint performance. Alex identifies four key ways teams can work with the strengths of their members.

Role fluidity

Role fluidity is about having flexible and fluid boundaries between roles. When roles are fluid, who does what, when, is not fixed in advance. Instead, people see what needs to be done and the person best suited, or with the time or energy, does it. To be effective this approach requires a shared understanding of the objective and a certain attentiveness or mindfulness. Many organizations are very role-bound and find the idea of role fluidity very challenging. This is frequently reflected in how they approach self-organizing tasks.

During formal management development events it is not unusual to set groups going on time-bound tasks, only to hear them spending valuable minutes discussing the need to allocate roles, usually timekeeper, chairperson and recorder. They then allocate these roles in a completely arbitrary way or people volunteer just to get this part of the process over and to move on to the discussion. What often then happens is that every five minutes the timekeeper looks at their watch, gets anxious and tells everyone to hurry up; the chairperson withdraws from the discussion so they can 'chair'; while the recorder waits poised by the flipchart until someone tells them to write something. The resource of three people is lost to the discussion. At the same time the levels of frustration in the group rise as the 'natural recorder' gets frustrated by the nominated recorder's inability to 'hear' what needs recording; or a member of the discussion group finds themselves itching to chair the conversation because it is being allowed to wander unproductively; while the timekeeper completely forgets their nominated role as they engage energetically in the discussion, causing others to become frustrated with their lack of adherence to role. No one in this scenario, which is not uncommon, is playing to his or her strengths.

In other groups they just start. When the need to record something occurs to someone, they either start to do it or they bring the need to the group's attention. They 'self-chair' their discussion, and occasionally someone realizes that time is passing and checks how much. All present are engaged in the discussion and in ensuring that what needs to happen does happen. This is the difference between role-rigid and role-fluid group working. Both can work well or badly. For role fluidity to work well there needs to be a common understanding of the desired outcome, a certain diversity of members, a willingness to volunteer for things for which people have a particular strength and an attentiveness to the needs of the group and the task. At its best role fluidity allows people to use their strengths in a combined way to ensure that the job is done and that anyone's individual weaknesses become irrelevant.

Role-shaping

Teams can also exercise role-shaping. This means redefining the role around the person rather than making the person fit the designated role. I used to work in the recruitment industry and it struck me then that when a vacancy arose, many organizations were looking for the person who had just left to fill the resultant organizational hole. It was as if the organization was a jigsaw puzzle and any piece that was removed had to be replaced by a piece that was exactly the same size, shape and pattern. How much more flexible to recruit for the absolute core skills essential to the role (e.g., a facility with numbers for accountants or a certain amount of emotional intelligence for social workers) and then define the boundaries of the job and the 'how' of delivery around the person's strengths.

Complementary pairings

A team can work out complementary pairings. This is where people are paired so that together their strengths cover the job. Many leaders and their deputies are excellent complementary pairings, as bosses and personal assistants can also be. In a project I worked on recently the internal commissioner, good at forward planning, hot on detail and highly methodical and organized, made an excellent partner to my strengths. I could rest assured that all the detail around the event would be attended to and that anything that I needed to be aware of would be brought to my attention. He in turn could relax from having to think about the actual process for the day, taking comfort from my confidence and inclusive way of working, even if the detail seemed a bit hazy to him. It was a very positive experience for both of us and one that could have gone very differently if we hadn't quickly recognized the complementarities of our approaches to the task.

Allocating roles by strengths

Finally, a team can go all the way and allocate team roles and tasks on the basis of individual strengths. You might wonder about how to deal with the team tasks that don't play to anyone's strengths. The short answer is first, to check that these tasks really don't play to anyone's strengths, it's not just your assumption, based on the fact that they don't play to your strengths, that is the issue; second, if there are tasks everyone dislikes, make sure they are shared out fairly; third, ensure that people only have to do the disliked task in short bursts; and, finally, be sure to give people recovery time doing something that energizes them afterwards. The more long-term answer is to assemble teams with a great and diverse set of strengths, as all the tasks will appeal to someone, however unlikely that might seem. Alternatively, find someone or some organization to which to outsource the task, preferably someone who has a known strength in this area. When teams are truly able to realize and utilize their strengths, the effects on productivity can be galvanizing, as George Karseras's account shows (see Supplement 7.1).

Supplement 7.1   Team Strengths

We ran a programme of change with 220 employees of a major software provider who wanted to change their culture from one that was based on conformity and fitting in, to one where people felt more prepared to take action they felt would move the business forward without fear of retribution. One major feature of the design of this programme was building a strong leadership community out of the existing separate groups of team leaders. Another feature was identifying the beliefs that were responsible for enduring success. These included being decisive under pressure and being positive and optimistic despite the challenges of the day.

Soon after one of these workshops a group of team leaders from the R&D team decided to get together to solve a long-standing problem. This was not their normal practice but, following a series of workshops that focused on building strong positive relationships, they felt comfortable in coming together to tackle a joint problem without senior leader sign off or presence.

A number of teams contribute to the production of a new software product. Before such a product can be released it needs to be tested. This means all the bits of software written by the different teams have to be assembled into one final product. The problem was that it was taking them too long to do, and they ran out of time. This meant that either the product was released with bugs or the release date would be delayed. The challenge was to speed up the pre-testing assembly process. The team leader takes up the story.

We were finding that every time we produced a new build, it would take about a week to get it into a state for testing. Ordinarily we would never have got together as a team of team leaders outside of our normal array of individual team meetings. The changes we introduced to the testing process made such common sense it was amazing we hadn't done it before. We were all so busy doing our thing, we'd never stopped to think about it. But we realised we had strong relationships we could utilise and through these we found collective strength to solve this long standing problem.

Following this meeting one person took responsibility for coordinating the entire build for all the teams, rather than each team being responsible for their own bit.

This person simply notified in advance all team leads when a build was due. This allowed each team to ensure any changes were ready in advance. Each team provided an out-of-hours contact if help was needed. The work we had done earlier helped them identify the strengths in their relationships, their ability to be optimistic and positive, and gave them the confidence to draw on these strengths to get together in a self-organizing way without waiting for leadership direction to solve this problem.

Contributed by George Karseras

It has to be said that some people really do struggle with this idea of role-shaping. Somehow the notion of everyone doing things they enjoy all the time is seen as inappropriately hedonistic for a work setting. They also struggle with the idea that other people might enjoy doing things they don't, seeing attempts to achieve this task reallocation as a selfish offloading of unpleasant tasks by the powerful to the less powerful. It is as if work can't be work unless there is an element of self-flagellation and martyrdom involved: 'Well, of course, I don't enjoy this part of the job but someone has to do it.' To which the only answer is: 'Well let that someone be someone who enjoys doing it!' They doubt such a person exists. I remember a story told to me years ago by someone who had been involved in some work at a ball bearings factory. He was sympathizing with, as he saw it, the poor person whose boring, soul-destroying job it was to inspect thousands

of ball bearings rolling off the production line. The ball bearing inspector looked at him with pity, took him aside, put an arm around him, and said: 'What you don't understand is, every ball bearing is different. It's a fascinating job.' He returned to his place in the line, shaking his head over the tragedy of this fascinating work being denied to this poor consultant. There truly is a job for everyone if only we can find it.

We can now identify various ways of enhancing positive working relationships within teams (see Supplement 7.2). However, not all work relationships begin and end at team boundaries. Most people have to work across team boundaries, some people don't belong to any team and some people are only temporary members of the organization. What do we know about what helps them to experience positive relationships at work?

High Quality Working Relationships

1) The nature of high quality connections

Dutton and Heaphy (2003) have investigated a particular form of positive work relationships, one they call a 'high quality connection'. A connection

---

**Supplement 7.2   Summary of Positive
Generative Team Working**

- Utilize strengths through role fluidity, role crafting, complementary pairing and role allocation.
- Be aware of, and attend to, the pattern of team dynamics, ensuring that move, follow, oppose and bystand acts are all present, honoured and helpful.
- Be aware of, and attend to, the positivity ratio in the group, recognizing that the greatest productivity, connectivity and generativity tends to occur at ratios between 6:1 and 11:1.

---

refers to a brief moment of contact, in contrast to a long-standing relationship. These relational micro-moments have their own distinct quality and can be high quality (positive), low quality (negative) or neutral in nature. High quality connections are experienced as life-enhancing; they promote trust and respect. The experience of such a high quality connection can leave people feeling more energized and richer than before they met. These connections can occur across organizational boundaries as well as within teams. Dutton and Heaphy's research suggests that three features define high quality connections: their ability to handle emotions, their ability to bounce back from setbacks and their degree of connectivity.

Positive connections can handle more emotions and in a better way than low quality connections. They have what is called a higher emotional carrying capacity. This means they can better withstand the expression of strong emotions of different hues: they are better able to accommodate expressions of joy and despair. For example, when experiencing a high quality connection we can risk exposing more of our true feelings, which means that less energy has to be invested in disguising our emotions. It also means that the people involved have access to the emotional information and can use that to divert the course of the conversation, if appropriate. I remember when my youngest son was about 10 he was under pressure from a couple of older boys, good friends of his, who had started smoking and were encouraging him to smoke too. I got them all together and started on an 'I'm very disappointed' speech to these two swaggering young lads. To my astonishment within seconds their eyes were filling with tears. This emotional feedback was crucial to letting me know how much more impact I was having than I had anticipated, or indeed desired, and allowed me to ease off and switch into forgiving and repairing mode, emphasizing how we all make mistakes and I knew they were good boys and good friends to my son, and so on. This was exceptionally strong feedback, but it demonstrates the emotional-carrying load of a good connection and the value that adds to the interaction.

The second characteristic of a positive connection is its ability to withstand strain and to function in a variety of circumstances. A high quality connection is able to bounce back after a setback. In other words, in our high quality connection we are able to sort out misunderstandings or losses of control that led to hurt, feelings of affront, etc. relatively quickly.

The third defining characteristic of high quality connections is that they create a high degree of connectivity. Connectivity refers to the ability of the connection to convey information of all kinds back and forth, and to generate new ideas. It is the feeling of a conversation that both flows easily between those involved and builds something new, often accompanied by mounting excitement. Such a connection is generative: it has an ability to incorporate change, new ideas or influence and create something new.

High quality connections are a subjective experience. When we are experiencing a high quality connection we feel vital and alive. We are also likely to have a sense of being known or 'coming home'. This feeling of familiarity and relaxation can be instantaneous. Interestingly, it has been found that this empathic and vital feeling can be detected physiologically as a form of unconscious resonance of neural engrams (brain patterns) between two people (Lewis, Amini and Lannan, 2000). Finally, when we are in a high quality connection, we are engaged and actively participating. We both feel to some extent vulnerable and responsive: there is a connection.

Unfortunately, not all connections in organizations, or indeed life, are high quality in this life-enhancing way. Poor quality connections have been described as toxic, each a little death for those involved. In organizations, poor quality interactions have a cost attached. They can be life-depleting, leaving people feeling diminished, frustrated, demotivated, demoralized, disrespected or worse: revengeful, despairing or annihilated. One short, low quality connection may have this effect; many over time almost certainly will. Repeated exposure to low quality connections can be a punitive experience. In any environment characterized by these low quality connections, people shrink psychologically: they take fewer risks, they absent themselves, they become less brave and outgoing, and less innovative (Sidman, 2000). If we have sufficient low quality or negative interactions with someone we shall try to avoid them, even if they have information or knowledge that might be useful to us. While low quality connections cost organizations, high quality connections add value. They are good for you too.

Research shows that having high quality connections with others is key to healthy living. So promoting high quality connections between people at work not only benefits work through the performance impact, but is also good for the individual. As with positive relationships, high quality connections mitigate stress, and are associated with a stronger immune system, longer life, lower blood pressure and a reduced risk of death. When in a moment of positive connection we experience a release of endogenous opioid peptides, which acts to reduce stress levels, our systolic blood pressure falls. High quality connections are good for us and good for the organization. High quality connections increase organizational capability in four key ways.

2) The effect of high quality connections

First, they facilitate the exchange of valuable resources within the organization (e.g., knowledge). They also build valuable resources, such as trust and influence. Trust is a great cost-reducer, allowing more to be done with less, while influence increases the likelihood of players who hold necessary information, but perhaps are not formally connected to a project, to influence decision-making positively.

Second, they facilitate the development of positive meaning-making and personal identities within the workplace. Organizations are often very ambivalent places with poor feedback loops, and the questions every individual experiences from time to time – 'What am I doing here?' 'What difference do I make?' – frequently need to be addressed. High quality connections help the organization as a whole answer and re-answer these questions as people see their value and contribution reflected in their connections with others. They also help people experiment with new identities so they are constantly growing and adapting.

Third, they assist with growth and development. High quality connections can allow people to hear difficult things that may be crucial for the organization. Leaders particularly need to have high quality connections with messengers who have immunity from being shot when they bring bad news. I remember when as a relatively new leader I inadvertently offended a number of people through a throw-away comment at a full site meeting. One of my reports was able to tell me what I had done and the reaction I had elicited. She and my boss encouraged me to name the mistake and apologize at the next meeting; encouraging me to believe that this would strengthen rather than weaken my not yet secure leadership position. The apology allowed me to undo the negativity I had created. Having received a genuine apology offered with humility, people were able to experience forgiveness and so release themselves from dealing with the negative feelings I had carelessly provoked. They could redirect their energy to the organizational task. I came to rely on this direct report particularly to alert me to the unintentional damage I did so I could undo it. We developed an ability to repeatedly form a high quality connection.

Fourth, high quality connections facilitate effective learning. It has been found that in these connections knowledge that is passed from one person to another is absorbed faster and more completely. At the same time, the relationship or connection is enhanced by the interaction so that both parties feel they have gained from the interaction rather than that one has given away something 'valuable' to the other. New knowledge is often generated in the course of these interactions. Equally exciting is the idea that high quality connections are a foundation for creating positive spirals of meaning about the organization and its work. As we saw in Chapter 3, the meaningfulness of work is important for employee engagement.

3) Temporary work relationships

One group of workers who are particularly vulnerable to experiencing poor quality connections and relationships at work are temporary workers, who are frequently excluded from established organizational socialization procedures that help make people feel they belong. Not seen as being really part of the organization, and so not worth investing in, they often miss out on proper induction, team days and training opportunities. In addition, in a more personal way, established organization members may withhold from forming any meaningful relationship with a temporary member, reserving such investment for their established colleagues, with whom they anticipate a long working future. The experience of the temporary worker can be lonely, isolated and alienating. However it doesn't have to be.

Blatt and Camden (2009) were interested to see what made it possible for this frequently disenfranchised group to develop a sense of community. To this end they interviewed 30 temporary agency workers, men and women, across a range of functions about their positive experiences of temporary work. Their interviewees ranged in age from 24 years to 73, and had been temporary workers from 16 months to 15 years. In particular they asked them when they had felt part of a community. They found everyone had at least one good story to tell and some several, suggesting that people find ways of negotiating the obstacles to achieving a sense of belonging on a temporary tenure. Their research revealed that positive connections were a key factor in promoting a sense of community in this group of workers.

A positive connection was defined by the participants as a subjective experience, located viscerally in the here and now. In other words, positive connections refer to the felt quality of an interaction, not to its outcome. These fleeting moments act to bind the temporary employees to their colleagues, creating both a sense of community and facilitating task performance. These relational micro-events have one or more of four qualities. They generate a sense of inclusion. They allow people to feel recognized and important for whom they are. There is a sense of mutual benefit to the connection. They facilitate shared emotions. Exchanging jokes, sharing moans, comforting someone who is distressed all help people feel less alone.

These brief moments of positive connection occur in the context of ongoing work, not at special events. They create a sense of community and solidarity. The sense of community generated among these temporary workers by tiny moments of interaction boosts people's motivation to come to work. They also increase the likelihood of the worker staying in the face of offers of alternative employment. It is the quality of this day-to-day interaction with co-workers that makes work attractive and a pleasant experience, counteracting the dangers of temporary work, such as alienation, depression and loneliness. They enhance the motivation to do a good job and the ability to communicate and collaborate with others. The quality of daily interactions in organizations makes a huge difference to people's experience of the organization and their levels of engagement and motivation.

4) Relational coordination

High quality connections also enhance work coordination, as Gittell's (2003) work shows. Work coordination is particularly important in situations like that described in my opening story, where the work extends across organizational boundaries. Typically, work coordination is seen as a management or information-processing problem. However, as we saw, when managers aren't available, it quickly becomes clear it is a relational process. The two key factors that make a difference are the quality of the

Supplement 7.3   Enhancing Temporary Workers' Experience

- Recognize the value of 'private' interactions at work and allow some slack.
- Develop organizational skills in fostering positive relationships quickly.
- Develop organizational skills in creating positive micro-moments of interaction.
- Encourage strong attachments to the organization, while also making it easy for people to detach.
- Encourage a mental model of the organization that accommodates both temporary and permanent staff – melding the workforce into more integrated communities.

From Blatt and Camden (2009)

relationship and the communication, and they in turn are related. In Chapter 4 we highlighted the communication process; here we want to focus on the relational aspect of this boundary-crossing, brief coordination. Gittell's work highlights the importance of the strength of a sense of shared goals across the process. In my opening story it would seem that the strength of shared goals may have, on occasion, been strong between peers, but not perhaps aligned with management goals. Shared goals allow people to act with regard to the overall work process.

This relational coordination along a process pathway is the opposite of the much cited 'silo-working', where each function operates as if it were in a separate world with responsibilities that ceased at the boundary of the function. In this situation work is often poorly coordinated, and when problems arise, abandonment or blame ensues. Also, as we saw in my example, timely communication does not occur. Gittell suggests that the point of organization development activity is not to create more structures through which information could (but probably won't) flow, but to build high quality connections.

The transformational collaborative methods we examine in Chapter 8 help with both of these challenges to achieving effective relational coordination: communication and relationship. Paying some attention to the relational skills of role-holders in boundary-spanning and supervisory roles can also be a good investment. Mapping out routines also facilitates increased fluidity as people understand the key interdependencies in the process, and so are alert to who needs to know what, when, especially when things change unexpectedly. It is suggested that as the nature of work changes, relational coordination processes will replace structure as the main means of coordinating work activity. We increasingly see this in fluid structure organizations, such as matrix-based organizations.

5) High energy networks

Researchers from a more sociological perspective have also been exploring the impact of positive relationships on organizational capabilities. They were interested to see to what extent positive organizational outcomes, such as empowerment, high performance or improved wellbeing, might relate to positive relationships. Baker, Cross and Wooten (2003) studied 'the extent to which interpersonal relationships generated or depleted a subjective feeling of energy' (p. 331). Their research covered seven organizations across six sectors, looking at how the network of energizing (or de-energizing) relationships mapped onto networks of information flow, controlling for variables such as how long they had been with the organization, gender and hierarchical level. In addition, they conducted semi-structured interviews with 63 people from across the organizations.

These people described what an energizing relationship felt like. They described feeling stimulated, 'up', intense and animated. They described how they were cognitively engaged and attentive to what was being said. They felt their thought processes were quick and responsive. They felt they made connections quickly, allowing the conversation to have give-and-take and to build up to new ideas or information. They felt enthused and drawn in. They described being committed to the interaction, willing to devote discretionary time to the issue after the interaction. One of the things people find exciting about these conversations is the sense of the creation of possibility or hope. Such conversations appear to be a pervasive feature of organizational life. Energizing relationships would seem to be very similar to high quality connections. What is interesting about this research is what it reveals about the patterns of such interactions.

By mapping the networks of energizing and de-energizing relationships it is possible to see who is in the centre of energy creation and those who sap energy. Early research in this area reveals that some people are much more central to energizing or de-energizing relationships than others. There are some people who are great at motivation, at giving people a lift when they're down. These people are well recognized by others. In a powerfully energizing network people can be energized to work on tasks they do not enjoy and with people they do not like. There are other people who are experienced as being a drain on energy, excellent at spreading hopelessness, despair and other de-motivating emotions. Again, the cost to organizations of de-energizing networks is as important as the benefit that accrues with energizing networks. Once the people at the centre of the de-energizing networks are known, interventions can be made to make the interactions more energizing.

For example, in one of Baker's companies, the de-energizing relationships centred on supervisors who were following standard procedures. Their strict adherence to these procedures bred resentment among their workers of being 'micro-managed'. The supervisors were unaware of the effect their perfectly correct organizational behaviour was having. Once this was known, action was taken to review procedures, roles and organization design with clear benefit.

Baker and colleagues suggest that as the stability of formal structures diminishes, as a result of repeated downsizing, less long-term organizational commitment and increasing matrix and team-based working, so the structural source of power and influence may be shifting. Where once such power arose from a powerful position in a stable network, it now might lie in an ability to attract, engage and energize others in the network. Early work on the relationship between energy networks, information flow networks and performance seems to support this proposition. Baker and colleagues found that performance was better predicted by people's place in the energy network than by their place in the information network. This suggests that, for performance, being able to energize others may be more important than occupying certain organizational positions in an information and communication network.

Summary

In this chapter we have considered how positive psychology enhances our understanding of, and ability to create, powerful working relationships. We have examined what is known about how positive relationships can be created in teams, among temporary workers, in short-lived interactions and by energizing networks. We have found that positive relationships at work can take many different forms; what they share in common is the value they add to the organization. Positive working relationships enhance productivity, the generation of new ideas, problem-solving, information and resource flow, and build social capital. They are also very good for our health.

Further Reading

Dutton, J. and Ragins, B. (Eds.) (2009) *Explaining Positive Relationships at Work: Building a Theoretical and Research Foundation*. Hove: Psychology Press.
This is a sociologically-oriented academic text only for those keen to explore this area in great theoretical depth.

8

Positive Transformation

Recently, I spent the day working with a group of adult and children's service providers from an English county council in a large marquee at a country house hotel. Almost 150 people had come together for the conference. They were senior decision-makers from the county council, the health service and numerous voluntary sector organizations. The conference was to create a strategy for a new initiative called Think Family. I had been asked to assist the planning group to make the event 'strengths-based', although they weren't sure what that might entail when they asked for it.

The day was designed to have a short opening session, after which people would form groups to share stories of excellent work in the past where they had really helped people make a difference to their lives by 'thinking family'. We would share some of these with the whole group and then people would again work in groups to imagine a future in two years' time where Think Family was an integral part of the county landscape. They would come back with visual, creative and impact-full images of this future to share. Finally, people would work in groups on any topic relevant to the theme to start working out how to move things forward. After the initial half hour the chairs would never again be facing forward in 'conference' style, but would be constantly rearranged as the system in the room took different shapes.

In the run-up to the day we had three planning meetings. The people at the meetings were going to be facilitators, working with me to help people through the process we designed. We never had the whole facilitator team together at once, and we were still recruiting facilitators the day before the event. The facilitators were not experts in Appreciative Inquiry, nor were they necessarily

Positive Psychology at Work: How Positive Leadership and Appreciative Inquiry Create Inspiring Organizations, First Edition. Sarah Lewis.
© 2011 Sarah Lewis. Published 2011 by John Wiley & Sons, Ltd.

experienced facilitators. While the success of the day clearly owes a great deal to the boldness, courage and skill of our facilitators in working under these less than ideal preparation conditions, it is also highly illuminative of the resilience of these positive, transformative, collaborative processes.

The first big round where we came together to share stories was a revelation of excellent practice. We heard about whole families being rallied to help struggling members, we heard about individual workers taking it upon themselves to solve practical problems, we heard about children getting back into education, coming off at-risk lists and gaining confidence. We heard about troubled young mothers becoming mentors to others, about travellers hungry for knowledge taking it and teaching each other about life-saving childcare. We heard again and again about lives transformed in a sustainable way by thinking 'family' not just individual 'service users'. These stories of family hardship and transformation were extremely moving: clearly 'think family' was already present in this system.

The 'images of the future' session was just as alive. People presented collages or models, and used words, songs and stories to convey aspects of the future that were important to them. I have worked in these Appreciative Inquiry-based ways for a long time and I never cease to be amazed and delighted at the inherent creativity in people and groups, and the energy such creativity generates. In the last discussion of the day people coalesced around themes. Many of these groups were people taking the opportunity to find out more about related services. Some were about how to help other parts of the system engage with what was being discovered today about what worked. Some were tentative discussions about reconfigurations of service delivery.

During the day people discovered the strengths and resources that already existed within their system. They increased their connectedness – indeed, that was one of the most commented upon features of the day. They discovered that they had ideas and aspirations in common. They began to develop a more coherent map of the system. They started to create some collective energy to do more. This knowledgeable and experienced system found out for themselves and from each other what works and what makes a difference.

The system changed during the day. Whatever happens now at the giddy heights of strategic planning, things have changed on the ground. People have made new connections and their mental maps of the world have shifted. They have shared positive and meaningful experiences about things that are important to them. They stand more solidly together. They know different things and they know things differently. There is more social capital, more positivity and a greater awareness of strengths and resources in the system. They will act differently and Think Family will become more a lived part of their ways of thinking and acting.

Introduction

In this chapter we shall review the key theme of the book: the power of positive psychology and Appreciative Inquiry to create flourishing and inspiring places to work. We shall identify some of the key processes that support these outcomes: social capital and relational reserves; the beneficial effects of positive emotions; strengths; and understanding the organization as a complex adaptive system. We shall note that while few standard approaches to organizational change recognize or utilize the value of these themes, there are some new approaches to change that do. However, bringing them into an organization has some challenges which we shall explore. We shall go on to consider these approaches and why they are so effective, looking at the key features of organizational life through which they create possibilities for change. We shall outline a few of the key methods and include a few case studies that illuminate their effect.

Key Processes of Flourishing and Inspiring Workplaces

1) Social capital and relational reserves

Throughout this book we have made reference to the value to organizations of social capital and relational reserves. Cameron and his colleagues' (2004) work demonstrates that the affirmative bias and virtuous practices found in the most exceptional of organizations build up reserves of social capital that help the organization produce exceptional performance and to recover more quickly from setbacks. Similarly Baker and colleagues (2003) have demonstrated the value added to the organization by positive energy networks where people will freely offer discretionary effort to achieve tasks and work with others. Gittell (2003) has researched how the quality of the relationships that people have, even the most fleeting, affects the quality of many aspects of organizational life, particularly the flow of information, the generation of new knowledge and ideas and the quick and timely solving of problems. The pattern and quality of organizational relationships, an organization's social capital, are key to creating flourishing and inspiring places to work.

2) Positive emotions

Another recurrent theme of this book has been the beneficial influence of positive emotions. Losada and Heaphy's (2004) research makes clear that the emotional bias of discussion directly affects the degree of connection and so the quality of innovation. Fredrickson and Cameron both refer to the contagion effects of positive acts and emotions: virtuous circles can develop within groups and organizations of increasingly positive behaviour. They also refer to the restorative effects of positivity: feeling good undoes the damaging effects of feeling bad. Fredrickson's broaden and build theory (Fredrickson and Branigan, 2005) illuminates how skills and resources developed during times of feeling good aid resilience by creating resources that can be called on in difficult times. People are less insular, are more able to reach out to others, when they are feeling good. Positivity in itself helps to create social capital amongst groups of people. Positivity is key to creating flourishing and inspiring places to work.

3) Strengths

A third theme has been the benefits for organizations of enabling people to play to their strengths. We have seen how when people are able to spend more time working in ways that energize them, that create experiences of flow and that call on well-developed strengths, they are more motivated, self-directed and become capable of excellent performance. When people are playing to their strengths they tend also to feel positive and so are more likely to be building social capital with others. Identifying and working with individual, group and organizational strengths help to create workplaces that people find inspiring.

4) Organizations as complex adaptive systems

A fourth theme has been the effect of viewing organizations through the prism or lens of the complex adaptive system. Viewing organizations this way, we see the big effects that can be produced by small changes and the importance of noticing them. We can see the value in a system of ambivalence and redundancy, and the important role every participant plays in forming and re-forming the organization. Viewing organizations as complex adaptive systems helps us see how changing patterns of communication and relating changes organizations. All of these ideas – social capital, positivity and strengths, and the organization as a complex adaptive system – offer ways of intervening in organizational life to move things towards a more positive state. However, standard approaches to organizational change make little use of them.

Instead, such approaches are wedded to the view of the organization as a complicated, yet ultimately predictable, machine, led from the top and powered by rationality. As Rowland and Higgs' (2008) work demonstrates, the planned and directive approach to change is doomed to failure for anything other than very local, low-impact change. Emergent change is a much more productive approach to change. Interestingly, there are ways of working with organizations that embrace and celebrate the emergent nature of change, rather than seeing it as a sign of failure of planned change; that pull on and create three phenomena (positivity, strengths, social capital) and that recognize the organization as a socially created, complex, living system. At present, though, they are called on as the exception rather than the rule.

These emergent ways of working with organizations are known, collectively, as large group technologies, strategic collaboration methods, transformative collaboration, whole-system working and large group participation methodologies. There are a number of specific, well-established approaches, some of which we outline below, collectively referred to by the terms above. They have been used across private and public organizations in different parts of the world. Calling on the combined intelligence of the organization, they offer rapid, collective change. The challenges of getting buy-in and overcoming resistance to change dissolve. They can be undertaken in-house or with minimal external support. All in all, they offer excellent value for money and potential return on investment compared to more traditional approaches to organizational change and development. Yet they are rarely an organization's first port of call. Why? Because working in this way challenges a number of organizational assumptions and shibboleths.

Why Organizations Ignore the Transformative Collaboration Approach to Change

1) They don't promise to achieve a predetermined outcome

By definition these approaches accept change as the emergent outcome of simultaneous combined action. They work by recognizing that when the patterns of interaction in an organization change, the organization is changed. In this way change is an emergent property of the system. These ways of working, rather than focusing on a single, predetermined outcome, work to create possibilities. They are focused on creating different ways of being now that will lead to better ways of being in the future. The future is conceptualized as emerging from the actions of the present. This presents a challenge to any leader who understands their job to be to lead their organization to a future predetermined by them.

2) They aren't based on the power of logical problem-solving

While these methods may call on the analytic and problem-solving skills of the participants, their power resides in the effect they have on emotions, relationships, system understanding and knowledge. In other words, the source of change is the motivating effect of feeling good and of finding common ground with others. When we find such common ground, when we find we have shared values and desired outcomes, then our relationships are positively affected and we are motivated to achieve desired futures. This means that analytic power is no longer privileged. The 'normal' organizational hierarchy is upset.

3) Change doesn't happen in sequential, linear steps

With these ways of working change happens 'in the moment' as people come together to find out about themselves and their organization. The big changes in mental models, orientation, joint understanding, perception, relationships and collective energy happen as people work together. Of course, after any collective event there will be follow-on actions, but they are a consequence of the collective event, not a top-down directive. This means the ownership, energy and execution are likely to be different. The sources of change are vision, energy and co-coordinated effort. Plans exist only to support these things. This is a reversal of the usual order where plans are seen to 'drive' change. These ways of working mean that planning becomes a supplementary activity, not a driving force.

4) Information is not neutral, decisions are not impartial

With these transformative collaborative ways of working, certain information is positively sought. The questions asked are biased to create particular pools of knowledge and positive feelings. By the same token others are deliberately ignored. It is not a balanced investigation; it is a positively biased inquiry. So we want to know what works, not what doesn't. We want to consider the best possible future, not the most likely future. There is no pretence that actions are dictated by bigger forces, such as 'logic dictates' or 'market forces demand that ...'. Rather, there is a recognition that although we operate in a world of affordances and constraints, there are many possibilities for action that can be created. This means that no one can claim to have the whole picture or a monopoly on 'the truth'. For those who think they are paid on this basis, this is hard.

5) The role of the leader is not to be omniscient about the past, present and future

These ways of working do not credit the leader with a monopoly on knowledge, vision, account, intelligence, leadership or truth. These are recognized as assets that exist throughout the organization which can be brought into the open to the benefit of everyone in the organization. Within the organization lie the knowledge, wisdom, relationships and intelligence to create attractive futures. The leadership perspective is one among many that create the organization. Leaders are uniquely positioned within the system, as is everyone, within a complex network of privilege and vulnerability. This requires a very different understanding of the role, power and influence of the organizational leader.

6) The vision of the future is co-created not dictated

When I enter an organization, I am frequently told that the vision or strategy has been created and the challenge now is to sell it to the organization. This represents a missed opportunity. The organization could have saved itself so much time, money, conflict and mistakes if it had co-created its vision or strategy with its people: there would then be no need to sell it; costly mistakes would have been avoided as people could have pointed out the unfeasibility of some of the bright ideas as they were being formulated; and people would understand what was needed to create the vision and would already be working to achieve it. These ways of working offer people the opportunity to co-create visions, plans and aspirations for the future that they feel part of and are inspired to achieve. To achieve this means involving others early in the process. It is this need to involve others that

makes this way of working seem very slow, not to mention risky, to those used to 'the usual way', whereby a small group draws up the strategic plan and then tells others about it.

7) *Imagination is a valid source of information*

Organizations tend to have a continuing love affair with facts as both recorders of the world and as fortune-tellers. Facts are used to support positions and argue for resources. They are seen as a fundamental resource for building the future. These alternative ways of working privilege imagination as a very powerful source of ideas, strategy, visions of the future and motivation. They work with metaphor and 'dreams', with pictures and other representations of how things 'could be' to create a resource to inform decision-making in the present. Using the imagination as an effective resource is considered suspect when applied beyond a small group of 'creatives'. It sounds dangerously close to daydreaming and other ways of avoiding 'action', not to mention hopelessly woolly and fuzzy. Many organizations and leaders find this a challenge to their security in the idea of hard facts as the key source of influence and change.

8) *There is a big initial impetus, then it runs itself*

These transformative, collaborative ways of working tend to involve a lot of people early in the process of change. This is an inversion of the normal way of proceeding whereby a small group researches and plans the change, and then a big effort is involved at the implementation stage. In these alternative ways of working the challenge for the organization is to coordinate the effort and energy that flow from the event, to create coherence as the energy flows through the organization, rather than the more usual challenge of driving and embedding the change. Many organizations find these apparently big, up-front costs difficult to contemplate as they are used to the bugle in the pipe, as it were, occurring later in the process. These new ways of working with their high-impact start offer a challenge to those used to a gradual curve of increasing involvement.

9) They aren't tidy and efficient

These processes are messy and iterative. They are resource-hungry in that they require physical bodies to be present, not representatives. Self-organizing can be slower and look messier than pre-set ordering. For example, in this way of working we would invite people to sort themselves into multi-stakeholder groups as opposed to designating seats beforehand. Why? Because it means people have to relate, be proactive, engage with the world to become organized to respond to the challenge. This models what they are going to have to do to engage with the change, where no one is going to give them the answer. How things are done is as important as getting something done: the process, the journey, is as important as the outcome. Collective self-organizing can be deeply uncomfortable for those used to efficiency as a first and primary consideration.

10) They involve taking a risk

These events can release huge amounts of energy and initiative. As people engage with the challenge and start to use their initiative, they can move in unexpected directions, produce unexpected ideas and act in unanticipated ways. For such events to be effective, leaders need to relinquish any illusions of having control of the organization and its destiny. To engage with an organization in these ways takes faith and courage. Working in this way is a bold and courageous act. Not all leaders are in a situation where they are able to display such courage. Given the many challenges of these ways of working to most organizations' status quo, it is perhaps not surprising that there isn't always a rush to abandon established approaches. For those who do though, the rewards are many.

Transformative Collaboration

Transformative collaboration events are interventions that energize the organization collectively to find positive ways forward to positive ends. They create opportunities for people to talk and work together about the things that matter. These events are based on an understanding of many of the ideas we have explored in this book. For example, they create: a sense of wellbeing or positive affect as people concentrate on discovering the best of the organization; energy and solidarity as people discover common ground; purpose and meaning as people explore what they want to achieve; positive decision-making and communication as people make decisions together about what is important and meaningful in their work; and they start to evolve towards a more positive workplace culture by the way they work together. They have their beneficial effects on the organization by effecting change in the processes of organizational life that are so prevalent that we barely notice them: the patterns of organizational life.

Patterns of Organizational Life

The patterns of organizational life are those of communication, relationship and behaviour. This is the material that already exists within the organization: it is the fabric of organizational life. These day-to-day processes are the elements of organizational life that are so commonplace we pay them little heed when we are thinking of change. When we think of change we tend to think change demands something big, new and different. We overlook the potential inherent in existing organizational patterns of interaction. To affect the patterns we affect the processes inherent in, formative of and consequent to the patterns. These are processes of conversation, connection, relating, sense-making, imagination, emotions and attention. Interestingly, this way of considering organizations and organizational change leads us well away from the familiar organizational undue concern about what goes on within people – their personality – encouraging instead a much less familiar focus on what happens between people – their relationships.

1) Conversation

Conversation is so endemic to organizational life we hardly notice it. Yet it is important, for it is in conversation and other forms of interaction that we recreate or change our organization. Conversation is a source of micro-diversity in the organizational system. The quality of conversation within an organization can be seen to run on a continuum from repetitive to transformational. Transformational conversation is that in which novelty arises or is created. Such conversation generates new possibilities in the world: it is the source of evolution. Transformative collaboration interventions recognize conversation as a key change process: by helping people have different conversations with different people about different things in different ways, they create change. Such conversations help the system to evolve purposively. In Supplements 8.1 and 8.2 Martin and Mario share two experiences of conversations that affected organizational destiny.

Supplement 8.1   Conversations That Matter Using an AI Approach to Facilitate Renewal and Cohesion

A head of a large academic department asked me to facilitate an 'Away Day'. The Department of 35 academic staff, like the rest of the university (and indeed Ireland itself), has grown exponentially over the last decade. This growth has come to an abrupt halt with the death of the Celtic Tiger. The organizational mantra is now very much *doing more with less*, resulting in the department having to reduce staff numbers while increasing student intake. The Away Day, I was informed, had to be a half-day and on campus. So, now *I* had to model the way of doing more with less!

The head of department wanted time for her colleagues to consider how best to move forward given the challenging environment they would now be operating in. Discussion with the head also revealed that a section within the department felt that they could function and thrive more if they left the existing department structures and created their own department. The mood in the department could be described as apprehensive and unsettled.

We agreed that the objectives for the Away Day would be to create a better shared understanding of the department's strengths and purpose and consider how they could move forward given the changed climate. The head felt the issue of the 'split' should not be highlighted as the issue was controversial for the department and given the time restrictions there might not be sufficient time to deal with it.

The design of the session was going to be crucial given the limited time, relatively large numbers and the issues involved. I was mindful of

Continued

Supplement 8.1   *Continued*

the proverbial Pandora's box being opened with insufficient time to deal with what flew out of it! I was confident that Appreciative Inquiry methodology was appropriate, but needed to give some thought to the workshop process which would be needed to allow the objectives of the day to be met.

I decided to use a hybrid form of *World Café*, a design where large groups can have conversations on issues that matter to that group. I wanted to enable this large group to have concurrent and multiple conversations around, in this instance, appreciative questions, e.g., *What were your impressions of the Department when you joined? What were the challenges then? What are the most important things to preserve through this period of uncertainty?* The design of the session was intended to allow a natural conversation style to emerge and I hoped would allow for some difficult things to be said and heard. I gave the Away Day a working title: *Conversations that Matter*.

A conversation did take place that mattered! The issue about the split did emerge. The design of the day allowed the 'story' of the department to be constructed by the participants through sharing of the department's folklore. What emerged was a greater understanding of their strengths, their collective identity and how this contributed to their success over some very difficult years. Also, it allowed the department to articulate its values (diversity with shared purpose), which they identified as contributing to the past successes of the department and would contribute to its success in the future. Those who were considering leaving the department gained an appreciation of what they brought to the whole department and, in turn, what the department brought to them. The issue of the split was taken off the agenda at that point. Maybe what the department learnt most was that when difficult things can be said and heard, solutions and a sense of what is possible emerge.

Contributed by Martin Leavy

2) Connectivity

People within organizations can be more or less connected. Typically, some groups are quite tightly and densely connected, and then there are loose and sparse connections across organizational boundaries such as between divisions, between the centre and the satellites and between the

Supplement 8.2   Conversation Changes Things

Lucio, a warehouse manager in his forties, sitting in a circle with his old and new colleagues, shares a thought: 'Now I do realize where I really belong. I had never had such an awareness of the extraordinary quality of all of you, and of this new organization that is taking shape thanks to all of our efforts!'

The circle was made by some 40 managers of two businesses that had been merged and had been experiencing a serious struggle. The usual things: people belonging to the two groups were blaming each other, and the management. These new issues were becoming meshed with older ones, while things had been becoming difficult to bear.

Earlier we had found ourselves consultants, board and managers, in a hotel in Sardinia, doing an AI summit during two consecutive Saturdays.

The Discovery phase really was a discovery in many ways, as many of them weren't in the habit of going in search of positive experiences, and some storytelling by some of them really started breaking the ice and making them feel part of the whole.

We went on with a playful Dream phase, and followed with some hard and deep conversations in the Design and Destiny phases. The paradigm of conversation shifted from the usual reciprocal blame, with very much cautiousness and defensiveness, to supportive conversations where these middle managers started to express concerns for issues that were afflicting their colleagues in other departments and in the other organization being merged.

One of the topics had to do with the supposed low proactivity by the managers. A whole-group conversation ended with the family-run board agreeing to allow much more autonomy to people working in the organization. To some different extent they had been micro-managing their people and realized it in the conversation. No one actually 'taught' them.

Some 50 days later we had a celebratory event where one story emerged, among many, as more meaningful and many people were competing to narrate it.

Luigi, one of the managers, said that, after agreeing in advance with the CEO, Massimo, he called a meeting. He prepared the content in advance, invited the right people and shared some complicated issues with them. He underlined the constructiveness of all of them. They came up with an innovative solution in 1½ hours and were all aligned and motivated. 'It took just 90 minutes!'

Continued

Supplement 8.2 *Continued*

They all recounted that in the past those issues would have wasted hours and hours of one-on-one conversations at the coffee machine, without making any progress. I asked what had made it possible for something different to happen this time. Luigi said: 'Well ... the experiences of conversation we had during those days [i.e., our AI summit] made it very easy for me to shift to that same approach for new and different conversations on organizational issues. We discovered then that we could talk in a very productive way. Why not do it again and again?'

Contributed by Mario Gastaldi

organization and its suppliers or consumers. The degree and pattern of connectivity affect how information flows around the system; it also affects any particular individual's ability to act. Connectivity creates possibilities of both cooperation and conflict (Stacey, Griffin and Shaw, 2000). Any individual is in relationship with a greater or lesser number of people. If they have fewer relationships they have greater independence, but their behaviour may be less well coordinated with the rest of the system. If they are in a dense mass of connections, they may find that they are caught up in a network of conflicting obligations, limiting their ability to act. By affecting these patterns of connection we can affect the ability of the system to act in a coherent, connected and coordinated way.

This pattern of freedoms and obligations is a big cultural pattern often overlooked by senior leaders attempting to engineer change. When the web of contradictory obligations within which they exist immobilizes people or groups, they can appear to be obstructive or resistant to change. Similarly, if they are only very loosely connected, they fail to feel any obligation to change. The solution to the impasse is usually seen as being to deal with the individual, often delivered as 'Shape up or ship out!' Our understanding of the organization suggests that an alternative is to pay attention to the patterns of relationship within the organization. Transformative collaboration events create an opportunity for the relationship pattern to realign itself to better fit the demands, requirements and aspirations of the present and future. The very events invite different patterns to form as they privilege interest and passion over seniority and fixed-form discussion. The decisions made about the organization often also require some later more formal structural realignment, through a change in lines of accountability or organizational structure.

3) Sense-making

Meaning or sense-making is a constant organizational activity. People deliberate over how to 'read the runes' of what the top people are up to. In the American TV series *The West Wing*, the President's staff huddle together trying to decide what the President actually meant when he said, 'Don't anyone tell my wife.' Did he mean that, or did he actually want someone to dispatch someone to tell his wife? Had they read the signs right? This behaviour goes on in all organizations. When the organization announces 'There will be no redundancies', immediately some people start to wonder why they said that and to deduce that it's time to brush down their CV. We cannot legislate for sense-making. Therefore, we have to be part of the conversations where sense is being made to be able to influence the sense that is being made. Transformative, collaborative events allow people to make sense together and to influence each other's sense-making. Sense-making is an iterative process, and transformative collaboration recognizes that collective sense and meaning-making is a continual organizational activity.

4) Relationships

People relate to others in the organization all the time and in many different ways: friendly, hostile, neutral, coldly, impatiently, aggressively, generously, arrogantly, with humility, anxiously, excitedly ... the list seems endless. These micro-experiences on a daily basis of relating to others, how that is experienced, makes up our experience of the organization, our lived experience of its culture. Never mind what the fancy words say on the value statement or 'our promise to our staff', it's the lived quality of our daily encounters that constitutes the organizational water in which we swim. By helping people have different experiences of each other, we can affect the quality of organizational life.

Not so long ago I designed and ran a team day for two project teams who would be working together on a huge IT project. One team consisted of people from the finance department; the other was made up from people

" Mr Blenkinsopp you're
needed at reception "

in logistics. The people from logistics had resigned themselves to working with those 'accountant types'. During the day we got both teams to create a collage of the timeline of this project, from where we were to the point of celebration, using pictures and words from magazines. They presented these to each other. They were both very funny. It is astonishing the images that can be found in seemingly innocuous magazines. The logistics guys just couldn't get over it. In the final feedback one man in particular, in trying to express his delight and disbelief that these finance guys had a sense of humour, wit, a sense of the raunchiness of life, just kept digging a bigger hole for himself as he revealed his expectations of how dull and boring these guys, and so the event, would be.

Transformative, collaborative events have this quality. People have meaningful conversations about things that matter. They have fun together, they create things together and they reveal themselves to each other, including their passion, excitement and joy at work. They reveal hidden talents as poets or singers, magicians and artists, actors and storytellers. In this way unhelpful prejudices and stereotypes are challenged by personal experience. Through these experiences social capital is built as knowledge, trust and information-sharing grow.

5) *Imagination*

Whether we are aware of it or not, our brains are in a constant state of anticipation about what is going to happen next. They imagine the future. And we act on the basis of our expectations, our imagination. Often we only realize this when something happens that surprises us, something other than expected. If we didn't have something in mind, some imagined scenario, then we wouldn't be surprised. Our images of the future guide our present actions. Frequently, our expectations of the future are unarticulated and unchallenged. The same applies to organizations. As living entities they too are always acting into an imagined future; the question is how much time does our organizational system spend consciously imagining different futures?

Normally, the energy devoted to conscious organizational imagining is minimal, preoccupied as we are with the problems of today and yesterday. Transformative collaborative interventions create opportunities to co-create positive images of the future through the connected use of imagination. To talk about what we hazily imagine is to breathe life into it. Once expressed verbally, or in another outward expression such as images, others can connect to our imagination. From the imagination can come things that have not yet happened: novelty of possibility and action. Until they are brought forth they cannot be considered as options. If we can't imagine our positive workplace, positive culture or positive future, we certainly can't create it. Boniwell and Zimbardo's (2004) work on temporal bias highlights how important a densely imagined future state is for healthy living and well being. The same is likely to be true for organizations. By helping organizations imagine positive future states, transformative collaboration events help them move towards them.

6) *Emotions*

Life is full of emotion, therefore organizational life is full of emotion. Emotions affect behaviour. There will be a pattern to the emotional life of an organization, most importantly the ratio of positive to negative emotions. An organization that is able to create many opportunities for people to feel good is going to reap extraordinary benefit in terms of helpful and virtuous organizational behaviour. Transformative, collaborative events create positive emotions in the moment, focusing on peak positive experiences from the past and imagined positive futures they create emotional states such as pride, joy, happiness, wellbeing, passion, excitement, interest, engagement, flow and satisfaction. The creation of positive emotion and energy is seen as one of the key processes that facilitate an organization's purposeful evolution towards ever-more positive states.

7) Attention

Attention is a finite resource. We cannot attend to everything that happens. We make choices, with full consciousness or otherwise, of what to attend to. Attention is a precious organizational asset. Very often organizations pay lots of attention to failure, unwanted behaviour and problems, but very little to success, achievement, desired behaviour and smooth running. Their world becomes full of problems, failures and unwanted behaviours. So, there is little to celebrate. The way to send the circle spinning the other way isn't to wait for something stunning to happen which you can then celebrate, but to attend to daily successes and achievements and celebrate them, as brilliantly illustrated in Clive Hutchinson's account of recognizing success (see Chapter 2). If you don't look for success, you won't find it. Transformative, collaborative events influence where the organization directs its attention and so influences the lived experience of being in the organization (i.e., the culture).

8) Mindfulness

When we are mindful we become sensitive to context and are situated in the present. We have a flexible state of mind, we are open to novelty and we engage in the process of actively drawing novel distinctions. We are alert to the possibility of change.

The more unstable the world, the more we need to be mindful. Mindfulness enhances adaptive behaviour. Transformative, collaborative events encourage mindful attending to certain features of organizational life – for example, what works, what is good, what is happening when the best things happen. By focusing attention in this deliberate and mindful way, it becomes possible for the system to notice small but significant details about what makes the difference between good and excellent, which can be the basis for adaptive behaviour in a changing world.

" Constable, I think I may have a clue "

Transformative Collaboration Approaches

Transformative, collaborative events work through the processes we have just outlined. It is possible to work in transformative ways in organizations using this awareness to help locate useful points of intervention. Patricia Shaw (2002) gives a wonderfully readable account of working as a 'free-range' change agent who understands the organization as a complex adaptive system and works to help it purposefully evolve through influencing the processes we have identified. There are also a number of more formal change approaches or methodologies: they understand the organization as a complex adaptive system; work through the organizational patterns; affect the organization at a cultural level; are likely to help the organization evolve towards virtuousness; and give us some tangible starting points for action. Below we outline a few: Appreciative Inquiry, Open Space and World Café.

1) Appreciative Inquiry

Appreciative Inquiry (Cooperrider and Whitney, 2001) is an inquiry into some aspect of organizational life. The inquiry is appreciative in nature: focused on the best of the present and past. In this way it identifies a strong base from which to build towards a positive future. Appreciative Inquiry is based on four key processes: discovering the best of the present; co-creating attractive futures; redesigning the organization in the light of the first two processes; and working with the energy generated by the process to make things happen. It can take place over a two- or three-day workshop, or can be incorporated into ongoing organizational life. Within any specific design it is imperative that many voices across the organization are involved collectively. The benefits of this inclusive approach become evident as the costs all too frequently associated with change (e.g., resistance, lack of buy-in, poor traction) are largely absent. Instead, the challenge for the leadership often becomes to keep pace with the energy and enthusiasm of the workforce for change.

Appreciative Inquiry is based on five key psychological principles: positive energy is a great engine for change; organizations are social systems, co-created by all members; the social world is socially constructed, so change happens as people's understanding of the world and its possibilities changes; as living systems, organizations grow towards attractive futures; and finally, that to ask a question is to effect change. There is also one other principle: that positive change is sustainable, at an individual, organizational and world level.

The fundamental process is built around a 4D model of intervention (see Figure 2.3): discover, dream, design and destiny. This represents an iterative circle of inquiry. First, a topic for inquiry is defined. In essence this will be what the organization wants to grow more of. Second, the organization inquires into the best of the past relevant to the topic to discover the resources and strengths that already exist in the system. Next, the organization imagines how it could be if it were able to bring these resources and strengths into play more often. From here the organization identifies what needs to change to make growth in the direction of the most desirable futures more likely. Finally, the organization moves towards its desired future. This movement is supported by a variety of consciously managed, formal working processes such as project groups, and by less consciously managed self-organized adjustments. There are many excellent guides to the practice of Appreciative Inquiry now available, some of which are listed at the end of the chapter.

2) Open Space

The Open Space process allows people to contribute to conversations that interest and energize them. It ensures that all topics that need to be discussed are discussed. It allows people to add value to the discussions in a way that works for them. It disrupts established patterns of organizational behaviour, allowing new voices, views, opinions and perspectives to be heard and developed.

People are invited to come together around a topic of key business importance. Once assembled, they are invited individually to put forward ideas for discussion which they believe are important to the overall topic. Different rooms at different times are assigned for the different discussions. Each discussion has a host, who needs to ensure a written record of the discussion is produced. Once the agenda is created, each person decides for him- or herself which discussion they wish to be part of. Some people choose not to join any discussion, some flit from one to another. Between rounds, the group reassembles to share the discussions so far and to identify further subjects or questions. In this way many aspects of a topic can be explored, defined, outlined or resolved by people who are interested to be in the discussion.

There are a few key rules that allow the process to work well. First, everyone has a right and a responsibility to bring out the things they believe merit discussion. This makes it unlikely that 'unmentionables' will remain so. Second, people have an obligation to ensure that they are somewhere where they are either learning or contributing; if not, they are obliged to take themselves elsewhere. This reduces the abuse of a captive audience scenario. Third, the group is formed through voluntary self-selection; there are no disruptive 'prisoners' or 'pressed men'.

Within the sessions there are four key principles: whoever comes are the right people; whatever happens is the only thing that could have happened; whenever it starts is the right time; and when it's over, it's over. These principles make it less likely that time and energy will be wasted on what 'might have been'. It also means that when a discussion reaches a natural conclusion, people are free to move on to something else. (See Harrison Owen's (1997) text for more detail.)

3) World Café

World Café (Brown and Isaacs, 2005) is a process to facilitate collaborative organizational conversation about things that really matter to the organization and its future. Based on the idea of café-style conversation (relaxed, intense, with changing members) it creates opportunities for small conversational groups to form and re-form around key topics, or questions, within a connected larger conversation. World Café creates a positive, hospitable environment within which rich conversation can unfold. Ideally, there are small tables with table cloths, maybe flowers, perhaps ambient music and readily available refreshments.

The café works to a pattern of rounds of discussions. After each round one person remains seated as a host while the others form new groups for the next round. The tables have paper table cloths so notes of the conversation can be made as the discussion progresses. Hosts act to link successive discussions, while travellers act to spread and connect different ideas. Between rounds some conversation between the tables usually takes place to connect conversations at a bigger system level.

The process is based on certain principles: clarify the purpose of the café; create a hospitable space; explore questions that matter; encourage everyone's contributions; connect diverse perspectives; listen for insights and share discoveries. The heart of World Café lies in well-crafted questions that attract energy and focus attention on what really counts. People attending the café are encouraged to: focus on what matters; contribute their thinking; speak their heart and mind; listen to understand; link and connect ideas; listen together for insights and deeper questions; and play, doodle, draw on the table cloths.

Appreciative Inquiry is unique in having a clear affirmative bias. However, the other two approaches discussed here can be integrated within a general appreciative approach so that they too have an affirmative bias. All recognize the power of inquiry and conversation. Below we give a few longer case studies that illuminate the use of these methodologies together or separately in different organizational settings. Lesley Moore's account of how a group of social care providers moved from being below-average to way out head in the national league tables in just six months illustrates the power of questions and language to change behaviour. Her work called on Appreciative Inquiry (see Supplement 8.3). Helen Higson's

Supplement 8.3   Working with the Positives in Plymouth

When stakeholders providing and receiving social care in Plymouth first came together in August 2009 to map their journey towards 'Putting People 1st', the city council were considered to be behind in the national league tables. By February 2010, just six months later, they were in the lead: recording their progress on film, enabling others across the city and beyond to quickly understand what was happening, and how to join in and contribute.

Together we reframed their challenges from deficits into possibilities. Under the banner of 'Everyone's a Winner', the focus emerged as Achieving Aspirations through self-directed support.

In four shared workshops the language people used changed the way in which they understood how to enable people requiring support and their carers to take control of their lives, think about what they wanted to achieve, then choose and manage the means of support that would enable them to do this.

From Them	To Us
Service 'users'	People being supported to live normal lives
Overwhelming needs	Achieving aspirations
Off-the-shelf services	Customized access to activities in communities
Employed 'carers' with fixed roles	People across the sector, both employed and voluntary, with flexible support roles
Increasing demands	Sharing responsibility for allocating limited resources

How did we work?

Using Appreciative Inquiry and other strengths-based dialogue and design tools we involved people who use services (carers, service providers and commissioners) from across the city from the outset. Participants began with storytelling, answering questions like:

1. Tell a story about a time when you were successfully supported to achieve an aspiration, something that you really wanted to do. What happened? What did you do? What did others do? How did people behave? What made this so exceptional?
2. What do you value most about the ways in which you are currently supported?

Continued

Supplement 8.3 *Continued*

3. If you had three wishes about the way you would really like to be supported in the future, what would they be?
4. You are already enjoying a renewed independence and are fulfilling all your own aspirations, & those of your family, friends and employer.
5. What are you doing? Who is involved? How is everyone behaving? How does it feel? What does it look like?

The principle of simultaneity – change begins from the first fateful question that we ask – played a big part in how quickly people moved forward together, supported by the positive and anticipatory principles: positive emotions stretched people's thoughts and actions, helping to identify and build enduring resources for the future, at personal, organizational and systems levels.

Creating an enduring impact

People reflecting in the film of this innovative work talk about how rediscovering their own strengths and resources, the things that they could and loved to do, enabled them to find new ways to become the active determinants of their lives. Their stories continue acting as powerful and inspirational drivers for others.

Contributed by Lesley Moore

account of how Aston Business School incorporated an Appreciative Inquiry approach into their annual community day demonstrates the approach's versatility. The aim of the day was to enhance the creativity and innovation within the department. By running the day in a way that called on people's creativity and innovation, they enhanced the sense of their own power both on the day and subsequently (Supplement 8.4).

Supplement 8.4   Appreciative Inquiry: A Case Study from Aston Business School

Aston Business School (ABS) is a large research-led business school based in the centre of Birmingham. ABS has about 3,000 undergraduate students, 1,000 taught postgraduate and 150 PhD students.

Each January ABS runs an Away Day for academics, administrative staff and other key university links. Members of its Advisory Board are also invited. In January 2009 the ABS Management Team decided that the theme should be to enhance the School's ability 'to become the most inspiring and innovative business school in Europe'. We decided to use an Appreciative Inquiry approach. We had experienced Away Days which had declined into opportunities for a good moan and wanted this one to be different.

Our facilitator, Sarah Lewis, met with a team from ABS to refine the Appreciative Inquiry approach, relate it to the School's environment, ensure that all voices had an input, identify key appreciative questions for the discovery interviews, and to design an 'appreciatively informed' process for the day.

When the team had reached agreement on these issues papers were circulated to all the participants outlining the aim and objectives of the day.

The success of the Away Day is dependent on everyone's willingness to bring their creativity, their playfulness, their best inspiration, and their most innovative self, their imagination, their goodwill, their bravery and their generosity to the event to enable themselves and others to make the best of the opportunity provided by the structure of the day.

Participants were also posed five questions on which they were asked to reflect in advance. These were:

Continued

Supplement 8.4 *Continued*

- What do you love best about working at ABS?
- What have been some of your best experiences at ABS?
- What valuable things in ABS culture would you like to see continued?
- When you think about the future of ABS, what are you most passionate about?
- What is your biggest, boldest dream for what ABS could be like in the future?

The day started with some quiet reflection when participants were asked to reflect on great and almost great stories. The participants then divided into five streams of 24 (working in three groups of eight) and shared these inspirationally new and different stories. The groups then tried to identify 'the difference that made a difference'. Each stream was asked to feed back their outstanding stories and also what had been the difference between great and almost great. One particularly heart-warming story was the experience of volunteering to teach a child to read. Participants were enthused by the difference another lecturer had made by innovative use of technology to create an even more inspiring learning experience. The groups were then asked to imagine that they were in ABS in 2012 and to describe what it was like to be a member of staff, student or customer of the School. They were also asked to imagine what a day in the life of this imagined School would be like. From there we created 'dreams of the future' of our best-ever vision of ABS and Aston University and put that shared dream into a visual representation. The representation could take any form. This is where the participants showed their greatest creativity. One group re-enacted *Dr Who*, another gave us an art appreciation class, a third sang an unforgettable song about our future. We came away with the impression that we would now work more effectively in cross-disciplinary teams towards a shared vision of the School's future.

At the end of the Away Day individuals and groups made a personal commitment to the actions that they would take following the day. These included each person writing on a postcard the action they would take. These were collected and posted up on the wall. The effect of this was to create a longer-lasting effect beyond the Away Day and to stimulate both an individual responsibility towards making a difference as well as a collective one.

Some of the activities were filmed throughout the day in order to preserve some of the highlights which could be shared with those unable to attend and to facilitate the follow-up actions agreed. For example, people said that it had been great 'to put faces to names' and 'Don't assume that because it has not been done before, it can't be done'.

Participants were given a chance to rate the day and these were overwhelmingly positive.

Following the Away Day, the video was circulated to staff and the postcards were delivered about a month later and staff asked to reflect on whether they had taken their actions. This revealed that many proposed actions were very similar and involved a commitment to improve communications. As one person reflected, 'a common sense of purpose' had been created and a belief that there was the space to experiment and take risks.

Some of the sustainable outcomes from the day have been a series of cross-School projects, some of which are already successfully completed. The Appreciative Inquiry approach used has also influenced further ABS events, which have reflected a more collective attitude towards change and have been much more positive and participative.

Contributed by Helen Higson and Jane Filby

Finally, we have Tim Slack's account of how the creative health council, part of the Liverpool Year of Culture, decided to break out of the conventional conference format by incorporating elements of Appreciative Inquiry and World Café. Working with the whole system and drawing on the resources of this creative group, they were able to engage the whole system in the creation and delivery of the conference in new and innovative ways (Supplement 8.5).

Summary

In this chapter we have pulled out the key theme of the book: the power of positive psychology and Appreciative Inquiry to create flourishing and inspiring places to work. We identified that some of the key processes that support these outcomes are: the creation of social capital and relational reserves; the power of positivity to positively affect so many aspects of organizational life; the benefits of taking a strengths approach to individual and organizational development; and the insights unleashed when we

Supplement 8.5   A Big Conversation, 5 December 2008

How a vision to adopt an alternative approach to conferencing was realized.

This is the story of *The Big Conversation*, one of the closing events in Liverpool's successful year as European Capital of Culture in 2008 – its visioning, development and realization. For the final Creative Health Conference in 2008, the intention was to build on the momentum of previous years and make a valuable contribution to the 2008 legacy. Rather than a traditional conference format, a more radical approach was courted.

Approach, philosophy and methodology

With a growing interest in Appreciative Inquiry and its potential for application in her field, Julie Hanna, Creative Health Manager, and I began a series of conversations. Our vision was to include artists, health workers and stakeholders in designing and developing the event. The design of these preliminary processes would reflect our belief that:

- The design, development process and event itself should all apply the philosophy and foundations of Appreciative Inquiry; and that
- There would be a series of planning events involving artists, funders and health staff, possibly including an AI interview project with stakeholders, to provide information and narratives to inform the final design.

We considered the use of whole-systems thinking, with its capacity to encourage change, key to the development of the event. Whole-systems thinking is based on two powerful foundation assumptions: high involvement, which means engaging people in changing their own system, and systemic design, which refers to a conscious choice to include the people, functions and ideas that can affect or be affected by the work. The presence of all stakeholders is a prerequisite for an effective whole-systems event.

Marvin Weisbord and Sandra Janoff, creators of one of the leading whole-systems methods, Future Search, recommend that a whole-system event should contain participants with **ARE IN:**

Authority to act (e.g., decision-making responsibility in an organization or community)
Resources, such as contacts, time or money

Expertise in the issues to be considered
Information about the topic that no others have; and the
Need to be involved because they will be affected by the outcome and
    can speak to the consequences

There was a concerted effort to ensure that ARE IN participation was achieved for *The Big Conversation*. Time taken on this proved crucial in achieving the breadth of experience and expertise on the day.

Whilst ARE IN was an integral element of delivery, Appreciative Inquiry provided the overall framework for the planning and development phase of *The Big Conversation* as well as feeding into the World Café element of the day itself.

Guiding principles of the development process

During the development process a set of guiding principles began to emerge:

- Development was to be organic, following AI principles of working from strengths, sharing stories. It was to be flexible and free-flowing.
- All planning meetings and artist design sessions would use components of the approaches and techniques planned for the final event.
- Emphasis placed throughout on a strengths-based, non-deficit process in a culture of openness and collaboration.
- Emphasis placed on co-creating the event by maximizing people's engagement in the process.
- Commitment to hold on to the core principles of a dialogue-based, whole-systems event.

Development process

As well as normal administration and logistics support, there were a number of stages that followed the guiding principles outlined above:

- **Half-day workshop** A group of artists using the Discovery and Dream stages of AI discovered from their experience what form their ideal event would take, informing conference content and style.
- **Afternoon workshop** A group of artists contributed to the design of the artist brief for *The Big Conversation* by using elements of World Café. Divided into groups and changing tables halfway their insights built on each other's contributions to produce an innovative artist brief.

Continued

Supplement 8.5 *Continued*

- **Operations group meetings** Drawn from Appreciating People (my organization) and Liverpool Culture Company to manage, coordinate and develop the event, the organization team underwent basic Appreciative Inquiry training and employed the use of the Time to Think process. This enabled difficult issues and concerns to be aired whilst maximizing work output. Meetings led by Appreciating People concentrated on developing an effective team with a high set of values, openness, trust and self-responsibility.
- **Funders' and sponsors' meetings** maximized the opportunity to learn from attendees' unique and diverse experience and engaged them in the process of event development. The meetings that proved most effective were those that adopted techniques later applied to *The Big Conversation*.
- **Appreciative Inquiry interviews** with key arts and health stakeholders helped raise awareness of *The Big Conversation* and also provided valuable information that fed into the content of the day.

Event format

The morning session concentrated on the arts and health story, past and present, with the afternoon focusing on the future: legacy and transition. To help the dialogue process, a specialist drama company performed dramatic sketches to highlight some of the issues throughout the day.

Arrivals, networking and creative activity

The opening 45 minutes encouraged participants to network in a creative environment.

Morning World Café

After a short introduction, delegates, 10 to each table, considered:

What is the connection between art, creativity, culture and health and well-being?
How do I know it has worked?

Delegates changed tables twice in each session, writing comments directly on the table cloths.

The World Café Process, the links between arts, culture, health and wellbeing. How amazing people are and the amazing work that is going on all the time – people's capacity to be positive.
Table host at *The Big Conversation*

Keynote speakers: Phil Redmond, Creative Director of Liverpool Culture Company, and Ruth Hussey, Director of Public Health for NW.

After lunch Drum Planet led an energizing drumming workshop. This was followed by the chair of Liverpool NHS PCT, Gideon Ben Tovim, who set out potential legacy and transition proposals.

Afternoon World Café

Questions for the afternoon session were:

If this was 2012 and you were looking back at the success of the arts and health practice, what would it look like? Describe what had been achieved.
If you were asked to suggest simple and effective arts and health actions, what would they be and what would be your contribution?
The biggest learning was the power of conversation – on a personal level I have been asked to go to a meeting in January to possibly progress a new initiative!
Table host at *The Big Conversation*

Event closure

The event closed with a drama sketch devised from comments collected during the day's conversations, highlighting themes and future hopes of those present.

Recording the event

A comprehensive pictorial record of the event was created by illustrator Dai Owen and photographer Matthew Sephton.

Ten learning points for similar events

1. Hold the vision and commitment to a whole-systems event even when people and funders want to stay in the comfort zones of more traditional approaches.

Continued

Supplement 8.5 *Continued*

2. Maximize the engagement of potential participants in the design and development process and use whole-systems techniques such as World Café, Appreciative Inquiry and Time to Think for development and design meetings and pre-events. Ensure that the right people are in the space (see ARE IN).
3. Operate within the operations group a culture of openness, delegation and trust.
4. Accept that such events need to be flexible, grow organically and not be afraid of change and adding ideas at the late stages.
5. Always aim to create an event that combines participation and fun.
6. For the creation of a successful event and maximum participation plan, prepare well and allocate Time to Think. Reflect.
7. Prepare the hosts well and consider pre-training if they are not conversant with whole-systems events.
8. Use different approaches and activities, such as drama, group activities and drumming, to create energy and innovation!
9. Create an environment that is welcoming, open and creative (e.g., good food, lots of flowers or candles) to create a comfortable space.
10. Remember the power of conversation and dialogue.

Summary

For *The Big Conversation* the design process became as important to the event's success as the day itself. The techniques employed encouraged high levels of energy during all stages and particularly during the conference. Feedback pointed to fledgling relationships and networks developing as a result of new ideas created and shared during the event. Comments and suggestions collected from participants during the conference were transcribed from the table cloths, analysed and recorded in a separate publication, *Creative Health Talks.*

A memorable event, this alternative approach to conferencing provided a collaborative space in which artists, health professionals, service users and representatives from voluntary and community organizations could come together. They gathered to celebrate the achievements and strengths of the arts and health programme in the run-up and during 2008. They acknowledged the value and importance of art's contribution to health and wellbeing but more significantly they succeeded in the identification of its legacy and together set out a foundation for potential future transition.

Contributed by Tim Slack

consider the organization as a complex adaptive system. We noted that transformative collaboration approaches to organizational development incorporate all of these key processes: building social capital and positivity; recognizing strengths and resources; and understanding the organization as a complex adaptive system. We identified the organizational processes through which they work. We also noted that despite the clear benefits of working this way, many organizations find these approaches hard to adopt because they challenge the accepted ways of doing things. For those that are able to make the shift we outlined three approaches: Appreciative Inquiry, World Café and Open Space. Finally, we presented a few case studies to illuminate the transformational power of these ways of working.

Further Reading

Lewis, S., Passmore, J. and Cantore, S. (2007) *Appreciative Inquiry for Change Management*. London: Kogan Page.
This book explains both the default way of thinking of organizations, as machines, and the alternative way, as living systems. It offers detailed guidance on Appreciative Inquiry-based practice.

Hammond, K. (consulting) (1996) *The Thin Book of Appreciative Inquiry*. Plano, TX: Thin Book Publishing.
A much-loved, brief, yet rich introduction to Appreciative Inquiry.

Cooperrider, D., Sorensen, P., Yaeger, T. and Whitney, D. (Eds.) (2001) *Appreciative Inquiry: An Emerging Direction for Organizational Development*. Champaign, IL: Stipes.
This edited text includes the original Appreciative Inquiry papers and a variety of case studies. A book for those who like to start at the source.

Harrison, O. and Koehler, B. (1997) *Open Space Technology, a User Guide*. San Francisco: Berrett-*Koehler* Publishers, Inc.
This book does exactly what it says on the tin: a complete, clear, comprehensive guide to doing Open Space from a master practitioner.

Brown, J. and Isaacs, D. (2005) *The World Café, Shaping Our Futures through Conversations that Matter (video)*.
The how-to guide for World Café, full of practice guidance and tips and accounts of events.

Other Things You Need to Know

How to Live a Happy and Meaningful Life

- Be part of a close family.
- Be enmeshed in a community of friends.
- Know your personal values and live them.
- Know your personal strengths and find a way to exercise them every day.
- Develop an optimistic thinking style.
- Make enough money.
- Be in work, or retire with sufficient money and health and all the above.
- Look after your health.

This list is pulled together from various sources. Genetics and upbringing also make a difference, but since we can't do too much about those I haven't included them in this list.

How to Have a Better Quality Old Age

- Eat real food, not too much, mostly plants.
- Exercise regularly: include aerobic, resistance, flexibility and balance exercise.
- Drink alcohol in moderation (this is probably some research aberration, but it is statistically better than not drinking alcohol at all).
- Don't smoke.

All things being equal, these four things make 14 years' difference to life expectancy, and, as importantly, the quality of life of those extra years.

Thanks to Raymond Fowler at the International Positive Psychology Congress 2009 for this useful distillation of the research.

Positive Psychology at Work: How Positive Leadership and Appreciative Inquiry Create Inspiring Organizations, First Edition. Sarah Lewis.
© 2011 Sarah Lewis. Published 2011 by John Wiley & Sons, Ltd.

References

Adams, V. H., Synder, C. R., Rand, K. L., King, E. A., Sigmon, D. R. and Pulvers, K. M. (2002) Hope In The Workplace (pp. 367–377). In R. Giacolone and C. Jurkiewicz (Eds.), *Handbook of Workplace Spirituality and Organization Performance*. New York: Sharpe.

Adler, P. S. and Kwon, S. W. (2002) Social Capital: Prospects for a New Concept. *Academy of Management Review 27*(1): 17–40.

Ancona, D. and Isaacs, W. (2009) Structural Balance in Teams. In J. Dutton and B. Ragins (Eds.), *Exploring Positive Relationships at Work: Building a Theoretical and Research Foundation*. New York: Psychology Press.

Avolio, B., Griffith, J., Wernsing, T. S. and Walumbwa, F. O. (2010) What is Authentic Leadership Development? In P. Linley, A. S. Harrington and N. Garcea (Eds.), *Oxford Handbook of Positive Psychology and Work*. Oxford: Oxford University Press.

Avolio, B. J. and Luthans, F. (2006) *The High Impact Leader: Authentic, Resilient Leadership That Gets Results and Sustains Growth*. New York: McGraw-Hill.

Babiak, P. and Hare, R. (2006) *Snakes In Suits: When Psychopaths Go to Work*. New York: HarperCollins.

Baker, W., Cross, R. and Wooten. M. (2003) Positive Organisational Network Analysis and Energizing Relationships. In K. Cameron, J. Dutton and R. Quinn (Eds.), *Positive Organizational Scholarship: Foundations of a New Discipline*. San Francisco: Berrett-Koehler.

Baltes, P., Gluck, J. and Kunzmann, U. (2005) Wisdom, Its Structure and Function in Regulating Successful Life Span Development. In C. R. Snyder and S. J. Lopez (Eds.), *Handbook of Positive Psychology*. Oxford: Oxford University Press.

Positive Psychology at Work: How Positive Leadership and Appreciative Inquiry Create Inspiring Organizations, First Edition. Sarah Lewis.
© 2011 Sarah Lewis. Published 2011 by John Wiley & Sons, Ltd.

Bandura, A. and Walters, R. H. (1963) *Social Learning and Personality Development*. New York: Holt, Rinehart & Winston.

Bateman, T. and Porath, C. (2003) Transcendent Behavior. In K. Cameron, J. Dutton and R. Quinn, R. (Eds.), *Positive Organizational Scholarship: Foundations of a New Discipline*. San Francisco: Berrett-Koehler.

Baumeister, R. and Leavy, M. (1995) The need to belong: desire for interpersonal attachments as a fundamental human motivation. *Psychological Bulletin 117*(3): 497–529.

Biswas-Diener, R. and Dean, B. (2007) *Positive Psychology Coaching: Putting the Science of Happiness to Work for Your Clients*. Hoboken, NJ: Wiley.

Blatt, R. and Camden, C. (2009) Positive Relationships and Cultivating Community. In J. Dutton and B. Ragins (Eds.), *Exploring Positive Relationships at Work: Building a Theoretical and Research Foundation*. New York: Psychology Press.

Bolchover, D. (2005) *The Living Dead. Switched Off, Zoned Out: The Shocking Truth About Office Life*. Chichester: Capstone.

Boniwell, I. (2008) *Positive Psychology in a Nutshell: A Balanced Introduction to the Science of Optimal Functioning* (2nd Edition). London: Personal Well Being Centre.

Boniwell, I. and Zimbardo, P. (2004) Balancing Time Perspective in Pursuit of Optimal Functioning. In A. Linley and S. Joseph (Eds.), *Positive Psychology in Practice*. Hoboken, NJ: Wiley.

Britt, T., Dickinson, J., Greene-Shortridge, T. and Mckibben, E. (2007) Self-Engagement at Work. In D. Nelson and C. Cooper (Eds.), *Positive Organizational Behavior*. London: Sage.

Brown, J. and Issacs, D. (2005) *The World Café, Shaping Our Futures Through Conversations That Matter*. San Francisco: Berrett-Koehler.

Buckingham, M. and Clifton, D. (2002) *Now, Discover Your Strengths: How to Develop Your Talents and Those of the People You Manage*. New York: Freepress Business.

Buckingham, M. and Coffman, C. (2001) *First Break All The Rules*. London: Simon & Schuster.

Cameron, K. (1998) Strategic organizational downsizing: an extreme case. *Research in Organizational Behavior 20*: 185–229.

Cameron, K. (2003) Organizational Virtuousness and Performance. In K. Cameron, J. Dutton and R. Quinn (Eds.), *Positive Organizational Scholarship: Foundations of a New Discipline*. San Francisco: Berrett-Koehler.

Cameron, K. (2008a) *Positive Leadership: Strategies for Extraordinary Performance*. San Francisco: Berrett-Koehler.

Cameron, K. (2008b) Paradox in positive organizational change. *Journal of Applied Behavioral Science 44*(1): 7–24.

Cameron, K. (2009) Positive Psychology Leaders Series. *Webinar for the International Positive Psychology Association*, www.ippanetwork.org. Accessed 6 November 2009.

Cameron, K., Bright, D. and Caza, A. (2004) Exploring the relationships between organizational virtuousness and performance. *American Behavioural Scientist,* 47(6): 766–790.

Cameron, K., Dutton, J. and Quinn, R. (Eds.) (2003) *Positive Organizational Scholarship: Foundations of a New Discipline.* San Francisco: Berrett-Koehler.

Cameron, K., Kim, M. and Whetten, D. (1987) Organisational effects of turbulence and decline. *Administrative Quarterly* 32: 222–240.

Cameron, K. and Mora, C. (2008) Positive Practices and Organizational Performances, (Working Paper). Ann Arbor: Ross School of Business, University of Michigan.

Cameron, K., Mora, C. and Leutscher (unpublished) Cited in Cameron (2009).

Carr, D., Hard, K. and Trahant, W. (1996) *Managing the Change Process: A Field Book for Change Agents, Consultants, Team Leaders and Reengineering Managers.* New York: McGraw-Hill.

Clifton, D. and Nelson, P. (1992) *Soar With Your Strengths.* New York: Dell.

Connelly, J. (2002) All Together Now. *Gallup Management Journal* 2(1): 13–18.

Cooperrider, D. (2008) The 3-Circles of the Strengths Revolution. *Foreword to AI Practitioner Special Issue: Strengths-Based Organisations.* November: 8–11: www.aipractitioner.com.

Cooperrider, D. (2009) The Discovery and Design of Positive Institutions via Appreciative Inquiry. Paper presented at World Congress of the International Positive Psychology Association, June. Philadelphia.

Cooperrider, D. and Avital, M. (Eds.) (2004) *Constructive Discourse and Human Organizations: Advances in Appreciative Inquiry, 1.* Oxford: JAI Press.

Cooperrider, D. and Whitney, D. (2001) A Positive Revolution in Change: Appreciative Inquiry. In D. Cooperrider, P. F. Sorenson, Jnr., Y. Therese and W. Diana (Eds.), *Appreciative Inquiry: An Emerging Direction for Organizational Development.* Champaign, IL: Stipes.

Cooperrider, D., Sorenson, P. F. Jnr., Therese, Y. and Diana, W. (Eds.) (2001) *Appreciative Inquiry: An Emerging Direction for Organizational Development.* Champaign, IL: Stipes.

Csikszentmihalyi, M. (2002) *Flow: The Classic Work on How to Achieve Happiness.* London: Rider.

Csikszentmihalyi, M. (2010) Positive Psychology Leaders Series. *Webinar for the International Positive Psychology Association.* www.ippanetwork.org. Accessed 24 April 2010.

Damasio, A. (2005) *Descartes' Error: Emotion, Reason and the Human Brain.* New York: Penguin Books.

Daniels, A. (2000) *Bringing Out the Best in People: How to Apply the Astonishing Powers of Positive Reinforcement.* New York: McGraw-Hill.

Deal, T. and Kennedy, A. (1982) *Corporate Cultures: The Rites and Rituals of Corporate Life.* Reading, MA: Addison-Wesley.

Dutton, J. and Heaphy, E. (2003) The Power of High Quality Connections. In K. Cameron, J. Dutton and R. Quinn (Eds.), *Positive Organizational Scholarship: Foundations of a New Discipline*. San Francisco: Berrett-Koehler.

Ehrenreich, B. (2009) *Brightsided: How the Relentless Promotion of Positive Thinking Has Undermined America*. New York: Metropolitan Books.

Flade, P. (2003) Great Britain's workforce lacks inspiration. *Gallup Management Journal, 11*.

Fredrickson, B. (2005) Positive Emotions. In C. R. Synder and S. J. Lopez (Eds.), *Handbook of Positive Psychology*. Oxford: Oxford University Press.

Fredrickson, B. (2009) *Positivity*. New York: Crown.

Fredrickson, B. and Branigan, C. (2005) Positive emotions broaden the scope of attention and thought–action repertoires. *Cognition and Emotion 19*(3): 313–332.

Fredrickson, B. L. and Losada, M. F. (2005) Positive affect and the complex dynamics of human flourishing. *American Psychologist 60*: 678–686.

George, B. and Sims, P. (2007) *True North: Discover You Authentic Leadership*. San Francisco: Jossey-Bass.

Gittell, J. (2003) A Theory of Relational Coordination. In K. Cameron, J. Dutton and R. Quinn (Eds.), *Positive Organizational Scholarship: Foundations of a New Discipline*. San Francisco: Berrett-Koehler.

Gittell, J., Cameron, K. and Lim, S. (2006) Relationships, layoffs and organizational resilience: airline industry responses to September 11th. *Journal of Applied Behavioral Science 42*(3): 300–329.

Goffee, R. and Jones, G. (2006) Why Should Anyone Be Led By You? Keynote Presentation at CIPD Annual Conference, Harrogate. Seminar handbook.

Grant, A. M. and Spence, G. B. (2010) Using Coaching and Positive Psychology to Promote a Flourishing Workforce: A Model of Goal Striving and Mental Health. In P. Linley, S. A. Harrington and N. Garcea (Eds.), *Oxford Handbook of Positive Psychology and Work*. Oxford: Oxford University Press.

Harris, P. (2010) Police report gives first details of Arizona sweat lodge deaths. *The Observer*, 3 January.

Harter, J. K. and Blacksmith, N. (2010) Employee Engagement and the Psychology of Joining, Staying In, and Leaving Organizations. In P. Linley, S. A. Harrington and N. Garcea (Eds.), *Oxford Handbook of Positive Psychology and Work*. Oxford: Oxford University Press.

Harter, J., Schmidt, F. and Hayes, T. (2002) Business unit level relationship between employee satisfaction, employee engagement and business outcomes: a meta-analysis. *Journal of Applied Psychology 87*(2): 268–279.

Held, S. B. (2004) The negative side of positive psychology. *Journal of Humanistic Psychology 44*(9): 9–46.

Higgs, M. (2009) *The Good, the Bad, and the Ugly*. Presentation at City University, London, 16 February.

Higgs, M. (2010) Change and its Leadership: The Role of Positive Emotions. In A. Linley, S. Harrington and N. Garcea (Eds.), *Oxford Handbook of Positive Psychology and Work*. Oxford: Oxford University Press.

Higgs, M. and Rowland, D. (2005) All changes great and small: exploring approaches to change and its leadership. *Journal of Change Management* 5(2): 121–151.

Hodges, T. D. and Asplund, J. (2010) Strengths Development in the Workplace. In P. Linley, S. A. Harrington and N. Garcea (Eds.), *Oxford Handbook of Positive Psychology and Work*. Oxford: Oxford University Press.

Hooper, J. (2010) Roman Awayday Lands Firewalking Estate Agents in Hospital. guardian.co.uk/world/2010/jul/06/roman-firewalking-hospital-estate-agents. Accessed 6 July 2010.

Isen, A. (2005) A Role for Neuropsychology in Understanding the Facilitating Influence of Positive Affect on Social Behaviour and Cognitive Affect. In C. R. Synder and S. J. Lopez (Eds.), *Handbook of Positive Psychology*. Oxford: Oxford University Press.

Jaworski, J. (1998) *Synchronicity: The Inner Path of Leadership*. San Francisco: Berrett-Koehler.

Kaplan, R. E. and Kaiser, R. B. (2010) Towards a Positive Psychology for Leaders. In P. A. Linley, S. A. Harrington and N. Garcea (Eds.), *Oxford Handbook of Positive Psychology and Work*. Oxford: Oxford University Press.

Kennedy, L. (2002) KFC Bosses Aren't Chicken, But They Sure Are Tender. *The Age*. http://www.theage.com.au/articles/2002/02/27/1014704967158.html.

Kruger, J. and Dunning, D. (1999) Unskilled and unaware of it: how difficulties in recognising one's own incompetence lead to inflated self-assessments. *Journal of Personality and Social Psychology* 77: 1121–1134.

Langer, E. (2005) Wellbeing, Mindfulness vs. Positive Evaluation. In C. R. Synder, and S. J. Lopez (Eds.), *Handbook of Positive Psychology*. Oxford: Oxford University Press.

Lazslo, C. (2008) *Sustainable Value, How the World's Leading Companies are Doing Well By Doing Good*. Sheffield: Greenleaf.

Lewis, S. (2008) The place of goal setting in the coaching process: an exploration. *Selection and Development Review* 24(3), The British Psychological Society.

Lewis, S., Passmore, J. and Cantore, S. (2007) *Appreciative Inquiry for Change Management: Using AI to Facilitate Organisational Development*. London: Kogan Page.

Lewis, T., Amini, F. and Lannan, R. (2000) *A General Theory of Love*. New York: Random House.

Linley, A. (2008) *Average to A+: Realising Strengths in Yourself and Others*. Warwick: CAPP Press.

Linley, P. A., Harrington, S. A. and Garcea, N. (Eds.) (2010) *Oxford Handbook of Positive Psychology and Work*. Oxford: Oxford University Press.

Losada, M. and Heaphy, E. (2004) The role of positivity and connectivity in the performance of business teams: a nonlinear model. *American Behavioral Scientist 47*: 740–765.

Luthans, F., Avery, J. B., Avolio, D. J., Norman, S. and Combs, G. (2006) Psychological capital development. Toward a micro-intervention. *Journal of Organizational Behaviour 27*: 387–393.

Luthans, F., Youssef, C. and Avolio, B. (2007) *Psychological Capital: Developing The Human Capital Edge*. Oxford: Oxford University Press.

Morris, D. and Garrett, J. (2010) Strengths: Your Leading Edge. In P. A. Linley, S. A. Harrington and N. Garcea (Eds.), *Oxford Handbook of Positive Psychology and Work*. Oxford: Oxford University Press.

Mulhern, C. (2010) Methods in Strategic Collaboration Workshop, Snowdonia, Wales.

O'Reilly, C. and Pfeffer, J. (2000) *Hidden Value: How Great Companies Achieve Extraordinary Results with Ordinary People*. Cambridge, MA: Harvard Business School Press.

Owen, H. (1997) *Open Space Technology, a User's Guide*. San Francisco: Berrett-Koehler.

Pascale, R. and Athos, A. (1982) *The Art of Japanese Management: Applications for American Executives*. New York: Viking.

Patterson, C. M. and Newman, J. P. (1993) Reflectivity and learning from aversive events: towards a psychological mechanism for the syndromes of disinhibition. *Psychological Review 100*: 716–736.

Peters, T. and Wasserman, R. (1982) *In Search of Excellence: Lessons from America's Best Run Companies*. New York: Harper & Row.

Peterson, C. (2006) *A Primer in Positive Psychology*. Oxford: Oxford University Press.

Peterson, C. and Seligman, M. E. P. (2004) *Character Strengths and Virtues: A Handbook and Classification*. New York: Oxford University Press/Washington, DC: American Psychological Association.

Pickering, A. D. and Gray, J. A. (1999) The Neuroscience of Personality. In L. A. Pervin and O. P. John (Eds.), *Handbook of Personality* (2nd edition). *Theory and Research*. New York: Guilford Press.

Rath, T. (2007) *Strengthsfinder 2.0*. New York: Gallup Press.

Reynolds, C. (1987) Flocks, herds and schools: a disturbed behaviour model. Proceedings of SIGGRAPH 87. *Computer Graphics 21*(4): 25–34.

Richardson, J. and West, M. (2010) Dream Teams: Towards a Positive Psychology of Team Working. In P. A. Linley, S. A. Harrington and N. Garcea (Eds.), *Oxford Handbook of Positive Psychology and Work*. Oxford: Oxford University Press.

Rowland, R. and Higgs, M. (2008) *Sustaining Change: Leadership That Works.* Chichester: Jossey-Bass.

Seligman, M. E. P. (2002) *Authentic Happiness.* New York: Free Press.

Seligman, M. (1999) Presidential address, delivered in Boston at the American Psychological Association's 107th Annual Convention on 21 August.

Seligman, M. (2006a) *Authentic Happiness, Using the New Positive Psychology to Realize Your Potential for Lasting Fulfilment.* London: Nicholas Brealey.

Seligman, M. (2006b) *Learned Optimism: How to Change Your Mind and Your Life.* New York: Vintage.

Senge, P. (1993) *The Fifth Discipline: The Art and Practice of the Learning Organization.* London: Century Business.

Shaw, P. (2002) *Changing Conversations in Organizations: A Complexity Approach to Change.* London: Routledge.

Sidman, M. (2000) *Coercion and its Fallout.* Boston, MA: Authors Cooperative Inc.

Stacey, R. (1996) Management and the science of complexity: if organisational life is non-linear, can business strategies prevail? *Research and Technology Management 39*(3): 2–5.

Stacey, R., Griffin, D. and Shaw, P. (2000) *Complexity and Management: Fad or Radical Challenge to Systems Thinking?* New York: Routledge.

Stairs, M. and Gilpin, M. (2010) Positive Engagement: From Employee Engagement to Work Place Happiness. In P. A. Linley, S. A. Harrington and N. Garcea (Eds.), *Oxford Handbook of Positive Psychology and Work.* Oxford: Oxford University Press.

Steger, M. and Dik, B. (2010) Work as Meaning: Individual and Organizational Benefits of Engaging in Meaningful Work. In P. A. Linley, S. A. Harrington and N. Garcea (Eds.), *Oxford Handbook of Positive Psychology and Work.* Oxford: Oxford University Press.

Stravos, J., Cooperrider, D. and Kelley, D. L. (2003) Strategic Inquiry, Appreciative Intent: Inspiration to Soar. a New Framework for Strategic Planning. *Aipractitioner*, November. www.aipractitioner.com.

Synder, C. (2000) *Handbook of Hope.* San Diego: Academic Press.

Weick, K. (2006) The Role of Values In High-Risk Organizations. In E. Hess and K. Cameron (Eds.), *Leading Wwth Values: Positivity, Virtue and High Performance.* Cambridge: Cambridge University Press.

Weick, K. and Sutcliffe, K. (2007) *Managing the Unexpected: Resilient Performance in an Age of Uncertainty.* San Francisco: Jossey-Bass.

Wheatley, M. J. (2007) *Finding Our Way, Leadership for an Uncertain Time.* San Francisco: Berrett-Koehler.

Williams, M., Teasdale, J., Segal, Z. and Kabat-Zinn, J. (2007) *The Mindful Way Through Depression.* New York: Guildford Press.

Wooten, L. P. and Cameron, K. S. (2010) Enablers of a Strategy: Positively Deviant Leadership. In P. A. Linley, S. A. Harrington and N. Garcea (Eds.),

Oxford Handbook of Positive Psychology and Work. Oxford: Oxford University Press.

Wrzesniewski, A. (2003) Finding Positive Meaning in Work. In K. Cameron, J. Dutton and R. Quinn (Eds.), *Positive Organizational Scholarship: Foundations of a New Discipline*. San Francisco: Berrett-Koehler.

Yerkes, R. and Dodson, J. (1907) The dancing mouse, a study in animal behaviour. *Journal of Comparative Neurology and Psychology 18*: 459–482.

Youssef, C. and Luthans, F. (2010) An Integrated Model of Psychological Capital in the Workplace. In P. A. Linley, S. A. Harrington and N. Garcea (Eds.), *Oxford Handbook of Positive Psychology and Work*. Oxford: Oxford University Press.

Index

abundance bridge 15, 169
abundance culture 15–16, 24
active engagement 42, 47
adaptive self-reflection 110–15
affirmative bias 9, 17–20
AI, *see* Appreciative Inquiry
airlines, after attack on World Trade
    Center 17, 105–7
ambivalence 9, 28, 30, 97–8
Appreciative Inquiry (AI) 8–9, 33,
    214–15
  and creativity 219–20
  and organizational change 158–62
  and positive workplaces 34–8
  and resilience 153, 154–5
  and sustainable growth 158–68
  dream phase 88, 149, 165
  key principles 35
*Appreciative Inquiry for Change
    Management* 162
appreciative leadership 121–4
approach goals 57–8
Arnott, Alastair 145–6
arousal 149–50
asset-focused strategies 153
Aston Business School 111, 219–21

attention 212
authentic followers 117
authenticity 8, 46, 117; *see also*
    authentic leadership
authentic leadership 102–17, 124
  defined 102
  distinguished from psychopathic
    leadership 107–10
Average to A+ 45
avoidance goals 57–8

balanced processing 115–17
behavioural activation/inhibition
    systems 54–6
best self-feedback 79–83
  benefits 83
Big Conversation, The 222–6
black humour 156
Bolchover, David 41
brain connections 44
brain behavioural systems 54–6
Branch Davidians 103
Bright-sided 2
Bringing out the Best in People 59
broaden and build theory 167, 198
Butcher, James 36, 37, 120–1

Positive Psychology at Work: How Positive Leadership and Appreciative Inquiry Create Inspiring Organizations, First Edition. Sarah Lewis.
© 2011 Sarah Lewis. Published 2011 by John Wiley & Sons, Ltd.

CPSIA information can be obtained at www.ICGtesting.com
Printed in the USA
BVOW06*2138140815

413149BV00002B/2/P